Those Inner Cities

Reconciling the Economic and Social Aims of Urban Policy

BRIAN ROBSON

CLARENDON PRESS · OXFORD
1988

Oxford University Press, Walton Street, Oxford OX2 6DP
Oxford New York Toronto
Delhi Bombay Calcutta Madras Karachi
Petaling Jaya Singapore Hong Kong Tokyo
Nairobi Dar es Salaam Cape Town
Melbourne Auckland
and associated companies in
Berlin Ibadan

Oxford is a trade mark of Oxford University Press

Published in the United States
by Oxford University Press, New York

British Library Cataloguing in Publication Data
Robson, B.T. (Brian Turnbull), 1939–
Those inner cities. Reconciling the economic and social aims of urban policy.
1. Great Britain. Cities. Inner cities.
Social planning
I. Title
307'.12'0941
ISBN 0–19–874148–0
ISBN 0–19–874149–9 (pbk.)

Library of Congress Cataloging in Publication Data
Robson, Brian T. (Brian Turnbull), 1939–
Those inner cities.
Bibliography: p. Includes index.
1. Urban policy—Great Britain.
2. Central business districts—Great Britain.
3. Urban renewal—Great Britain. I. Title.
HT133.R595 1988 307.3'42'0941 88–17900
ISBN 0–19–874148–0
ISBN 0–19–874149–9 (pbk.)

Set by Hope Services, Abingdon
Printed in Great Britain
at the University Printing House, Oxford
by David Stanford
Printer to the University

To Glenna

Preface

In the early hours of the morning after the General Election in 1987 and ebullient from her victory, the Prime Minister stood on the stairs of Conservative Central Office to address her party workers. Her first words were about the inner cities: 'So no-one must slack . . . On Monday, we have a big job to do in some of those inner cities.' Whether this was meant as a presage of new policy or merely a political message is open to interpretation. What is certain is that, for a while at least, the media were to focus on the inner cities as *the* matter of the moment and the government, in its turn, gave some sustained attention to an issue which has now fitfully been on the political agenda for over two decades. It led to the establishment of a Cabinet subcommittee and to the appointment of Kenneth Clarke as Minister for the Inner Cities. Both are signs of intent—of the government's recognition of the need to co-ordinate its policy more effectively and of its need to respond to the interpretation of the prime ministerial message: a long-promised White Paper has been transmogrified in the glossy opuscule *Action for Cities* (Cabinet Office, 1988). What also is of interest in any exegesis of the Prime Minister's statement is its distancing from the inner cities themselves; 'some' could be taken by those of more machiavellian persuasion as a covert threat; and 'those' is hardly a term of endearment or indeed of familiarity. Such are and have been strands in the elucidation of inner-city policy.

Inner cities have indeed been on the political agenda only fitfully for the last two decades. An 'urban programme' was first announced (largely it is said as a matter of accident) by Harold Wilson in 1968; the enhanced Urban Programme, responding to the publication of the Inner Area Studies of London, Birmingham, and Liverpool, began in 1977/8. But the heart beat of official concern about the fortunes of inner areas has been prompted as much by events like urban riots as by any deeper-seated and longer-term governmental commitment. For a brief while it seemed that every organization and every interest group had common cause in developing an inner-city perspective to its work. Reports and working parties proliferated: the archbishop's *Faith in the City*, pronouncements from the Town and Country Planning Association, the Royal Town Planning Institute, Mr Rod Hackney. The Confederation of British Industry set up a working party. The problem with dancing to the tune of ministerial and prime ministerial pronouncements is that, like the old-time dances, their rhythm is slow-slow-quick-quick-slow. Yet if, as seems plain, British cities are experiencing a crisis of governance, of funding, of economic rationale, and of social tractability, then a more sustained concern seems called for.

In writing this book, I have pitched my concern very broadly, as seems appropriate to the issues. The urban question is not simply a matter of evaluating current policy approaches to the city and thinking about alternatives; the issues presuppose a view both on whether the city is worth 'saving' and what future rationale cities might have in a post-industrial world; hence my apparent digressions into broader discussions in the initial and final chapters. I have consciously stuck rather narrowly to a concern with the practicalities of policy and eschewed a wider discussion of theory and the role of the system of capital in generating the problems of cities. Such debate has been extensively explored in much of the recent geographical, political-science, and sociological literature and has greatly deepened our understanding. If I have a particular experience to offer it is that of someone who has been fairly close to policy issues over the last decade; so I make no apology for this emphasis. I am also a firm believer in that grand old geographical practice of basing views on direct experience and knowledge of issues 'on the ground'—a view now greatly sustained by our growing realization of the way in which the different inheritances of different cities produce variety and individuality in their experiences and in their consequent ability to respond to the broader process of economic and social change. What I say is almost wholly drawn from English examples—despite the temptation to draw more solidly on the United States, from whose policies we have drawn perhaps too liberally without considering the structural differences between the two sides of the Atlantic. Nor (although I discuss the successes achieved north of the border) have I looked in detail at the Scottish experience, since the legislative framework is subtly different in Scotland; indeed I argue that it is from such differences that English policy has much to learn. Much, indeed, of what I say is drawn from the very local context of Greater Manchester, an area which has been surprisingly neglected by academics. I came to Manchester in 1977 at the start of the enhanced Urban Programme and the ten years of working in the area have been a humbling and a privileged experience. In tackling local research and in my role as Chairman of the Manchester Council for Voluntary Services, which has provided an entry point to many of the activities of local groups, I have learned a great deal about the complexities and the uniqueness of how things happen in a local area. Many of the examples on which I draw are taken from this local Manchester experience and it has coloured much of my own views of what the problems are and of the successes and failures of policy.

I am aware of how much I owe to and how heavily I have drawn on the recent series of research reports on the inner city and of the debt that I owe to many of their authors for the stimulus of having discussed ideas with them. Not least among those researchers have been Victor Hausner, Ken Spencer, Martin Boddy, John Goddard, Duncan Maclennan, Ken Young, Ian Gordon, Bill Lever, Ray Pahl, David Donnison, Derek Diamond, Doreen Massey, Noel Boaden, Phil Cooke, Peter Hall, Judith Marquand, Chris Hamnett; the list could and should be longer. I am also conscious of the debt that I owe to discussions with many civil servants both in Manchester and in London and with many members of community groups in Manchester. Equally, I have benefited from endless help from within my own Department. Discussions with Robert Barr, Michael Bradford, Richard Thomas, Richard Nutter, Alan Steward, and Sarah Scobie—all fellow members of the Centre for Urban Policy Studies—have broadened my familiarity with literature and ideas, as have discussions with Peter Lloyd and Peter Dicken, John Shutt and Jamie Peck. In particular—and as ever—the professional skills of Graham Bowden and Nick Scarle in producing the illustrations have been invaluable. Since I have little doubt that some of what I say will not be what others would have written, the disclaimer that the views are my own should be taken seriously.

Contents

List of Figures xiii
List of Tables xv
List of abbreviations xvi

1. What is the Problem? *A Pitiless Indicator* 1
The urban and regional dimensions of distress 2
Individual and contextual dimensions of well-being 6
Monitoring the spatial patterns of well-being 9
Urban and regional interplay 16
Demographic loss 17
Social polarization 23
Economic collapse 25
Unemployment 29
House-price changes 31
Environmental degradation 35
Crime and unrest 37
Conclusion 39

2. Why Bother? *The Measure of a Man* 41
Equity and efficiency 42
Down with the city! 49
Up with the city! 54

3. What are the Causes? *Clarity of Vision* 58
Economic restructuring 62
Industrial mix 67
Factor costs 70
Labour 70
Land and premises 74
Capital 83
Environmental perception 84
Residential preference 84
Demographic trends 85
Gigantism 87
Locality-specific arguments 89
Local politics 89
New investment and small firms 92
Conclusion 94

4. What has been Done? *There is no Health in us* 96
Spatial targeting 101
Designated areas 103
Garden Festivals 111
Enterprise Zones 111
Partnership 116
Central–local partnership 116
Public–private partnership 117
Urban Development Grant 118
Urban Renewal Grant 120
Private housing and privatizing housing 121
New agencies 124
Urban Development Corporations 124
City Action Teams and Task Forces 134
Local authority economic development activity 136
The voluntary sector 140

5. With what Success? *Like the Curate's Egg* 143
The Greater Manchester experience 143
Assessing the employment impacts 150
The case of Tyne and Wear 153
Social frustrations 160
The successes and limitations of policy 164
Consistency 166
The broader impacts of unintended conflicts 172
The ineffectiveness of targeting 175
The assumption of development capacity 177
The spatial scales of development 178

6. What might now be done? *The Flower of Civilization* 181
The principles for policy 184
The need for coherence and consensus 185
Poverty, low pay, and unemployment 188
Employment strategies 189
Targeting the deprived 192
Scales of governance 196
Regional co-ordination 197
The community scale 202
Party politics 207
Infrastructure and resources 212
Future scenarios 218

BIBLIOGRAPHY 227
INDEX 237

List of Figures

1.1.	Determinants of well-being	6
1.2.	Distribution of the percentages of unemployed men aged 15–64 for the wards of Hackney, Liverpool, Birmingham, and Manchester	10
1.3.	Economic performance of functional groupings of towns	15
1.4.	Urban decline across the EEC in the 1970s and early 1980s	20
1.5.	The decline of large towns. The relationship between density and population change 1971–1981 in English towns of over 50,000 inhabitants	21
1.6.	Employment change by sector, Great Britain and the North West, 1971–1986	26
1.7.	Employment change in rural and urban areas, Great Britain 1951–1981	28
1.8.	Male unemployment in Manchester, 1986	30
1.9.	Employment balance sheets for Greater London, West Midlands, Tyneside, Clydeside, and Bristol, 1951–1981	32
1.10.	Rates of change in average house prices in Greater London and the North West, 1977–1987	34
3.1.	Varying perspectives on 'the urban problem'	60
3.2.	The dual labour market: the search for flexibility	73
3.3.	Industrial rents in Britain	75
3.4.	Changes in manufacturing employment and industrial premises	80
3.5.	Changes in manufacturing employment and industrial premises: (*a*) by regions; (*b*) by type of settlement	81
4.1.	Urban Programme resources, 1973/1974–1985/1986	97
4.2.	Changes in expenditure for categories within the Urban Programme, 1979/1980–1985/1986	97

4.3. Priority areas in the Urban Programme, England 1986 104
4.4. Urban Programme expenditure by category in the Newcastle metropolitan area: (*a*) by category of overall expenditure; (*b*) by categories within expenditure on economic development 108
4.5. Urban regeneration schemes in Manchester, Salford, and Trafford 114
4.6. Salford Quays: developments and future plans 130
4.7. Recently declared Urban Development Corporations in West Midlands, Greater Manchester, Teesside, and Tyneside 132–3

5.1. Castlefield, Manchester: an urban heritage site 145
5.2. Size of assisted establishments by source of public funding in the Newcastle area 155

6.1. Housing investment resources, Manchester, 1979/1980–1985/1986 214
6.2. Alternative scenarios 218

List of Tables

1.1 The 27 most deprived areas, 1981, according to Begg and Eversley 12
1.2. The highest and lowest scores on Champion's index of economic performance 13
1.3. Recent population change in large cities 22
1.4. Regional prices for semi-detached houses, first quarter 1987 35
1.5. Derelict land in the seven English conurbations, 1974–1982 36
1.6. Indices of population and employment change in urban and rural areas 40

3.1. Imperial Tobacco Limited: employment change 1980–1984 65
3.2. Shift-share analysis of employment trends, 1971–1978 and 1978–1981 68
3.3. Residual valuation of two vacant sites in Salford 77

4.1. The changing balance of expenditure on economic, environmental, and social projects, 1979/1980–1984/1985 99
4.2. Urban Programme allocations, 1987–1988 and 1988–1989 105
4.3. Enterprise Zones in England, Wales, and Scotland 112
4.4. Impacts of Enterprise Zones on rentals and capital values 115
4.5. Urban Development Grant gearing ratios 118

5.1. Financial assistance for economic development, Newcastle area, 1974–1984 155
5.2. 'Cost per job' from public assistance in the Newcastle area, 1985 158
5.3. Defence procurement and regional assistance, 1974/1975–1977/1978 173

List of Abbreviations

ALURE	Alternative Land-uses for Rural Areas
BiC	Business in the Community
BSC	British Steel Corporation
BTG	British Technology Group
CAT	City Action Team
CURDS	Centre for Urban and Regional Development Studies
DE	Department of Employment
DES	Department of Education and Science
DLG	Derelict Land Grant
DoE	Department of the Environment
DTI	Department of Trade and Industry
EE	English Estates
EEC	European Economic Community
EZ	Enterprise Zone
GEAR	Glasgow Eastern Area Renewal
GLC	Greater London Council
GLEB	Greater London Enterprise Board
GMC	Greater Manchester Council
ITL	Imperial Tobacco Limited
LA	Local authority
LDDC	London Docklands Development Corporation
LEL	Lancashire Enterprise Limited
LLMA	Local labour market area
MDC	Merseyside Development Corporation
MSC	Manpower Services Commission
MSCC	Manchester Ship Canal Company
NCP	New Commonwealth and Pakistan
OPCS	Office of Population Censuses and Surveys
RAWP	Resource Allocation Working Party
RDG	Regional Development Grant
RSA/NSA	Regional Selective Assistance/National Selective Assistance
RSG	Rate Support Grant
SDA	Scottish Development Agency
TCPA	Town and County Planning Association

UDC	Urban Development Corporation
UDG	Urban Development Grant
UP	Urban Programme
URG	Urban Renewal Grant
WDA	Welsh Development Agency
WDC	Washington Development Corporation
WMEB	West Midlands Enterprise Board
YTS	Youth Training Scheme

1

What is the Problem? *A Pitiless Indicator*

The building of cities is one of man's greatest achievements. The form of cities always has been and always will be a pitiless indicator of the state of his civilisation.

Edmund Bacon

All modern societies are kaleidoscopes, fragmented along a variety of economic, social, cultural, ethnic, and geographical dimensions. The kaleidoscope may be shaken—by economic and social developments over time, by changing policies, or by cataclysmic events like disease, social unrest, or war; all of which throw up new patterns and concentrate political and academic debate on one rather than another of the dimensions of the pattern. The focus of concern shifts as fashion dictates. *Tout passe, tout casse, tout lasse* has a hollowly realistic ring as modern Marxist scholars contemplate the passing of the bases on which their master built his theories.

Living in another period of great change, unable without benefit of hindsight to label it glibly 'industrial revolution' or 'agricultural revolution' or to determine with confidence whether we are in the fifth, sixth, or seventh Kondratieff, the putative policy-makers of our age struggle to describe, define, and analyse. Academics, politicians, and above all the self-styled media pundits whirl the kaleidoscope energetically, if often unhelpfully. 'Buzz-words' clog the air waves and the printing-presses and infest the conversation of the so-called chattering classes. In a country long besotted by its geographical uniqueness—'this sceptr'd isle . . . this precious stone set in a silver sea'—it should cause no surprise that a current obsession is with 'North' and 'South', with the creation and allocation of geographical unevenness in the welfare and well-being of society. The defining of these areas has become a national game which all can play (TCPA, 1987; Breheney *et al.*, 1987).

Inextricably interwoven in this debate are the themes of town and country, city and suburb, inner city and outer city. Some have attempted to suggest that the perceptual North is not a geographic North (Robson, 1985). Most strikingly, the bishop of Liverpool, the Right Revd David Sheppard, coined the phrase 'comfortable' Britain in a memorable Dimbleby lecture. Common sense, if not common currency, might suggest that the converse side, 'uncomfortable Britain', is neither a condition nor a place but an amalgam of both. Yet inexorably 'uncomfortable Britain' has become synonymous with the 'North' and with the 'inner city'. A wealth of statistics and research shows the inner areas of northern cities as having more than their fair share of economic and social problems. The scale of this misery may mask its lack of uniqueness, but that very lack, once recognized, leads to wider questions: can such problems be alleviated or even solved as part of a national social and economic programme or is there a historic inevitability about every period of change which claims its own victims? In practice, a period of world-wide recession coupled with the shifting fortunes of a de-industrializing Britain has seen a policy concentration on economic regeneration rather than social well-being. The one does not, alas, necessarily lead to the other.

THE URBAN AND REGIONAL DIMENSIONS OF DISTRESS

The social well-being of individuals in different areas has been endlessly charted and there can be little doubt that many of the dimensions of well-being are mutually reinforcing and conterminous. The indicators chosen to measure well-being differ from study to study, but the gross pattern of advantage and disadvantage remains, even though individual places may move somewhat up or down the league tables of different studies. Liverpool, Manchester, Glasgow, Newcastle, Hull, and some of the London boroughs consistently appear at one extreme of such tables, smaller southern towns and rural areas keep appearing at the other. It happens, as an accident of geology and geography and the course of early industrialization in Britain, that, with the exception of London, all of the large industrial towns in the country are north of the line running from the mouth of the Severn to the Wash. The urban dimension of poverty is therefore confounded with the regional dimension now crudely, if inaccurately, defined as the divide between North and South. Both make separate and independent contributions to the overall geography of well-being and ill-being in the country as a whole.

The costs and benefits of living in different areas are therefore a function partly of the size of place but partly of the region in which one lives. There are many members of comfortable Britain, like myself, who live in a 'southern-style' enclave within a ten-minute drive of the centre of a once-thriving industrial city. The industry that made Manchester has gone, but there is much to make life extremely pleasant for somebody with a professional job, paid at national rates, and with some long-term job security. There are the amenities of the city; theatre, music, restaurants, shops, night clubs, museums, art galleries, leisure centres, all of good quality and available at affordable prices. There is easy access to splendid countryside in the Peak District, the Pennines, the Lake District, and North Wales. It is possible to find solid Victorian and Edwardian houses at reasonable prices. Local labour is cheap and easy to find. Good hospitals and schools both public and private are easily accessible, as is the local airport with its through flights to Europe, the US, and the Far East. Of course there are costs associated with living in a large northern city rather than in a small town in the south. Opportunistic burglary is a local hazard as are occasional graffiti and vandalism, even though the tree-lined streets are kept free from litter and refuse is cleared regularly and without fuss. Within Manchester the cost of rates is unusually high, at a new rate poundage of 336p in the pound, and a not insignificant part of that rate income is spent on items which reflect the ideological priorities of a hard-left council. With house prices in the area being very low by the standards of southern England, most professionals are effectively locked into the housing market of the area since a move elsewhere would mean either starting at the bottom of the housing market or taking on levels of mortgage repayment which would be cripplingly high. Nevertheless, as a life-style it has much to recommend it.

In Manchester, cheek by jowl with such a pleasant city suburb lie the acres of inter-war council estates and the remaining streets of terraced houses. A surprising number of people living here still rate life as 'comfortable', but the apparently rising wave of crime and vandalism, coupled with the grim reality of rising unemployment, is gradually altering that. In the traditionally immigrant area of Moss Side, less than three miles away from the suburb, the view is much worse. Here hard work and an ambition to succeed have petered out in the futility of life in the 'inner city'. This is predominantly an area where West Indian immigrants settled: they came with dreams and hopes falsely fostered by the colonial experience and their belief in the 'mother country'. Some are owner-occupiers in whatever streets were left standing by the planners in the flamboyant destruction of the area in the 1960s and 1970s. Many have managed to work their way through the council housing lists to the more desirable recent low-rise council housing which reflects the change in building style of the 1980s; others still endure the difficulties of life in the notorious deck-access crescent blocks of Hulme. All share the fear and very real prospect that, if they are not already unemployed, they may well be made redundant; all know that their sons and daughters are discriminated against in education and in seeking employment. One such middle-aged man, recently made redundant as a result of the privatization of the Greater Manchester bus company, now spends much of his time in the West Indian Sports and Social Club which he helped to finance by mortgaging his house. That same house, well looked after, in a street of well-built Edwardian terraced houses, has little resale value. Around his home the legacies of an earlier townscape—the pubs, an old School Board building, an empty warehouse, and churches now colonized by black religious movements—sit eccentric to the geometry of the comprehensive planning of the 1960s; small patches planned as grassed-over public space now provide merely the focus for detritus, roaming dogs, and stripped-down abandoned cars. Despite the almost thirty years of his life given to the city and the country, he is now making plans to join kin in the United States and make a further fresh start. He is concerned for his younger children, boys of 19 and 17 and a girl of 16. His older children were reared in the West Indies and thus were unharmed by the vagaries of the English educational system, which they joined when they already had a good grounding. They are all in work, one back in the West Indies, one in the United States, and the other in London, but the prospects for the three younger children are poor. Unemployment in the Hulme area is distressingly high—for the young and especially for the young black it is close to 80 per cent—and the father is already alarmed by the political and criminal influences working on his family. Youth Training Schemes are dismissed as 'skivvy' labour; police harassment is a way of life, prejudging wrong-doing by skin colour. Prostitution and drugs both flourish in the area. As yet these youngsters remain loyal to the family values and attend their local New Testament Church of God, but his daughter has already been told by her school that she has no chance of following her mother into the nursing profession. Parental support and enthusiasm have been no match for years of interrupted education caused by industrial action and a rapid turnover of education gimmicks. The 19-year-old has succeeded in attaining some catering qualifications at a local technical college, but finds that he is offered nothing other than washing-up jobs. The 17-year-old has, at his father's persuading, gone on to a YTS scheme only to find that it is indeed lacking in any training element. Radicalized and rebellious, he is rapidly heading for the world of petty theft and handling, of lying in bed until noon and coming to life for the pub and the disco; a style of life that marks too many of his contemporaries, both black and white.

The members of this family are fortunate in inner-city terms in that they can and will move, but there are many who cannot. Trapped in this and other inner-city areas are old people, single parents, and unskilled workers, each of whom has their own version of 'hell is a city'. It may be shortage of money in a society where consumer spending rules; it may be lack of friends and family; it may be fear of assault and robbery; it may be actual experience of serious or petty crime; it may be environmental squalor; it may be the mean onslaught of racial attacks ranging from the harmless but hurtful graffiti to the burning petrol-soaked rag stuffed through the letter box. All live only a short distance from the lawyers, doctors, MPs, academics, and business men who people the suburb. In terms of well-being, they could be on different planets.

Individual and contextual dimensions of well-being

To disinter the numerous dimensions involved in establishing a calculus of well-being one would need to consider the respective fortunes of a very large number of households, since the elements that determine life-styles and life chances are numerous, but the point of the examples is to suggest the two principal sets of dimensions which have to be considered. On the one hand are the characteristics of individual people and families, and on the other are the contextual circumstances which play an important independent role in determining their prospects. Fig. 1.1 suggests a very simplified version of the interplay of some of the elements involved. The aggregate context of place is comprised of the region in which a family lives, the size of place in which it lives, and the industrial and occupational mix and history of the place. These, in turn, help to determine the political complexion of the locality and its economic buoyancy. The characteristics of the individuals—age, occupation, housing tenure, skills, ethnicity, and sex—are strong independent determinants of well-being. As Buck and Gordon (1987, p. 198) show, the probability of being unemployed is related both to personal characteristics *and* to the area in which people live. An unqualified, unmarried black man aged

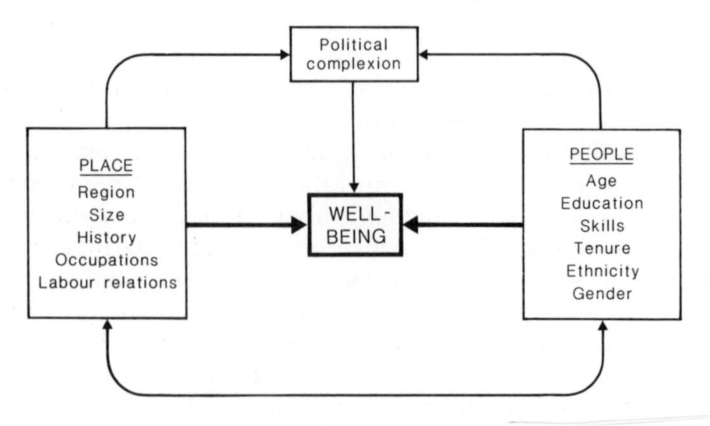

FIG. 1.1. Determinants of well-being

16–19, living in local authority tenure and with only unskilled manual work skills, is thirty times more likely to be unemployed than is a 'standard' male. But equally there is a contextual effect. The probability of being unemployed for a 'standard' male is 20 per cent greater if he lives in London and 70 per cent greater if he lives in some other metropolitan area. For the 'standard' woman these figures are 35 per cent and 60 per cent. The disadvantages are multiplicative. For example, educational performance may be affected by high levels of local unemployment which discourage pupils from trying to improve their levels of skills and formal qualifications. In the conurbations of the North and Midlands the pattern of cumulative disadvantages associated with employment decline means that more workers lack qualifications, that more of them are likely to occupy unstable jobs, and that there is a wider disparity in unemployment rates between those in stable and unstable employment. Such growing disparities have not been helped by inter-regional migration, since the moves of people have been socially selective, contributing little to any adjustment of the balance of supply and demand for unskilled workers and leaving behind in areas of net out-migration an increasing proportion of unskilled workers in the labour forces of the declining areas. In London, for example, while the unskilled comprise almost one-third of active men, they contribute only 10 per cent to the regional stream of out-migration to the rest of the South East (Buck, Gordon, and Young, 1986). The context within which a household lives and the personal characteristics of its members are therefore important additive contributors to the chances of that household's well-being. Place, as well as people, matters.

The political complexion of an area in such equations provides yet a further, albeit only partly independent, dimension. Increasingly the flavour of local politics is associated with the structural characteristics of localities. Conservatives have established ever stronger hegemony in the rural and small-town heartlands of the South; Labour has increasingly been reduced to the rump of its urban and industrial heartlands, the party of an urban underclass. At local-government level, Labour controls no fewer than twenty-eight of the thirty-six metropolitan districts; in seven there is no overall party control; the relatively affluent Solihull on the outskirts of Birmingham is the only metropolitan district in which the Conservatives maintain control. The same is true of only three of the London boroughs. At national-government level, Labour is firmly entrenched in all of the inner cities: it has all eleven of the constituencies in Glasgow; all of the five in Manchester; all of the six in Leeds; all of the three in both Newcastle and Hull; and all but one of the six in Liverpool and the six in Sheffield. Only in Birmingham is this virtual hegemony of political control of the large provincial cities incomplete, since there the eleven seats are split between six Labour and five Conservative members of parliament. The polarizing effect of the first-past-the-post electoral system has helped to exacerbate the political divide between a Labour party of the North and the large city, and a Conservative party of the South and the small-town and rural areas. Political control is important for a number of reasons, especially at local-government level. The legacy of inherited attitudes and patterns of political control goes some way to explain the details of the warp and woof of local circumstances: long-standing control by one or another political party helps to lock in a locality to predetermined ideological responses to change. The reactions of a perpetual Conservative authority—of a Hereford or a Solihull—or of a Labour area such as Salford or South Shields differ from those of areas in which political control has been more vacillating—such as Birmingham or indeed Liverpool. And, amongst Labour areas, differences are just as apparent between those in which conservative patriarchal Labour control has been maintained and those in which a 'new polycratic' culture has led to hard-left Labour dominance. Long-standing Labour control of a large city will have made more likely a higher pattern of local spending on social and welfare services, partly reflecting need but partly reflecting ideology. It will most probably be associated with a disproportionate supply of council housing and a stock of high-rise housing from the 1960s and 1970s, with all of the problems that such housing has subsequently brought in its train, but with the benefits of offering a stock of rented housing for the poor. Long-standing Conservative control will be associated with low spending and low rates and hence with less social-service provision. There are clear costs and benefits to different groups of people. Labour control brings with it on one hand the provision of good amenities; but on the other a generally unyielding entrenched bureaucracy and a legacy of financial problems now made more severe through rate-capping and the reduction of local-authority freedom to spend resources. Conservative control brings with it a less rich provision of public goods and services, but low levels of local taxes for those who have to meet them. Increasingly, in the context of economic decline, the nature of local political control has had effect on the *local* response to unemployment; with Labour authorities being more active in developing local economic initiatives and Conservative authorities being better placed to develop joint activities with the private sector.

Monitoring the spatial patterns of well-being

Such dimensions can clearly be seen in all of the many exercises in monitoring social well-being. They all suffer from the problems of uncertainty about what variables should best be used to measure the slippery concept of well-being, and about how the variables might best be aggregated into a single index. Further, there is the problem of how best to define a 'unit' of observation for which to take measurements. If there are consistent spatial differences, say between suburban and inner areas, then whether the spatial boundaries of an urban unit are defined generously or narrowly will clearly affect the value of the score that it shows. This is nowhere more so than in the case of how one handles London boroughs. In terms of absolute population size and for administrative purposes, London boroughs are equivalent to whole towns elsewhere. In functional terms, however, it is more logical to regard London as a single complex labour-market area. The London boroughs should therefore be compared with wards or small areas within the major provincial conurbations. This means that the oft-quoted suggestion that Hackney is the most deprived area in Britain (as for example in the Department of the Environment's own calculations in 1982) makes little sense, since it is but part of a larger and much more affluent labour-market area. In 1981, for example, Hackney, Liverpool, Manchester, and Birmingham all had high and not dissimilar levels of male unemployment. But the internal distribution of those unemployment rates showed clearly that Hackney is not a functional unit, since all of the unemployment rates for its constituent wards fell uniformly within a band between 15 and 20 per cent, whereas the large towns more closely—if still very imperfectly—approach the concept of functional labour markets, with some high and a few low rates across the set of wards. By comparing wards, it is clear that the provincial towns have areas of concentrated deprivation much more severe than any of those within Hackney (Fig. 1.2). In 1981, the highest rate in Liverpool was in Everton with 44 per cent; in Manchester, Hulme had 37 per cent; in Birmingham, Deritend had 34 per cent. By comparison, within Hackney the highest level was in King's Park with 22 per cent. Comparing like with like, the

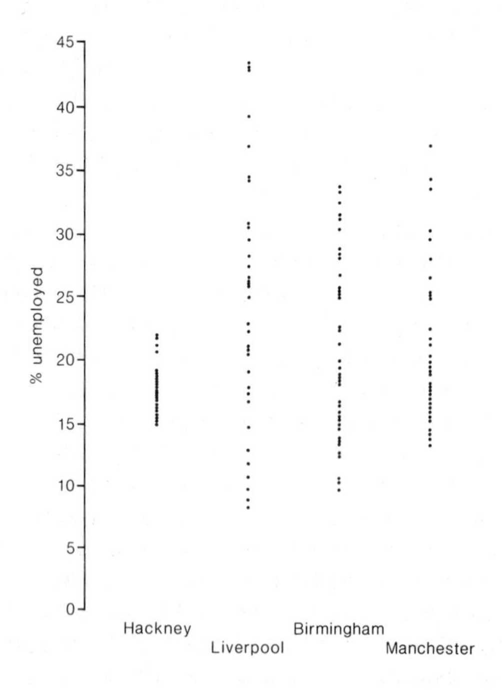

FIG. 1.2. Distribution of the percentages of unemployed men aged 15–64 for the wards of Hackney, Liverpool, Birmingham, and Manchester

Source: 1981 Census.

levels of distress are significantly higher in the big industrial cities of the North.

Nevertheless, for all of the difficulties of calculating indices, the results of social monitoring show great consistency. Two of the many sets of indicators show this to good effect. The first is from Begg and Eversley (1986), who based their calculations on 160 indicators measuring lack of choice and lack of opportunity in a set of 85 functional areas. The resulting lists of towns show that the most extreme cases of deprivation are uniformly found in the large old industrial cities. Their listing (shown in Table 1.1 for the 27 most deprived areas) ranks places on a combined list of favourable and unfavourable indicators and suggests that the degree of deprivation is more overwhelmingly severe in the conurbations than in the smaller free-standing cities. Wherever they compare the inner cores of large cities with the peripheral areas, it is consistently the inner urban areas which show the most marked symptoms of deprivation. The outer estates of council housing show an interesting pattern, since they are relatively advantaged in terms of housing, ethnic, and demographic indicators, but massively disadvantaged in terms of economic and social-class indicators. Some of the smaller cities, such as Plymouth or Stoke, have levels of deprivation not greatly dissimilar to those in the large conurbations, although the scale of the problem is smaller because of the relatively small size of the population involved. On the other hand, the tracts of inner London, such as Hackney, score relatively well partly because, on the favourable indicators, *all* London areas score quite well. Nevertheless the scale of the deprived population in London cannot be ignored. Indeed, there is much to be said for the view that it is worse to be deprived in an area of greater affluence.

Those places which score best, on the other hand, are the smaller, free-standing, and more rural areas. There is clearly a consistent gradient related to size and running from the small free-standing places to the large metropolitan areas. At the extreme, it is the metropolitan counties—Merseyside, Manchester, West Midlands, Tyneside, Clydeside, West Yorkshire, Teesside, and London—which show the worst features, with some of the other large towns such as Hull joining this list of deprivation.

TABLE 1.1. *The 27 most deprived areas, 1981, according to Begg and Eversley*

Ranking	Population
1. Glasgow core	181
2. Glasgow periphery	170
3. Birmingham core	235
4. Hull core	51
5. Derby core	54
6. Manchester–Salford core	289
7. Liverpool core	250
8. Nottingham core	70
9. Teesside core	236
10. Other W. Midlands cores	388
11. Other Strathclyde cores	74
12. Other Gt. Manchester cores	292
13. Leicester core	121
14. Merseyside periphery	51
15. W. Yorkshire cores	343
16. London Docklands	437
17. Plymouth core	34
18. Other Tyne and Wear cores	276
19. Sheffield core	228
20. Newcastle/Gateshead core	215
21. Other Merseyside cores	336
22. Other S. Yorkshire cores	132
23. Stoke core	48
24. Hull periphery	216
25. Hackney and Islington	337
26. Kensington, Chelsea, Haringey, Westminster	209
27. Lambeth	156

Note: The areas are ranked from most to least starkly deprived.

Source: Begg and Eversley (1986).

Such data clearly confirm the big-city dimension of disadvantage. Yet there is also an independent regional facet to deprivation. Begg and Eversley note two spatial belts of affluence; one along a line from the south coast to Lincolnshire and a second along a line from West London to Bristol. The second study—of booming towns—shows this spatial patterning to even better effect (Champion and Green, 1985). Champion and Green's measures are taken for functionally defined local labour-market areas (LLMAs) and they use only five indicators —two of employment change, one of population change, and two cross-sectional variables measuring unemployment and (as a proxy for affluence) households with two or more cars. The top fifteen most favourable scores are all found in towns within the South East and all but three are in the direct ambit of London, forming an almost unbroken arc of affluence around the western fringe of London from Crawley and Hayward's Heath in the south to Milton Keynes and Aylesbury in the north (Table 1.2). Significantly, almost all of these affluent areas have a high proportion of jobs in the financial sector. Those that lie outside the top octile of financial employment are the three towns outside the ambit of London—Winchester, Milton Keynes, and Aylesbury—together with Basingstoke and Crawley; four of which are New or Expanded Towns whose rapid growth is attributable largely to planned overspill from London. A diametrically opposite pattern describes the

TABLE 1.2. *The highest and lowest scores on Champion's index of economic performance*

1. Winchester	·
2. Horsham	·
3. Bracknell	·
4. Milton Keynes	266. Corby
5. Maidenhead	267. Middlesborough
6. Basingstoke	268. Peterlee
7. High Wycombe	269. Port Talbot
8. Aldershot	270. Greenock
9. Bishop's Stortford	271. Birkenhead
10. Aylesbury	272. Irvine
11. Hertford	273. Liverpool
12. Crawley	274. Bathgate
13. Haywards Heath	275. Sunderland
14. Woking	276. Hartlepool
15. Guildford	277. Coatbridge
·	278. South Shields
·	279. Mexborough
·	280. Consett

Source: Champion and Green (1985).

most deprived places. The worst 35 labour-market areas pick out the industrial heartlands of Central Scotland, Tyneside, Teesside, Merseyside, South Yorkshire, the West Midlands, and South Wales; with Corby in the East Midlands and the remoter parts of West Wales being outliers. In total, 55 of the top 70 labour markets are found in the South East and, of the 31 labour-market areas in the London Metropolitan Region, no fewer than 24 are in the top quartile. By this measure, an area in the London Region has over 5 times more chance of being in the top octile on the index than is the case for LLMAs nationally. This is the old North/South divide writ large, following the division long ago suggested by Sir Cyril Fox in his distinction between Highland and Lowland Britain which divided the country into areas south-east and north-west of the line from the Severn to the Wash. The most interesting of Champion and Green's findings is that the the North/South dimension is a stronger explanation of the differentiation of prosperous areas than is industrial structure *per se*. By dividing the labour-market areas into categories, it is clear that the North/South dimension overrides the structural characteristics of the 280 LLMAs. In virtually every case of comparable *types* of area, it is invariably those in northern regions which show worse circumstances: northern manufacturing towns are more deprived than southern manufacturing towns; northern commercial towns are worse than southern commercial towns; even northern rural areas are worse than southern (Fig. 1.3). Their subsequent updating of these patterns shows just as strong a regional and urban impact on what is clearly a highly divided Britain: even though there are 'brighter' places in the North, 'the place with the most dynamic record of change in the Northern region can manage only 74th place in the national rankings [of 280 places] and that for the North West only 85th place' (Champion and Green, 1988).

Such distinctions are of long standing within Britain. They were graphically described by Donnison and Soto (1980), in their attempt to discover the 'Good City', using 1971 data. They distinguished between 'new' and 'traditional' Britain: at one extreme, towns with a base of new industry, or New Towns or residential suburbs; at the other, those with a base of old heavy industry and textiles and those in Central Scotland

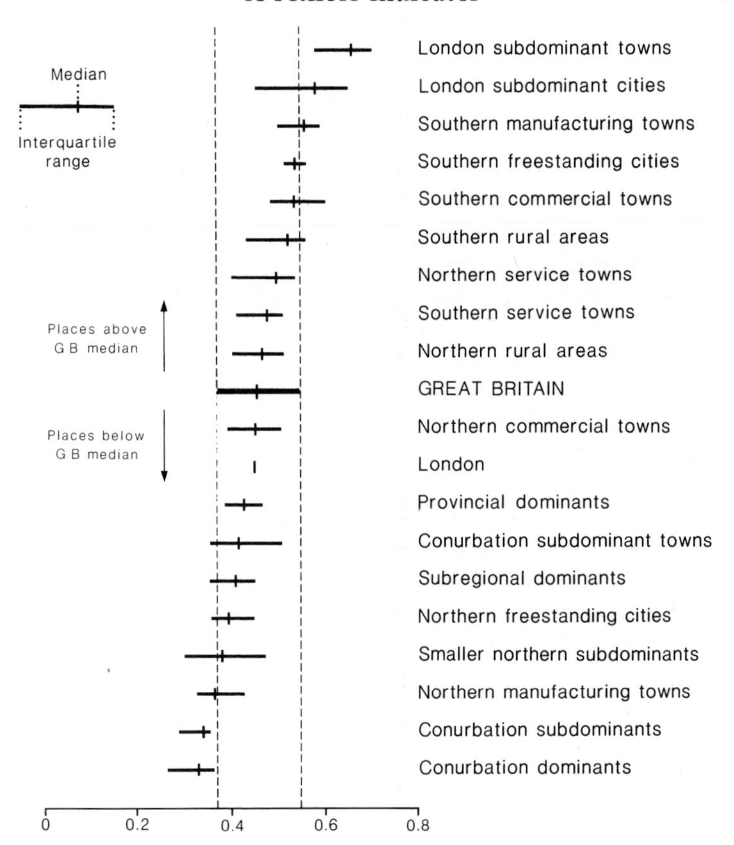

FIG. 1.3. Economic performance of functional groupings of towns

Note: For each category of town the median and interquartile range are shown. Better-performing towns lie above the GB median.

Source: Champion and Green (1985).

and the Welsh mining valleys. Like Champion and Green, they argued that such distinctions had a separate independent influence on the fortunes of those who lived in prosperous or depressed places. Levels of unemployment for similar occupational groups showed marked variations across the several categories of town, and the most vulnerable residents gained or lost most from the context in which they lived. As they comment, 'although all classes suffer from unemployment in the less prosperous towns, the least skilled suffer most; and although all gain from the prosperity of more fortunate towns, the least skilled gain most' (Donnison and Soto, 1980, p. 108).

Urban and regional interplay

It is clear, then, that there are two principal contextual dimensions, each of which has independent influence on the map of distress. There is an urban/non-urban dimension and a separate regional dimension along the line of the Severn/Wash. This dual impact of geography has grown stronger as recession has deepened. It is now not merely the inner areas of towns, not even whole town economies, which suffer. Rather, in the North, it is whole regions which have felt the impact of recession and its associated job loss and economic immiseration. This twin urban and regional pattern is not gainsaid by evidence that there are areas of relative prosperity in the North and deprivation in the South. The regional and urban well-being of the country has been likened to Emmental: more cheese in the South, more holes in the North. There are indeed areas of affluence in north Cheshire, or in areas such as the upper Tyne valley which are parts of the commuting hinterland of the professionals working in the large depressed conurbations; there are affluent enclaves within the big cities—Solihull or Edgbaston in Birmingham, Didsbury in Manchester, Gosforth in Newcastle. For those in employment in such enclaves, and particularly for those in professional employment, living standards are indeed high. Conversely, there are deprived areas in the South such as those in the Isle of Sheppey or in some of the inner boroughs of London and in inner areas of the larger cities such as Bristol, Portsmouth, or Plymouth. There are, of course, rich areas and rich people in Bangladesh or in Burundi, but that seems not to persuade us that the overall poverty of those countries cannot be distinguished from the affluence of such developed-world countries as Britain or the United States. The relative affluence and the scale of that affluence in the North of England never approach the levels or the scale of that in the South, while, running across this regional divide, the contrast between the large old cities and the smaller towns provides a recurrent motif of urban deprivation which reaches its apogee in the inner urban areas.

It is this broader national and regional context within which the distress of the inner urban areas needs to be set. The charting of these most deprived areas is helpful, but it has to be remembered that they are but part of a continuum of deprivation and affluence. There is a danger that over-preoccupation with the apparently most disadvantaged areas can become self-fulfilling prophecy. The image of the whingeing northerner constantly crying 'we wuz robbed' is not conducive to ameliorating the situation. In another—more optimistic—time, worse deprivation and greater disadvantage were tackled by robust reformers against backgrounds of variable economic fortunes. The goals were clear, the fields of play obscured and overgrown. From the first timid Factory Act of 1833 to the Welfare State of 1945–50 the aim was to make all of Britain 'comfortable'. Having conspicuously failed in that aim we now seem unsure whether we even want to go on trying. We made the cities and the conurbations; we allowed the polarization of the regions; we live in a socially and economically divided Britain. This is no time for a loss of nerve or a loss of will. What are the nettles we need to grasp?

DEMOGRAPHIC LOSS

Demographic loss of population was the first indicator of urban problems. Indeed, because of the selective nature of out-migration and the differential reduction in tax base, population loss has itself become a problem, not merely the indicator of a problem. Within Britain, loss of population from towns and particularly from the inner areas of towns is of long standing. The flight to the suburbs can be traced to the middle years of the nineteenth century with the move of the more affluent to such newly conceived and newly built suburban middle-class areas as the West End of London or Victoria Park in Manchester. In the inter-war years and in the decades after the Second World War, the suburban migration achieved major dimensions, and in the 1950s most of the large towns began an absolute loss of population. Between the 1951 and 1981 Censuses the largest towns lost on average of the order of one-third of their population, most dramatically so in their central areas.

Liverpool's population fell from 791,000 to 510,000, Manchester's from 709,000 to 449,000, London's from 3.7 million to 2.5 million. In each case, it is as though one in every three residents has disappeared. Some part of this loss was planned. The rash of huge out-of-town council estates which replaced the inner-area slums and housed the population of clearance areas was part of this. The building of New Towns dates from the same period. With some 100,000 houses per annum being cleared in the peak years of such programmes, the 1950s to early 1970s represented a time of profound physical restructuring of British cities; and the physical change entailed equally massive social and perceptual change. Communities were broken up and, added to the considerable social mobility of those affluent decades, populations which had long been physically and socially immobile were shaken loose in a process that was both liberating and traumatic. Looking back from the vantage-point of a generation later, it is clear that the process of slum clearance was on a scale which dwarfed all previous population movements. The hand of God had once wiped out whole villages through the bubonic plague, the hand of man had enticed people to the growing towns in the early nineteenth century, but only the clearance of poor housing areas to make way for railways in the late nineteenth-century cities can compare with the planned and organized upheaval of post-Second World War reconstruction and reorganization. In those post-war years, the whole map of the central areas of almost every major city was massively redrawn and new—and often discordant—street lines and building layouts were crudely superimposed through comprehensive renewal as planners tried to come to terms with the desire for new forms of transport and new scales of organizational structure, both in public housing and in business and commerce.

It would be wrong to stress the uniqueness of this British experience as a prompt to the massive out-migration of households in the post-war decades. Nevertheless, the role that formal planning played in Britain was an important trigger and stimulus to the timing of the change. Similar processes took place in America at the same time—and with similar results. Of Harlem, a novelist summed up the sense of bewildered disruption that ensued:

Sometimes she seemed . . . to be like a survivor of some incomprehensible war. Building after building where she found her small apartments had been torn down, and she had taken her things up and found another building only to have it destroyed in its turn. She had moved from one side of Harlem to another, never sure when she would be forced to move again, and never understanding what it was that was laying waste to building after building, block after block, the destruction as sudden and as complete as if there had been some kind of attack, with weapons so frightening that no one could bring themselves to talk about them. (Charters, 1986, p. 48.)

And where America and Britain led, European countries later followed. The pattern of population out-migration across a range of countries has followed a progression; America and Britain experiencing earliest loss, with Germany following, and now with signs of population loss evident in many of the cities of what Hall calls 'Atlantic Europe', but with urban population gain still occurring in many parts of Mediterranean Europe (Hall and Hay, 1980). The logic of the sequence is related roughly to the industrial longevity and maturity of the countries concerned. Urban population loss need not necessarily in itself be a problem, but where it is associated with the de-industrialization of old industrial urban economies the combination of demographic and urban decline entails severe social and economic problems (Cheshire, Carbonaro, and Hay, 1986). The pattern across Europe shows a concentration in a belt of old industrial cities stretching from Italy through Belgium, parts of Germany, and northern France to the northern parts of Britain (Fig. 1.4).

The lineaments of this urban population loss are now well established. The bigger and older the city the greater the loss. As Fig. 1.5 shows, there is a very clear relationship between population loss and the size of settlement. The diagram uses urban density as a proxy for the size and age of cities so as to avoid the difficulties of defining a 'true' boundary within which to measure the population size of cities. It shows a strikingly consistent pattern. with the partial and special exception of the New Towns, all the large cities have lost population massively; the only gains have been found in smaller places. In America the flight from the cities in the 1970–80 decade led to widespread debate about whether the

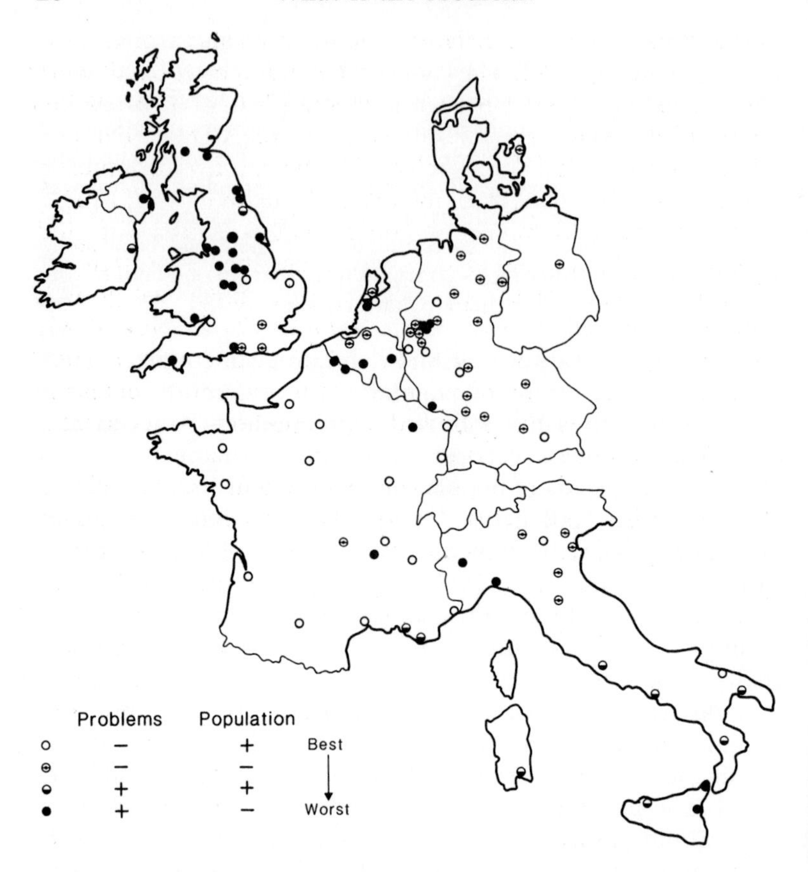

FIG. 1.4. Urban decline across the EEC in the 1970s and early 1980s

Note: Cities are arrayed on two dimensions: population change and urban problems. The extremes are shown as solid and as open circles: solid circles show severe population loss together with severe problems; open circles show little population loss (or population gain) and an absence of problems. The problems of urban decline are concentrated in a belt of older industrial cities from Turin in Italy to south-west Scotland.

Source: Cheshire, Carbonaro, and Hay (1986).

decade represented a 'clean break' in the settlement pattern, a turn-around in the trend of urbanization (Vining and Kontuly, 1978). An equally heated debate ensued on both sides of the Atlantic about whether one was dealing with 'counterurbanisation', 'deconcentration', or 'decentralisation' (Gordon, 1979, Fielding, 1982; Hamnett and Randolph, 1982; Roberts and Randolph, 1983). Between 1971 and 1981 every British city of over 250,000 lost population, with the exception of Plymouth, whereas many rural areas such as Norfolk, Cornwall, Somerset, Powys, and the Scottish Highlands and Islands grew by over 10 per cent, thereby reversing more than a century of rural population loss. The places which declined represent the familiar roll-call of the engines of earlier industrial growth; those that gained make an unfamiliar litany of the New Towns and erstwhile market towns. At the least, this reversal must change our perception of the prompts to growth. It represents an outward and visible sign of the profound structural shifts in the operation of the economy as a whole.

Interestingly, there are signs of a slow-down in the relative loss of urban population in the last few years. London's population loss has slowed in relative terms, as have those of

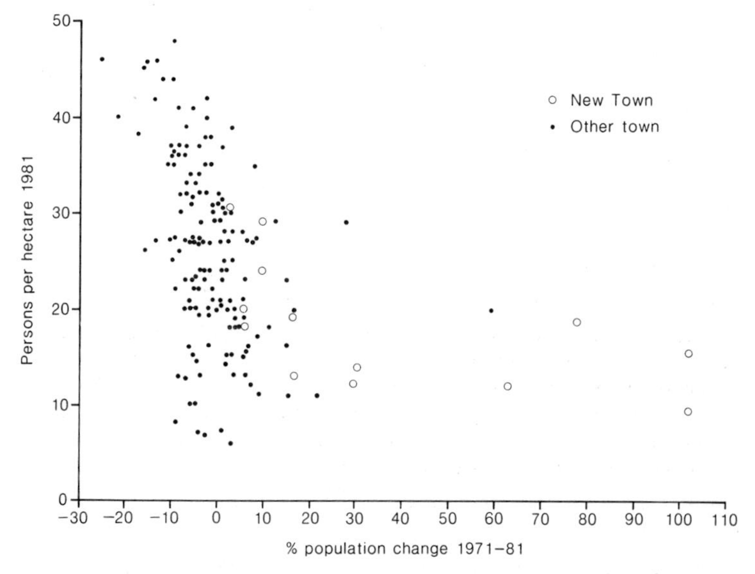

FIG. 1.5. The decline of large towns. The relationship between density and population change 1971–1981 in English towns of over 50,000 inhabitants

Note: New Towns are shown as open circles.

the large provincial cities. Champion has seen this as a reversal of the trend of the last three decades (Table 1.3), but talk of a renaissance of the population of London and other large towns seems premature. In recession—just as in the 1930s—it is clear that households become less mobile and, indeed, that some of the unemployed may return to their areas of origin where they can more readily seek the informal support of established networks of kin and contacts. Lower rates of overall mobility were evident in the reduction of residential mobility from around 11 per cent per annum in 1961–71 to less

TABLE 1.3 *Recent population change in large cities*

(*A*) Greater London	Population change (% per year)	
	Inner boroughs	Outer boroughs
1961–6	– 0.82	– 0.11
1966–71	– 1.93	– 0.21
1971–6	– 1.99	– 0.61
1976–81	– 1.49	– 0.36
1981–5	– 0.37	0.00
1981–2	– 1.32	– 0.13
1982–3	– 0.32	– 0.09
1983–4	0.01	0.03
1984–5	0.13	0.20

(*B*) Large cities	Population change (% per year)		
	1971–81	1981–5	Shift
Greater London	– 0.96	– 0.14	+ 0.82
Birmingham	– 0.68	– 0.33	+ 0.35
Glasgow	– 2.16	– 1.30	+ 0.86
Leeds	– 0.37	– 0.25	+ 0.12
Sheffield	– 0.51	– 0.41	+ 0.10
Liverpool	– 1.42	– 1.22	+ 0.20
Manchester	– 1.37	– 0.62	+ 0.75
Newcastle	– 0.89	– 0.17	+ 0.72
Great Britain	+ 0.08	+ 0.11	+ 0.03

Source: Champion (1987).

than 10 per cent in 1971–81. Mobility has declined in response to economic recession. If household mobility leads to outward movement, as it has over many decades, it is inevitable that any diminution in rates of movement will thereby slow down the *relative* rate of loss of urban population. The real question is what might happen when the economy recovers and mobility increases. Will this reopen the increasing flood of outward migrants from large cities to smaller towns and rural areas?

Social polarization

Associated with the population loss has been an increase in the poverty and deprivation of large cities as differential migration has re-sorted the social characteristics to the loss of inner urban households, on one hand, and the gain of suburban and small-town populations on the other. Migration has always been age- and ability-selective. Inevitably the re-sorting of population has changed its social composition in space. The piling up of the poor and deprived in urban areas is not as consistent as might popularly be thought, but there is no doubt that there has been a considerable relative polarization of the poor in inner areas. This has been exacerbated by the changes in the housing market in the post-war decades. The inexorable growth of owner-occupation and the growth and subsequent stabilization and decline of council renting has meant that there is now a much closer correlation between poverty and council tenancy and an increasing dominance of the stock of inner-area housing by council properties (Robson and Bradford, 1984). The polarization can equally be measured in terms of health, where all of the measures of morbidity and mortality suggest not only the extent of ill-health and premature death in inner areas, but the degree to which the disparities have widened over recent years (Department of Health and Social Security, 1980; Townsend, Phillimore, and Beattie, 1987). Housing policy has clearly exacerbated this polarization through the sale of council houses, the reduction in new building, and the financial incentives to climb the ladder of owner-occupation for those who are able to take the initial step of purchase (Bentham, 1986). Even in London, where the reverse trend of gentrification has been most marked, the overall pattern of social composition between 1961 and 1981 has shown an increasing polarization between an ever-more affluent suburban and outer area and an ever-increasing immiseration of the inner areas. The scale of reverse movement of the professional managerial and intermediate groups into inner London boroughs has not compensated for the loss of such groups from the traditional high-status areas of London. It is only very locally in the peripheral low-status areas such as Islington and Hammersmith that increases in owner-occupation have been accompanied by absolute increases in professional and managerial households (Hamnett and Randolph, 1986).

It would be an exaggeration to talk of a uniformly poor state-dependent population in inner urban areas, but it is nevertheless true that we have moved a considerable way towards this. For local councils in the large cities this can be both blessing and curse. It increases their dependence on central government for grants, but Labour councils have equally seen their large council tenancy as a fiefdom whose dependence helps to assure political support and legitimacy. The fact that Labour has consolidated its hold at local elections in most of the largest urban areas is a symptom of this symbiotic relationship between political master and dependent tenant.

If we were to caricature the ideal-type large old inner urban area it would be one which has lost population massively from its inner areas and, overall, has lost one-third of its people in the last three decades. The remaining households are predominantly poor and state-dependent, living in council housing and reliant on social-security benefits. The one demographically buoyant element in the population has been the ethnic groups which now form significant statistical proportions of urban populations, especially in their inner areas. They have brought both demographic expansion and some economic vitality to those areas. Given the younger age distribution and the higher, although now declining, fertility regimes of households of New Commonwealth and Pakistan origin (NCP), they make a disproportionate contribution to births; within the districts of Greater Manchester, for example, between 1971 and 1985 NCP births rose as a proportion of all births from 8 per cent to 17 per cent in Bolton, from 9 per cent to 12 per cent in Manchester, and from 5 per cent to 16 per cent in Oldham. Since between 65 per cent and 75 per cent of such groups live in metropolitan counties, this continuing fertility differential clearly has implications for the large cities. Households with origins in Pakistan, India, Bangladesh, China, Hong Kong, the West Indies, and West Africa have replaced the earlier immigrant-derived populations of Irish and central European origin, have introduced new religious groupings which have established themselves in the abandoned white churches, have brought an increasingly mature but nevertheless still fragile commercial presence into the fringe areas of the inner zone, and, with high rates of birth, have provided the one buoyant source of children to inner-city schools which have suffered disproportionate declines in their pupil rolls.

ECONOMIC COLLAPSE

The economic dimension of urban decline has been evident only more recently, but it has followed the same pattern as that of population loss; an outward ripple of contraction which has had its worst effects in inner cities and in northern regions. Nationally there have been major sectoral changes in the economy which have involved: a relative switch from manufacturing to service activity; a growing absolute loss of employment in manufacturing and, more recently, only the most minute gain in service employment; a switch from full-time to part-time employment, associated in large part with a growth in female activity rates; and a spatial re-sorting of employment so as to create what has been called a new spatial division of labour (Massey, 1984). The sectoral changes for Great Britain and for the North West are shown as an example in Fig. 1.6. As elsewhere, the only really consistent employment growth in all of these changes has been in the professional and scientific service jobs and in producer services such as banking, insurance, and finance. In all other sectors the losses have been considerable; and such changes have been accompanied by the spatial re-sorting of occupational groups throughout the country. The new spatial division of the labour force, based on differing occupational composition, can be seen as having replaced the older regional specialization based on industries. Whereas, for example, the North East once specialized in mining, shipbuilding

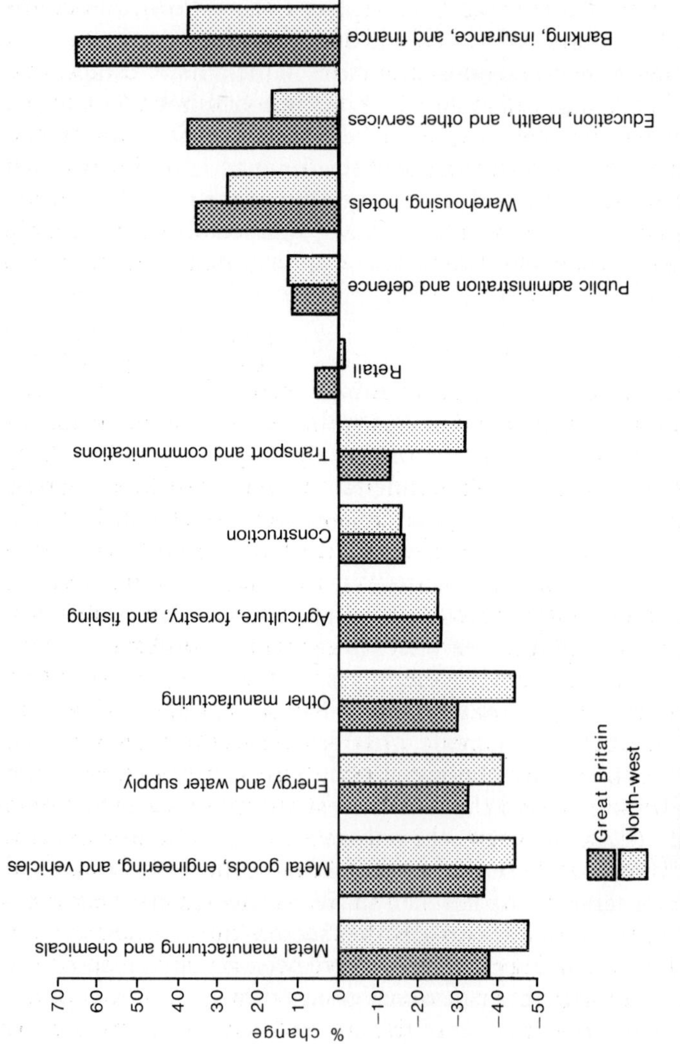

FIG. 1.6. Employment change by sector, Great Britain and the North West, 1971–1986

Source: Employment Gazette.

and ship repair, and steel, South Wales in coal and steel, the North West in textiles and mixed engineering, and the West Midlands in car production, now the pattern has become one in which research and development and higher-level managerial decision-making functions are concentrated in London and the South East, while lower-skilled routine production activities of all kinds have concentrated in more northern areas. It is this spatial division which has become self-reinforcing to create a decision-making, information-rich, affluent South and a routinized, low-skill, impoverished North. In all of such changes cities have lost out most dramatically. Again, the summary figures bear this out by showing the clear relationship between the size of settlement and the extent and nature of job loss (Fig. 1.7). There is a marked contrast both between large cities and small towns and between the inner and outer areas of the cities themselves. The pattern is again a widespread one, not restricted to Britain, with similar changes evident throughout most of Europe (Keeble, 1986) and in North America (Clark, 1984).

Case-studies of individual cities provide many graphic illustrations of this employment collapse in Britain's cities. Glasgow is one of the most dramatic (Lever and Moore, 1986). For the Clydeside conurbation as a whole, manufacturing employment fell from 387,000 in 1961 to 187,000 in 1981, with faster rates of loss in the 1960s (at 8,000 per year) and the late 1970s (at 23,000 per year). Service employment grew relatively fast in the 1960s from 315,000 to 407,000, but only slowly in the 1970s and hardly at all in the late 1970s, to reach 431,000 by 1981. In the inner city, manufacturing virtually collapsed from 227,000 in 1961 to a mere 90,000 in 1981. In the 1960s overall decline in the conurbation had been −6 per cent, with some employment growth in instrument and electrical engineering and with growth in all the service sectors apart from distribution; but in the 1970s the overall rate of loss increased to −13 per cent, with every manufacturing sector losing employment and with some, such as iron and steel, electrical engineering, textiles, and vehicles, being reduced to approximately one-half, and the only major growth in employment being found in financial, professional, and miscellaneous personal services. Since these data are for the whole conurbation,

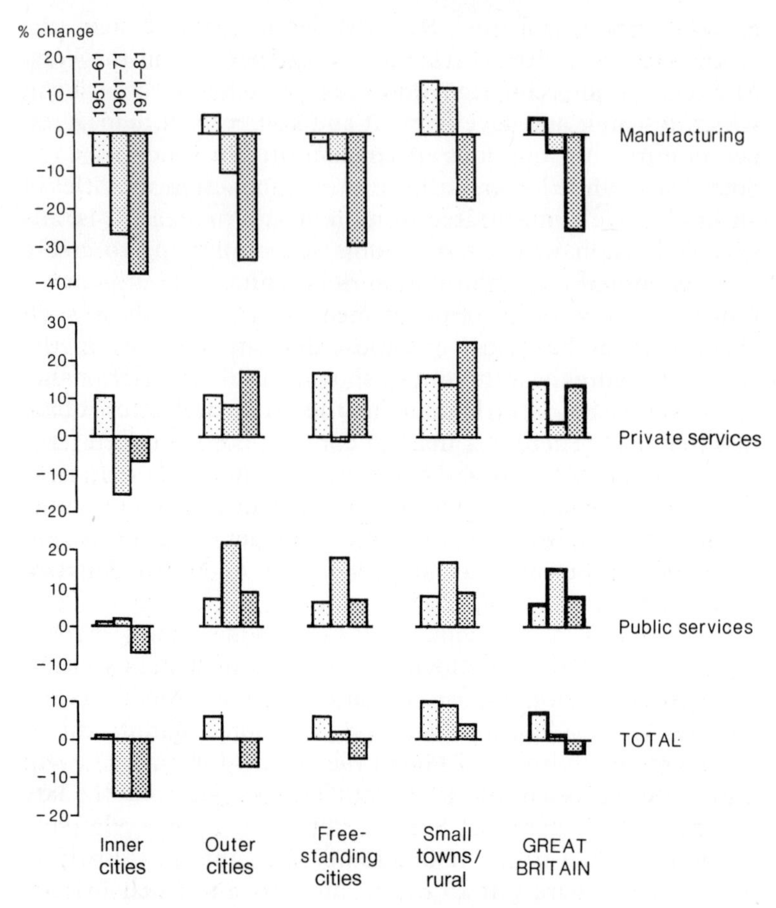

FIG. 1.7. Employment change in rural and urban areas, Great Britain 1951–1981

Note: Cities are the 6 conurbations of Greater London, West Midlands, Merseyside, Greater Manchester, Tyneside, and Clydeside. Freestanding towns are the 17 next largest cities.

Source: Begg, Moore, and Rhodes (1986).

such job losses cannot be attributed to short moves across the boundary to peripheral suburbs: they represent the closure or contraction of the existing traditional and newer activities of the conurbation's industrial base. Nor were the small increases in service jobs likely to have provided alternative employment for some of the massive losses in manufacturing, since the service jobs were clerical and professional non-manual, which favoured a much higher proportion of women. The West Midlands shows an even more dramatic turn-around from having been relatively buoyant in the post-war decades, to experiencing a massive industrial collapse in the 1970s (Spencer *et al.*, 1986). Between 1978 and 1981 its manufacturing jobs declined by 20 per cent. Between 1981 and 1983 the conurbation suffered 156,000 redundancies, over 85 per cent of which were in its five key manufacturing sectors of vehicles, metal goods, metal manufacture, and mechanical and electrical engineering. The Manchester case reinforces the patterns of such changes. Lloyd and Shutt (1985) are able to record no fewer than 22 industries which lost more than 20 per cent of their base-year employment in the period 1978–82. These include man-made fibres (which had lost 85 per cent of its 1978 employment), spinning and doubling of cotton (−46 per cent), electronic computers (−45 per cent), iron and steel (−34 per cent), paper and board (−29 per cent).

Unemployment

All the large provincial cities have suffered such contraction of employment since the onset of recession from the middle of the 1970s, and the losses grew progressively up to the deep recession in the early 1980s. Job loss has resulted not from the movement of firms away from cities, but largely from the shedding of labour from *in situ* plants or the closure of whole firms (Lloyd, 1980). The result has been horrendous levels of unemployment throughout the largest cities: levels which have only partly been ameliorated by the effects of net out-migration. These levels of unemployment clearly reinforce the picture of a gradient running outwards from inner areas to peripheral areas of the large cities. The only consistent distortion to the outward gradient is the appearance of outliers of high unemployment in most of the large peripheral council estates. In the case of Manchester, for example, the highest levels of unemployment are found in inner areas, where overall levels of over 30 per cent were found in 1986 in central wards with ethnically mixed populations such as Hulme (with 48 per cent) and Moss Side and in white inner areas which have suffered from the closure of traditional engineering firms such as Ardwick. The outer council estates in Wythenshawe, where levels of over 30 per cent were found, provide the exception to the othewise regular gradient of inner/outer differentiation (Fig. 1.8).

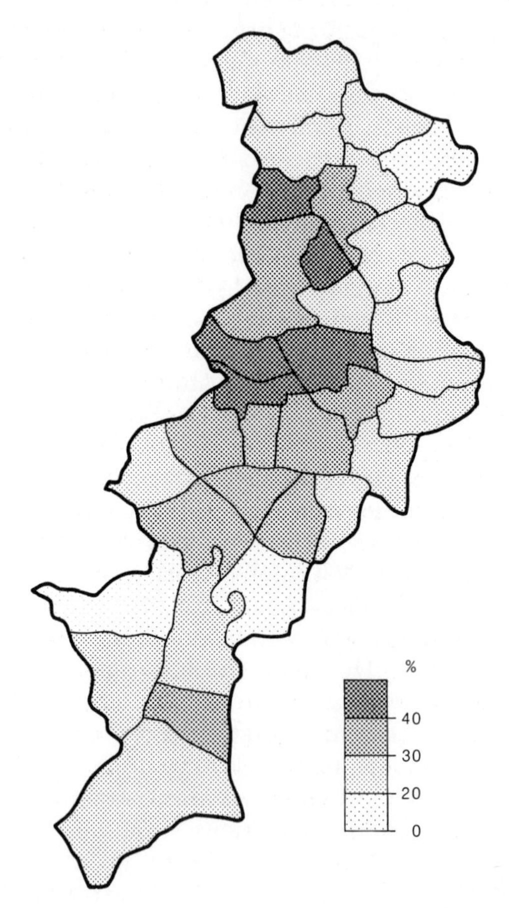

FIG. 1.8. Male unemployment in Manchester, 1986 (the inner/outer gradient)

Note: The peripheral council estate of Wythenshawe lies in the south of the city.

Source: Manchester City Council (1987).

There is considerable variability between different cities in the shape of their loss of employment. Two of the important determinants of that variability are the industrial or service base from which they started and the economic buoyancy of the region in which they lie. Labour-market balance sheets show how the different experiences of Bristol, London, Glasgow, Newcastle, and Birmingham were comprised (Fig. 1.9). In these five conurbations, the percentage increases in levels of unemployment were not dissimilar, varying from a low of 5 per cent in London to 11 per cent in the West Midlands, Tyneside, and Clydeside, but the balance sheets by which these figures were obtained differed markedly from place to place. Demographic change, change in the participation rate, and the level of commuting from suburban areas create the change on the labour-supply side and the net creation or loss of jobs creates the supply of employment opportunities. All have to be considered in understanding the balance of unemployment. Greater London and Clydeside are alike in having suffered large-scale loss of both labour supply and employment; the West Midlands and Tyneside are alike in having high increases in unemployment through growth in labour and loss of jobs, but the growth in labour has been arrived at by different means—with Tyneside's dramatic growth in activity rates being associated with its historically low initial level of female participation. Bristol illustrates in particular the role of commuting as a critical determinant of the relationship between job change and labour-force change since its growth in local employment was more than cancelled out by the high increase in labour supply through the impact of commuting from outside. The open nature of job markets is an important element in understanding the way in which growth or contraction are translated into the well-being or the immiseration of local residents.

House-price changes

The collapse of the economies of cities and the old industrial urban regions—concentrated as they are in the north of the country—has been most dramatically reflected in the differential changes in house prices in the last decade. This serves as perhaps the single most telling indicator of the joint effects of

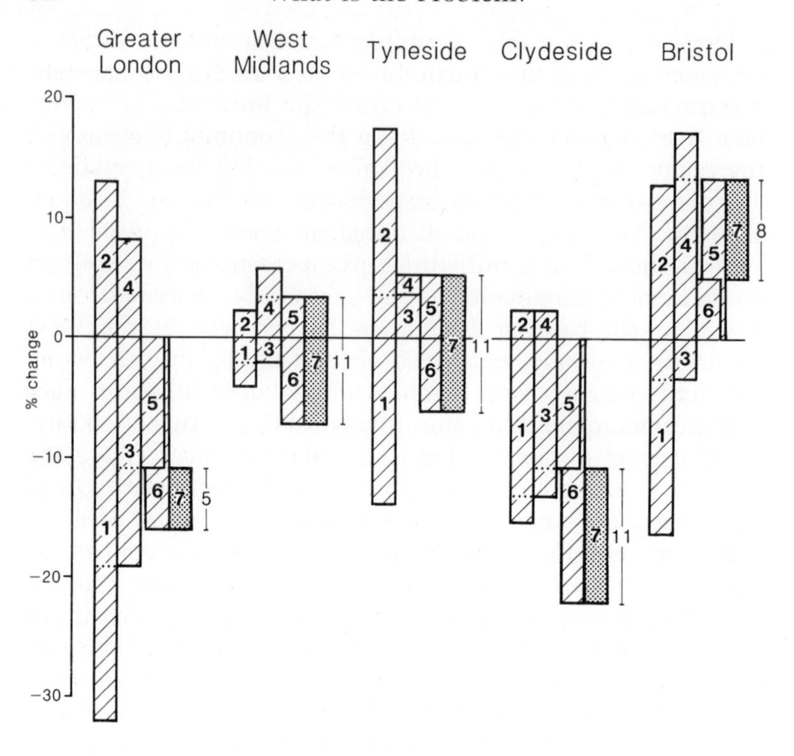

FIG. 1.9. Employment balance sheets for Greater London, West Midlands, Tyneside, Clydeside, and Bristol, 1951–1981

Note: Each numbered bar shows the positive or negative contribution of the components of change for the period 1951–81. The product of bars 1 and 2 = bar 3; 3 and 4 = 5; and 5 and 6 = 7. The resulting increases in unemployment are shown as percentage figures.

Source: Begg, Moore, and Rhodes (1986).

the social and economic divisions between North and South and urban and non-urban Britain, since price changes reflect the level of current and of expected future demand in an area. There has long been a regional distinction in house prices, with price rises first having effect in London and the South East. In the past there has been a tendency for regional prices to maintain an unequal equilibrium over time as northern prices have eventually partly caught up the rises in the South over a longer period (Hamnett, 1983).

The earlier pattern of price changes can be seen in the surge of the late 1970s for the two most urban regions, Greater London and the North West (Fig. 1.10). Inflation in house prices in that boom showed *relatively* close correspondence between the northern and southern areas; the levels of increase in Greater London were felt earlier and were consistently greater at the height of the increase, but this was partly compensated for by the later down-turn in the North West. Over the most recent cycle of house price recession and growth, however, there is no indication that the rise in the South in the years since the deep recession of 1980–1 has been reflected elsewhere in the country, fuelled as that South East rise has been by overseas investment and the impact of high salaries in the growing financial sector based on the City of London. The price surge in the 1980s has therefore shown a very different and much more sinister pattern, with no indication of the southern growth being echoed in the North West. The annual price rise for 1986–7 was 26 per cent in Greater London and 24 per cent in the South East, as against 7 per cent in the North West and 3 per cent in the North, and that differential has continued for some five years. The gap between the two has consequently grown progressively wider and the cumulative effect on absolute price levels has indeed been considerable. For the first quarter of 1987 the average national house price of £43,000 was greater by a substantial margin than the average of *every* region outside Greater London, East Anglia, and the South West (Table 1.4). The comfortable professional selling a detached house in any of the regions except the South East and East Anglia would be unable to afford the price of even a flat or a maisonette in Greater London and would be able to afford only a terraced house in the South East. If the population projections of OPCS are borne out to the end of the century—showing as they do a continuing net out-migration from the North and West—there is little indication that market pressure will provide a stimulus to reverse this growing disparity. Like the differential out-migration from cities, this exacerbates the process of 'locking-

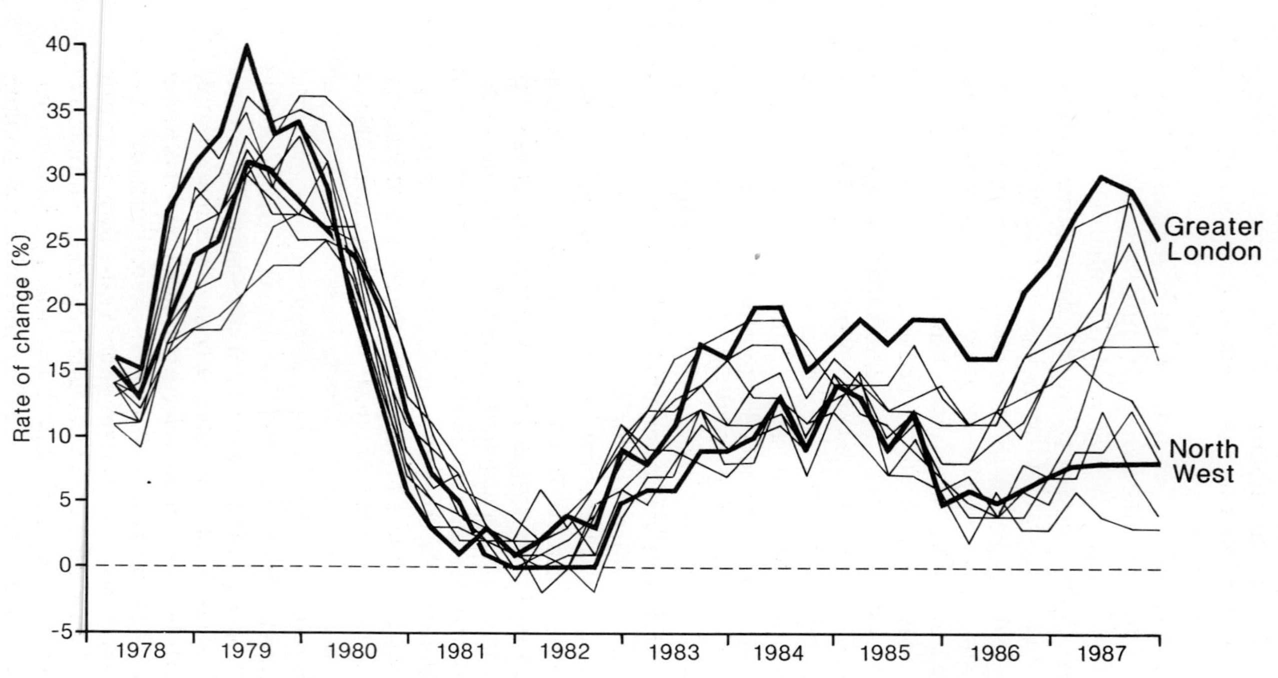

FIG. 1.10. Rates of change in average house prices in Greater London and the North West, 1977–1987

Note: The discrepancies between these two regions are echoed throughout the other regions in England, which are shown as background lines. East Anglia and the South East are similar to Greater London. Northern regions are similar to the North West.

Source: Nationwide Building Society.

TABLE 1.4. *Regional prices for semi-detached houses, first quarter 1987*

	£
North	28,750
North West	29,640
Yorks./Humberside	29,130
W. Midlands	30,190
E. Midlands	29,340
Wales	29,420
East Anglia	40,980
South West	41,190
Outer South East	49,710
Outer London	65,870
Greater London	80,940
United Kingdom	42,720

Note: Based on loans approved by the Nationwide Building Society.

Source: Nationwide Building Society (1987).

in' large numbers of families to areas of decline—either because of the constraints of the council-house sector which make cross-authority transfers difficult or because of the lack of equity in an existing house through which to trade up in the vastly more expensive housing market of southern areas. As a composite indicator of the economic disparities of the present, these growing differences presage a yet deeper future locking-in of the economic prospects of residents in northern cities.

ENVIRONMENTAL DEGRADATION

Environmental dereliction has been the seemingly inevitable element of urban decay which has accompanied the losses of population and employment. The withdrawal of investment from cities has left them with large tracts of despoiled and abandoned land, partly in private hands, but largely in the ownership of local authorities or statutory undertakings such as British Rail or the public utilities of water and electricity. The definition of derelict land provides problems; for example, the Department of the Environment's definition is of land 'so damaged by industrial or other development that it is incapable of beneficial use without further treatment' and therefore excludes a good deal of 'brownfield' that lies vacant (Chisholm and Kivell, 1987). Nevertheless, the national surveys by the DoE in 1974 and 1982 provide the best indication of the scale of dereliction and its concentration in the large cities. The surveys show that, of the English total of 43,273 hectares in 1974 and 45,683 in 1982, no less than 27 per cent was found in the seven major conurbations in 1974 and that the figure had risen to 32 per cent in 1982 (Table 1.5). Many of the cities had restored large acreages during the period, but still ended up with even more dereliction than they had started with. Add to this the empty, boarded-up housing of local authorities and private landlords, the partly abandoned, sometimes partly demolished, high-rise flats which are the legacy of the 1960s and early 1970s, and the collapsing infrastructure which dates from the last century in the form of sewers, utility lines, roads and pavements, and the like, and it is not surprising that the metaphor of wartime bombing is used so frequently in descriptions of large areas of cities such as Liverpool or Glasgow.

Alongside the physical decay have come the increasing vandalism and the litter and graffiti associated with affluence

TABLE 1.5. *Derelict land in the seven English conurbations, 1974–82*

	Area derelict (hectares)		Total area restored, 1974–82
	1974	1982	
Greater London	324	1,954	422
Greater Manchester	3,405	4,035	1,727
Merseyside	529	1,716	390
South Yorkshire	1,565	1,110	871
Tyne and Wear	1,314	1,458	1,000
West Midlands	1,535	1,833	1,104
West Yorkshire	2,857	2,640	1,104
TOTAL	11,529	14,746	6,348

Source: Chisholm and Kivell (1987), from official DoE surveys.

and the challenge to traditional authority during the last few decades. That Alice Coleman could use a measure such as density of faeces in her descriptive studies of the relationship between building design and social malaise speaks volumes for the decline in the physical environment of cities in today's recession by comparison with that of the 1930s (Coleman *et al.*, 1985). It is small consolation for those in the inner cities to know that the swirling garbage on their streets is a testament to the general affluence of a throwaway society. The contrast with many European (but not American) cities is instructive: even those European cities which suffer many of the same problems as those in Britain have managed to provide a better physical environment. There is more than the deceptively straightforward dimension of economic hardship to the environmental squalor of British cities. The lack of self-discipline and the failure to respond to exhortations about maintaining a clean environment are, perhaps, part of the general malaise which affects sections of the urban young.

Crime and unrest

Nothing in the squalor of inner cities commands more instant attention than urban riots. The major disturbances of 1981 and 1985 focused popular and official attention on the plight of cities. The riots undoubtedly reflected genuine economic distress, the casual violence of an alienated population, and above all the often merited hatred felt alike by black and white youths towards the police as emblems of an alien authority. The 1981 riots were analysed at official level in the Scarman report and in Manchester by the local Hytner report (Home Office, 1981; Greater Manchester Council, 1981). The more recent disturbances in 1985 in Handsworth, Brixton, and Broadwater Farm, triggered in each case by ill-judged behaviour by local police forces, did not merit national inquiries (although, like Manchester before, it, Birmingham set up its own local enquiry into the Handsworth unrest). They have been discussed at length by a variety of commentators (Benyon, 1984; Benyon and Solomos, 1987). It is clear that official responses to these later disturbances suggest a growing hardening of attitude. Government reactions were dominated by views of the criminality of the disturbances rather than by any more liberal concern for messages that riots might convey of hardship, disillusionment, and ill-treatment.

Less well publicized, but equally unnerving and distressing for those unwittingly involved, are the minor upsurges of violence which occur with monotonous regularity in some city areas. It should be noted, however, that such violence is something found with surprising frequency in small and more favoured free-standing towns. Despite the oft-repeated implication that 'urban' and 'riot' are synonymous, the frequency of disturbances in small towns ought to give pause for thought in any assumption that it is only cities that 'breed' violence. In the last few years, places as supposedly idyllic as Shrewsbury, Buckingham, Stroud, Chertsey in Surrey, Weston-super-Mare, Brighton, and Oxford have all experienced occasional or recurring incidents of white-led serious disturbances (Kilroy-Silk, 1987). The football hooligans of Cambridge can readily outdo the followers of Manchester United or Liverpool. Most tragically, the massacre at Hungerford ought to give the lie to the common impression that violence is a peculiarly urban phenomenon. Indeed, it would not take great effort to compile a tally of small-town violence which would put to shame the degree, if not the frequency, of urban turbulence.

The difference in small towns is that there the police have more time and manpower to deal with such outbreaks and that the media treat such occurrences as the exception, as in the Hungerford massacre, thereby reinforcing the stereotype that crime and violence are intrinsically urban. It is the frequency of 'trivial' disturbance which affects city residents, particularly in deprived areas. They may be nightly disturbed by violent, drunken youths only to find when their local community constable intervenes that he is beaten up since no back-up help is available. Even more are such residents concerned about the daily round of crime. In Manchester, interfering with cars or taking and driving them away is an almost minute-by-minute occurrence. Much of the breaking and entering, mugging, and the variety of petty theft is opportunistic crime. It affects those already deprived more harshly than those who can afford the luxury of alarms, strengthened glass, and good insurance. The impossibility of, or at the least the extra premiums associated with, insuring property in inner areas—and not least in areas of heavy ethnic business—have been widely recorded (Patel and Hamnett, 1987). Such problems reflect partly the reality and partly the stereotypes of the violence of inner areas. There has been a response from government through targeted assistance arranged through consortia of insurance companies, but the existence of the problem says much about the reality of living and working in such areas. It is probable that, despite the horrendous stories of attacks on elderly people, life in the city is now less violent than at the turn of the century. Nevertheless, our expectations, quite rightly, are for a life less shadowed by both fear and experience of crime. It is easy for academics to say piously that the 'hooligan has always been with us' (Pearson, 1981) or for penal reformers to quote the high figures for re-offending consequent on imprisonment. That is of no help to the pensioner bilked by the false official or the young single mother whose meter has been broken into. Of all the factors that affect the quality of life for those already under stress as members of the urban underclass, real or imagined crime is probably the worst.

CONCLUSION

The picture that emerges of the life and prospects of inner cities cannot be other than bleak. To summarize their recent experience, Table 1.6 draws together the contrasts between urban and rural areas by looking at indices for population loss, employment change, and levels of unemployment. For the inner cities of the six main conurbations in Britain, population by 1981 had fallen 35 per cent below the level of 1951; jobs had fallen by 45 per cent and unemployment, which had stood at 33 per cent above the national figure, stood at 51 per cent above by 1981. Such figures suggest something of the scale of the growing concentration of economic, social, and environmental distress of our major cities. The nettles to be grasped are indeed profuse and unpleasant. So far the palliatives offered have been of the dock-leaf variety, calculated to soothe if not to eradicate the cause of the sting. It might be suggested that a few nettle-beds in obscure places should be of little moment; that concern should lie with the healthy and attractive plants elsewhere. Keen gardeners know the flaw in that argument.

TABLE 1.6. *Indices of population and employment change in urban and rural areas* (Great Britain index = 100)

Residents of	1951	1961	1971	1981
(a) Changes in population of working age				
Inner cities	100	93	77	65
Outer cities	100	92	87	87
Free-standing cities	100	96	94	91
Towns and rural areas	100	106	114	117
(b) Changes in total employment				
Inner cities	100	89	71	55
Outer cities	100	97	97	93
Free-standing cities	100	93	91	85
Towns and rural areas	100	105	112	120
(c) Unemployment rates				
Inner cities	133	136	144	151
Outer cities	81	82	88	101
Free-standing cities	95	107	112	115
Towns and rural areas	95	93	90	90

Note: Inner and outer cities are London, Birmingham, Manchester, Liverpool, Newcastle, and Glasgow. Free-standing cities are the 17 next largest cities.

Source: Begg, Moore, and Rhodes (1986).

2
Why Bother?
The Measure of a Man

> The ultimate measure of a man is not where he stands in moments of comfort, but where he stands at times of challenge.
> *Martin Luther King*

The geographical location of 'uncomfortable' Britain is clearly more widespread than the snapshot of places defined by the terms 'North' and 'South', 'inner' and 'outer' city, however blurred may be their definition. The nettles in the garden of Britain, those distressing symptoms of change, encompassing decay and decline, are widely scattered. The inner-city areas do not have a monopoly of social, economic, and environmental distress, as is apparent in the decay of the outer estates such as Kirby in Liverpool or Wythenshawe in Manchester or Easterhouse and Drumchapel in Glasgow. Indeed, many would add that the problems of *rural* deprivation cannot readily be dismissed. The colonization of the countryside by the new footloose urban élite has undermined rural services such as transport and local shops and increased the isolation and immobility of the rural poor. Recently I took a visitor from Devon to see some of the inner areas of Liverpool and Manchester: her reaction was, 'There's nothing new in this. Come to the run-down estates and back streets of Plymouth, walk out into the idyllic villages of the West country and there's poverty, bad housing, and unemployment.' Sally Holtermann's pithy observation is still apposite: 'Most of the deprived do not live in deprived areas and most of those who live in deprived areas are not themselves deprived' (Holtermann, 1975). Yet, while it is clearly true that much deprivation is found outside inner areas, and indeed outside large towns as a whole, the large cities do represent concentrations of deprivation of a size and an intensity not found elsewhere. There are both larger numbers and higher densities of the poor and underprivileged in the Liverpools, Manchesters, Birminghams, and elsewhere than in smaller places or in rural areas.

But the question then arises, does it matter that there are such spatial concentrations. Poverty has long been with us; why bother that the poor are differentially concentrated in large cities? Should we not be channelling all of our energies and our resources into *general* policies to ameliorate disadvantage, wherever it may be found? Were we to lessen inequalities, the mere fact of their being concentrated in urban areas would consequently mean that effective policies to tackle poverty would have a differential benefit to urban areas. Many of the arguments about the genesis of urban problems do indeed emphasize the general nature of the processes which work against cities—that the problems are ones *in* but not necessarily *of* cities. By this token we could best attack the problems of cities not by developing specifically *urban* policy, but by developing *poverty* policy.

To a large extent this argument is irrefutable: whether they be called basic income support, negative income tax, tax credits, or unitary tax system, such universal approaches to poverty have to be an essential element of any serious attempt to address the problems of the poor and deprived. There are, however, many reasons why it is important that we consider the *urban* dimension and the case for saving cities *per se*, and therefore consider the justification for developing policy that is specifically urban.

EQUITY AND EFFICIENCY

The first argument is based on equity. We have to accept that not even the most dramatic poverty programme can eradicate relative deprivation. If the relatively poor are likely to remain relatively spatially concentrated, there are additional multiplier effects associated with that concentration which exacerbate their disadvantage and make it cumulative and self-reinforcing, thereby justifying a policy of affirmative action to offer such groups the opportunity to break out of that downward spiral. Even if this argument were to find little support, there is then the efficiency argument which asserts that equitable outcomes can most efficiently be achieved by the concentration of resources; that there are administrative advantages and the benefits of scale economies through concentrating assistance in limited areas where the poor are concentrated. Patch work, suitably co-ordinated, makes best use of housing resources, of primary health-care facilities, of education, even of the all-too-often unpopular social workers. Spatial concentration should therefore be of concern in any policy-making which addresses issues of equity, over and above any general concern about well-being. Generations of schoolchildren used to be taught the unpleasant adage used by Robert Lowe when introducing 'payment by results' into education in 1861: 'if the system is not efficient it will be cheap, if it is not cheap it will be efficient.' It may well be that the spirit of our age would be ready to respond to the suggestion that spatially directed policy would at least be efficient and that thereby it could create the conditions for more equitable outcomes.

It is not hard to enumerate the prompts through which a spiral of self-reinforcing decay sets in. Poor people mean less investment in local shops and higher prices within those shops; lower expectations of pupils' performance in schools; less willingness by employers to recruit from the area; higher expectations of criminal behaviour and hence less tolerance from or more stereotyping by the police; less willingness by insurance companies to insure properties and businesses against vandalism or damage, or at best the charging of higher premiums for that insurance; less willingness by banks to invest in the potential of entrepreneurial ideas; more competition and fewer opportunities to develop alternative incomes from the informal economy. There is ample evidence that all of such attitudes and behaviour can be and have been found applied to concentrated areas of disadvantage and they militate against the likelihood of the poor family in a poor area being able to pull itself up by its bootstraps. For those who begin to make some headway, the millstone of stereotyping hangs round their necks by nature of the address they give. There can, in fact, be a multiplicative disadvantage suffered by those who live in areas of deprivation.

The counter-argument to this is that the poor who live in areas of affluence face greater costs and greater loss of self-esteem than those who are surrounded by others who are equally poor: that to be poor in Winchester is worse than to be poor in Wigan since life is more expensive, there are fewer fellow sufferers through whom to seek support, and the visibility of the affluence of others increases the stigma and sense of inadequacy of those who are poor. Even though most of the really poor who live in affluent areas may have the benefit of council housing, there are indeed additional costs which they face by virtue of living in rich areas. Public transport is often infrequent and expensive in areas where the two-car family is the norm. The higher cost of private housing both creates more marginal home owners—for whom the increasing level of repossession through mortgage defaulting suggests the growing extent of the problem—and increases the levels of homelessness in areas which have attracted large net immigration but have too few council houses and privately rented houses to offer accessible accommodation. Against these disadvantages has to be set the greater possibility of employment in an area of some economic growth.

Some of these latter views carry less weight than once they might have. It has been suggested that it is more galling and more shaming and more difficult to sustain one's poverty if the evidence of others' success is more immediately apparent. However, this is less convincing today when the images of affluence have more universally and insidiously penetrated the homes and the awareness of people through the impact of television. The relative affluence of much larger numbers of people and the increased social, economic, and geographic mobility that followed 1945 have rightly increased expectations; they have also increased greed and selfishness. It is fashionable to contrast the current 'I'm all right Jack' attitude exhibited by much of comfortable Britain with a supposedly idyllic earlier world of neighbourliness, community spirit, and unselfish sharing, where poor people lived together in a continuous glow of communal activities and popping-in to neighbours to borrow tea. Much of this is a mythical paradise much touted by those historians and sociologists who rely upon the dubious recollections of elderly people. It ignores the enthusiasm and the genuine relief of those who welcomed the chance to break out of the old ways and the mean streets. For every recollection of community spirit garnered by those with axes to grind there are memories of spite, jealousy, and violence. Then, as now, life was more difficult for those trapped in areas of disadvantage. Only an armchair theorist safely musing—preferably on a well-paid television programme—on the delights of poverty in the past as opposed to the present could suppose otherwise. The fact of cumulative disadvantage, demonstrated both by Buck and Gordon and by Donnison and Soto, is an argument for tackling social disadvantage on a concentrated urban basis, and this is reinforced by the greater efficiency of administration and delivery associated with tackling such problems in a concentrated fashion.

Lurking behind arguments about equity and efficiency is the very real anxiety about widespread social unrest. Such apprehension of the urban mob has a long history, as Stedman-Jones's (1971) study of the fear of social unrest in turn-of-the-century London has graphically shown. There may be some doubt about the novelty of urban disturbances in Britain; indeed Benyon's catalogue of violent incidents during the supposedly quiescent years of the 1930s shows the inter-war period to have been less tolerant, less law-abiding, and less pleasant than it is often nostalgically depicted. Rather, it supports the view of the 'devil's decade'. He gives the lie to suggestions that the experience of the 1980s was on a scale or of a nature unique to this century (Benyon and Solomos, 1987, pp. 38–41). There may also be doubt about the degree to which unrest is as exclusively an urban phenomenon as is popularly supposed, but there is no doubting the fact of the large-scale rioting in Bristol in 1980, in Liverpool, London, and Manchester in 1981, and in Birmingham's Handsworth and London's Brixton and Broadwater Farm in 1985. As yet, research suggests that these public disorders are only weakly associated with indicators of social malaise. Deprivation may be a necessary but not a sufficient condition for such disorder. Parry and Moyser, for example, looked at Moss Side in Manchester, Burngreave in Sheffield, and Glodwick in Oldham—areas whose overt degrees of material deprivation make them not dissimilar, yet amongst which it was only in Moss Side that serious rioting occurred in 1981 (Parry, Moyser, and Wagstaffe, 1985). Local knowledge of people and events in that area would confirm the implicit and explicit findings of the

Hytner report (GMC, 1981) that the policy and behaviour of the police were the most important factors in those disturbances. Trying to soften their more critical statements the members of the Hytner inquiry embedded in their detailed and helpful recommendations about the police the pious statement that 'we believe that the worst police force in the United Kingdom is preferable to the overwhelming majority of police elsewhere'. Unfortunately such soothing words have not prevented inept police policy, coupled with incompetent and possibly corrupt behaviour, from being the sparks which have set alight the tinder available in massed spatial deprivation; a view endorsed with some vigour by recent commentators on 'the roots of urban unrest' (Benyon and Solomos, 1987).

Much has been made of the fact that, in the later London disturbances, conditions on the Broadwater Farm estate had improved. But footloose youths, jobless and disgruntled, are easily roused to anger and violence. Deprivation, while causing suffering and creating tensions wherever it may be found, is clearly not a sufficient prompt to disturbance. Simmering resentment at unemployment, discrimination, and harrassment may smoulder for a long time, but their continued presence is a risk to be eliminated. 'We believe', said the Hytner report (p. 54):

> that the raw material for rioting is made where young people are left, rightly or wrongly, with the impression that they have nothing to gain from established society, *particularly where they have hitherto not yet gained any stake in it* [emphasis added]. Where this grievance is underlined by disappointed hopes, a belief that they are and will continue to be discriminated against and they are continually surrounded not only by the affluence of others, but also advertising pressures to engage in material acquisition, their resistance to lawless conduct will be that much weaker; the situation will deteriorate further if habits born of idleness bring them into conflict with the police.

The sad fact that too many of these young people are black is a further reflection on the racism endemic in our society. One of the more unpleasant facets of comment on the urban disturbances of the 1980s has been the suggestion that 'it only happens in cities and it only happens where there are blacks'. Given our history of urban *and* rural riot (the Gordon riots,

Captain Swing, Rebecca, Chartists, Blackshirts, *white*-led race riots in Liverpool and Cardiff in 1919 and 1946), such supposition is patently untrue. It is even untrue that the disturbances of the 1980s were uniquely urban—despite the impression created by the media that it was 'the city' which caused rioting. Less glamorous—or less glamorized—disturbances were found in places like Lincoln, High Wycombe, and Newport Pagnell. Indeed the recurrence of disorder in the latter small town must amount to a 'Newport Pagnell syndrome' which should make us beware of the myth of the inherent evil of the city (*Newport Pagnell and District Herald*, 9 January 1987). What *is* true is that many ethnic minorities are found in areas of disadvantage. Some stay despite economic success because they prefer to be near their own people, their own black-led church or mosque or temple, their own shops; others have to stay because they have been pushed into poverty and unemployment. Their future well-being must be part of the argument.

A further strand in the case for developing urban policy is the economic one of greater efficiency in the use of the existing resources and infrastructure in city areas. If, as the evidence suggests, there is a process of cumulative decay associated with inner-city dereliction, many serviceable buildings and much potentially valuable land will be drawn into the downward spiral of decline and hence represent a heavy net loss of resources for the nation as a whole. There are both direct and indirect costs entailed in this. On the one hand are the underuse and abandonment of the buildings, land, and services which exist in cities; on the other are the opportunity costs represented by the use which is made of the alternative areas which *are* developed—areas not currently used for residential or industrial or commercial uses and which could have been used for recreation, agriculture, forestry, and the like. In this, the hotly fought arguments about Green Belts come into play since the current disputes about the future use of rural areas are directly involved in the urban dilemma. With forecast levels of 20 per cent of agricultural land now being surplus to the needs of our efficient agricultural industry, the way appears open to encourage further large-scale development of rural areas for housing and other urban-related types of land use. The ALURE (Alternative Land-uses for Rural Areas) plan helped to open up a debate which has focused on a variety of possible rural land uses: development of housing and associated services, recreation in the form of golf courses and leisure parks, forestry, and new forms of non-intensive agriculture. Current indications are that central government has continued to offer some, but fluctuating, support to the concept of Green Belt protection and to planning restraint on development in rural areas; policies which have been among the mainstays of physical planning in post-war Britain, through which the containment of towns has been achieved. Tillingham Hall, the first of the many proposals for a new private New Town in southern rural areas and one which lay within the London Green Belt, was refused permission at the inquiry stage. Time will tell whether a more sympathetic hearing will be accorded to other of the proposals in the pipeline (such as Foxley Wood, Wilburton, Bishop's Park, Brenthall Park, Chafford Hundred, Leybourne, Maiden Bower, Southwater, Hook, Great Lea, Bracknell, Stone Bassett, and Caddington, which form a complete ring around London). Ominously, Berkshire, in an area of development pressure, has been unsuccessful in its attempt to limit housing approvals to 36,000 houses by 1996 since the Secretary of State for the Environment has ruled that the number should be increased to 43,500 (*Independent*, 30 January 1988). Despite the advocacy of non-plan which was represented by Peter Hall and Rayner Banham, who suggested in *New Society* in the late 1960s that all restraints should be lifted from the development of land, we are still faced with the fact of being a small and densely populated country in which open space and land for public access is at a premium. While it is true that the policy of urban containment has had a strong element of social unfairness, through its 'drawbridge' effect of preserving pleasant areas for those who already live in them, there is no guarantee that any new attempt to open up the countryside for further development would not be just as socially inequitable and would not merely draw yet sharper divides between the comfortable and uncomfortable in an extended form of social spatial segregation. Unless the proponents of rural development are able to suggest mechanisms to ensure a socially just means of development, history leaves one suspicious of the likely outcome of a hands-off process of rural development.

In this context decaying cities represent a potentially valuable resource—of buildings and infrastructure, of people and of land—which is currently underused and growing more so. And, contrary to the marginal adjustments posited by neoclassical economists, there is little evidence that the disparities reflected in house prices are growing any less, or that such spatial inequalities are attracting new investment to areas where factor costs are lower. Inflation nodes of intense activity in the South East can seemingly coexist with the swathes of depression elsewhere. The economy as a whole suffers when national resources remain underused.

There are, therefore, both social arguments based on equity and economic arguments based on efficiency which justify the development of a consciously urban policy. At heart, these arguments raise the question of the economic and social benefits of alternative forms of settlement system. Why save the cities? Or, more precisely, why bother with the decaying conurbations of declining regions?

DOWN WITH THE CITY!

One of the much-publicized myths, and one of particularly long standing, is the myth of rural virtue and urban vice. The city—seen as a necessary evil which 'causes' decay and disruption—has in this view little to commend it other than the central services which it provides. The ironical fact that those who retreat to rural fastnesses spend much of their time in cars returning to cities is seen as a mere and normal concomitant of the 'good life'. If households vote with their feet to move to areas of lower density away from cities, why should one do other than welcome the opening-up of opportunities to allow people to live where they will? Should market forces not simply enable, indeed encourage, whatever settlement system people choose to enjoy? This is a seductive argument. It is also a dishonest one since it begs the question of whether the existing trends are 'natural' and inevitable. To what extent is it correct to make the assumption that people and enterprise 'choose' locations in rural areas or small towns?

There is strong evidence that the attractions of rural areas are, in no small degree, manufactured by conscious or unconscious policy decisions. Formal planning policy in the post-war years itself consciously aimed to encourage New Towns and to attract people and enterprise from cities to the new settlements in a process of planned dispersal. Now that New Towns are no longer being built by the state, is that not an end to the anti-urban bias of policy? Indeed, now that it is private-sector interests in the shape of Consortium Developments Limited which are proposing to build private new towns, does this not betoken the end of state-dominated policies which might work to the disadvantage of the cities? That would only be so were there to be a financially neutral choice between locations in urban and non-urban areas. The proponents of 'non-plan' can only be convincing by adopting a very restrictive definition of what spatial planning is: they view it, in other words, as merely the conscious act of physical planners to permit or to forbid developments in certain areas in response to revealed demand and within the framework of planning ideology and practice. A more realistic definition would include all those financial and structural decisions which create a context of differentially attractive investment in different areas. Public investment in infrastructure and services has helped to create attractions in the small towns of the Thames Valley; uniform charging rates for postage and telephones and for public services such as gas and electricity clearly work to the benefit of rural areas. Taxation policies have, consciously or unconsciously, created a financial context which has done much to influence the spatial attractiveness of different regions and different types of area. For example, taxation law in the form of tax allowances on mortgage interest repayments has long encouraged owner-occupation and the building of new houses at the expense of the upgrading of old. Since developers have found it easier to develop greenfield sites, such tax incentives have added a powerful stimulus to outward population moves. Tax law has also encouraged the sale of family businesses and thereby encouraged the growth of large multi-corporate enterprise through offering an unequal choice between the use of heavy capital taxation on the realization of gains or inheritance and the competing attraction of deferred taxation for publicly quoted companies. Faced with such a choice, few owners of family firms have been able to resist the legislatively created financial logic of selling, thereby helping to create a degree of corporatism and gigantism in British industry and business which is without parallel in other European countries or in North America. This has therefore hastened the closure of many local urban-based firms as restructuring has proceeded and has weakened the connection between industry and the local area in which it operates. In 1984, finance policy, with one hand, gave £168 million for regional support in England, thereby helping northern cities; but, on the other, offered incentives to taxpayers of some £8,000 million which flowed to areas supported by the market and thereby dwarfed the impact of regional policy. Such financial currents are 'on a scale that overwhelms any regional programme ever seen in Britain' (Heseltine, 1987, p. 154.)

In such ways one can argue that a differential financial attraction has been created whereby urban areas have been set at a disadvantage. The free 'choice' of location has not been one made in a financially neutral context. Furthermore, the lure of the country has been stengthened by the hype of modern advertisers never averse to using false images for their own ends. 'Country fresh', 'natural goodness', 'peace and quiet'; every possible cliché is used and reused. The long-established strand of anti-urbanism in Britain continues just as strongly today. It stems from the goals of the social hierarchy developed in the context of nineteenth-century industrialism, taking as the visible tokens of its success the trappings of an earlier landed gentry. The scaled-down versions of the country property continue to act as powerful imagery which sustains a rural myth which is based on a false premiss. As yet the voices raised against it are still too few (Weiner, 1981).

Despite the falseness beneath the enticing mask of rural life there are other arguments why we might be persuaded not to pursue an urban policy and not to try to discourage the movement of people and investments from cities. First, land in rural areas and small towns is still cheaper than in large cities. The encouragement of development in non-urban areas will therefore help to reduce the costs of enterprises and increase the international competitiveness of industry and business, not least in a period when technical change has placed an increasing premium on space for capital-intensive production in industry. Likewise for housing, cheaper land would reduce the costs of building. If there are bottlenecks in construction through the lack of space available for development in certain parts of the country, the release of extra land would reduce the cost of housing. By so doing it would potentially open owner-occupation to many first-time buyers who currently find the costs prohibitive. Nevertheless such policies to encourage development outside the large cities would seem likely to do little to reduce the problems of the most deprived. If anything they would probably merely achieve marginal shifts in the boundaries between comfortable and uncomfortable Britain. Were rural development to lie in the hands of private developers it would be the middle rank of incomes which would seemingly have the best chance of being the principal beneficiaries, since only they would be able to generate the market demand to which developers would respond. The rural drawbridge might be let down, but only to broaden somewhat the social spectrum of rural and small-town society—for those with the necessary credit to join in relative privilege. The filtering-down of housing to the poor is a most imperfect mechanism for extending the benefits of mobility; not least because of the tenurial divisions in the housing market and the sheer mathematics of the pyramid of wealth which is involved. There would thus be no guarantee that the poor would achieve even second-round benefit from a large-scale opening-up of the rural areas. Even if rural development were to be in the hands of local authorities, it would seem likely that it would merely repeat the experience of the peripheral estates of the 1950s and 1960s; the creation of relatively isolated developments faced with above-average living costs, especially for those without private transport. The better prospect offered by the increasing pattern of decentralized jobs may not benefit those who start off from a base of being unskilled or semi-skilled.

The second argument against urban regeneration would be that opening up the rural areas for housing and associating that with an enhanced programme to upgrade roads and build motorways would maximize the freedom of movement for households. The closest parallel to this is the charter for private transport in the United States in the years after 1956 when the country embarked on its massive interstate freeway system. Such freedom of movement is, of course, highly selective socially. Those who do not have cars have little freedom; and this would include not only whole households who lack cars, but many of the wives and children of the one-car household. Their mobility would in practice be likely to be yet further reduced unless massive subsidies were applied to public transport in the less densely populated areas. Those with cars, on the other hand, would have the benefit of ready access to the dispersed facilities which would be attracted to rural areas—to new out-of-town shopping centres, to far-flung social, medical, recreational, and cultural facilities. Apart from the increasing misery thus inflicted on the already disadvantaged, there is an additional constraint in Britain where the ratio of population to land mass is so much higher than that of the United States.

Third is the argument that the cost of developing new infrastructure on greenfield sites is less expensive than that of redeveloping worn-out infrastructure on sites which have already been developed. Existing 'brownfield' urban sites present many problems: complex existing use-rights impose legal costs and uncertainty about ownership; the need to make good already-used sites increases construction costs for laying new infrastructure or upgrading old, for example converting existing lines to incorporate new technologies such as fibre optics; the uncertain foundations of older structures add to the cost of building on their base; land despoiled by industrial waste or by pollution through the storage of chemicals is expensive to stabilize to acceptable levels; developing new streetlines reorientated on top of an existing and discordant geometry of services such as sewers, whose mapping is in any case often imperfect, creates considerable additional costs. As yet, we know insufficient about the details of the relative costs of different sites and of different geometries of the overall settlement pattern to be able to say with any certainty what the order of magnitude of such differences might be. From what *is* known, such costs of urban regeneration can be considerable in the short term but may, of course, work out cheaper in the long term.

UP WITH THE CITY!

'God made the country and man made the town', wrote the eighteenth-century poet Cowper. He may indeed have been thinking of smaller urban entities than the products of nineteenth-century industrial Britain, but both the attitude and the fact remain. Sheer pride might encourage us to help the city to survive by adaptation. There are, fortunately, more practical arguments.

First is the use of existing resources. While much of the infrastructure of the large old cities is in desperate need of renewal, much is serviceable and—at the extreme—the wholesale abandonment of cities would leave an incalculable set of assets unused. Indeed, as the urge for conservation has spread and as the rallying cry of 'heritage' has gained voice, so the realization of the longer-term commercial potential of much of the legacy of urban and industrial buildings has been more widely appreciated. Even the land itself, despite the cost of developing it, has considerable value in this crowded island.

Second is the argument that relatively dense settlement makes most efficient use of a variety of resources. Publicly provided services are more efficient when supplied to a concentrated population; energy costs are minimized by supplying gas and electricity to small concentrated areas rather than to a dispersed population; efficient district heating schemes become feasible in more densely developed areas and in any case there is a net saving from neighbours enjoying the benefit of each others' wasted heat within an urban heat island; fuel costs are reduced when the use of private cars is minimized or journeys are shorter; and the delivery of social services is more efficient when they can benefit from the scale economies of concentration. It is this argument for which we need an updating of the kind of calculus which Stone (1973) provided in looking at the costs of urban construction in the 1960s. What is the balance of advantage in a settlement system which is dispersed against one which is concentrated; how do the construction costs and the running costs of each compare? This is a different argument from the questions about the use of rural and agricultural land for development, which have been so hotly fought over ever since the inter-war years. The arguments on the efficiency of concentrated settlement in terms of running costs and resource saving are difficult to challenge. It is interesting, for example, that there is some evidence that the rise in petrol costs in Australia has been accompanied by some voluntary movement of population back to the cities, even though generally the patterns of car use seem highly price inelastic.

There could be disagreement about the effectiveness, if not the efficiency, of large-scale supply of services to dense populations. Large size can bring with it an insensitivity which helps to alienate the users of services such as schools, hospitals, and the like. The value of the small village school and the cottage hospital (where they still flourish) is still a telling part of the idealized image of country life. This, however, is not an argument which is exclusively related to the rural/urban dimension, but one about organizational structure, regardless of whether the organization is rural or urban. There is no reason why the supply of goods and services to concentrated populations, benefiting from scale economies, should not be organized in ways which devolve much of their implementation to local levels. The amount of local feeling attached to certain buildings, institutions, and organizations is as apparent in an old city like Manchester as in any village. It is a question of finding the practical means to channel that emotion.

Third is the practicality of the greater-number thesis. There are more poor people trapped in the cities. Opening up the rural areas would continue to work to the advantage of the haves and would drive yet deeper the divide between comfortable and uncomfortable Britain. In everyday terms poor people are better off in cities. Many living costs are externalized to the public sector and, so long as the welfare state provides income-related benefits, the costs of such services do not fall directly on the poor. The provision of free services is maximized so that libraries, formal recreational amenities, and the like are in greater supply. Private goods are less expensive within cities—even though shops within the immediate neighbourhood of poor areas often have higher prices. Furthermore, the informal economy is more feasible as an alternative prop to those who are out of work, given the density of opportunities within the city. Pahl's (1984) work on the Isle of Sheppey argued to the contrary that those who most benefit from the informal economy are those who least depend on it—those in work. But anyone with direct experience of life in any large city must find such formal conclusions hard to accept. Casual and sub-legal work among the poor in deprived areas may be no substitute for the financial benefits of a regular income from paid employment, but in the large cities of the North its extent is widespread. It leaves one to suspect either that the labour market of Sheppey differs from those in large northern cities or that social surveys are not a likely medium through which to assess the scale, range, and incidence of illicit and semi-legal activities.

Fourth, and following from this, the large city still offers a dense mesh of opportunity and of stimulus. This may be difficult to quantify, but the force of the argument is hard to dispute. At present cities offer a wide range of cultural and recreational opportunities in the form of clusters of theatres, concert halls, galleries, libraries, museums, cinemas, all of which depend on access to a large potential market of consumers. Nor are they all beyond the resources of the less well-off, so long as some public support of such facilities continues. Manchester like most cities offers extensive free or low-priced entry to its amenities as do those theatres, concert-halls, and other places sponsored by public monies. Even a more extensive privatization of many such facilities may not erode the force of the argument since this same good practice is now being followed by some commercial organizations. The location of such amenities may partly be a residue of history, through the legacy of those ebullient nineteenth-century buildings in which many of them are housed. But they require a large clientele for their continued operation and they benefit from the agglomeration economies which continue to provide the rationale for the groupings of museums in London's Kensington or of theatres in the West End. The alternative model is the provision of new peripheral entertainment complexes such as are now developing in the Gateshead Metro Centre or in association with major out-of-town shopping complexes such as exist in Milton Keynes or are proposed for many of the outer areas of the large conurbations, or in such existing purpose-built entertainment centres as Alton Towers in Staffordshire. All but the last of these examples are of course already directly associated with a conurbation. Were we to plan a network of similar complexes it would be tantamount merely to reconstructing a new urban settlement pattern. As for truly rural theme parks of the kind characterized by Alton Towers, while they may indeed cater for one particular type of entertainment, they cannot re-create the sheer variety of stimulus which larger and more dense provision of a range of amenities can provide. It is the excitement and variety of their built form and the social and economic opportunities which they offer that continue to be among the chief attractions of large cities. If to this it is argued that this may only be telling for the young and single or for the staid and childless, I would quote Colin Ward's characteristically forthright view of the excitement that a lively and a potentially dangerous urban environment offers to the child and of the converse visual and social deprivation that one can argue restricts the development of the rural child (Ward, 1978). Marx's encomium of the city and his dismissal of the 'idiocy of rural life' still has force. The alertness, inventiveness, and articulateness of the urban child, whether Cockney, Scouse, or wherever, says much for the potential benefits of urban living if once relieved of the gnawing and dulling effects of poverty and deprivation.

All of this is not to argue a city-in-aspic view; that nostalgia demands a renewal of a once-familiar and now-endangered pattern of settlement. It is clear that the city needs to adapt and to respond to the very different economic and social circumstances of the end of the century. At the least, a lower overall density would offer scope for imaginative ways to recycle the inherited stock of urban land uses. It is, however, to argue that the wholesale abandonment of cities would put at risk the many advantages which accrue from relatively large and relatively dense settlement; and that the positive benefits of cities need to be harnessed in ways which do not put at even greater risk the uncomfortable poor who remain trapped in decaying cities and on whose shoulders the problems of that decline have rested. Failure to tackle those problems has been allied with a blinkered spirit of anti-urbanism. Both have to be reversed.

3
What are the Causes? *Clarity of Vision*

> As a rule, people have already made up their minds what they think about the present. About the past, they are more susceptible to clarity of vision.
>
> *J. G. Farrell*

Within the framework of policy—or the lack of a policy dictated by views imbued with anti-urbanism—can be seen the genesis of our present situation. Historically the large cities of Britain presented a Janus appearance: their grand and imposing central buildings reflected the confidence and financial power of industrial Britain in its heyday; their slums reflected the human cost of that wealth. The piecemeal effort to maintain the former while eradicating the latter reached its apogee in the twenty-odd years after 1945. It is now common and all too easy to condemn those peak years of slum clearance, of planning, and of New and Expanded Towns, of welfarism and universal benefits. As early as 1958 Malcolm Muggeridge wrote bitingly:

> this welfare state is a kind of zoo which keeps the inmates in ease and comfort, but makes them unfit for life in their natural habitat. Mangey and bleary-eyed they grumble and growl as they walk up and down in their cages waiting for slabs of welfare to be thrown to them at mealtimes.

Behind that criticism and the current dismissal of those policies lies a sense of bitter disappointment. Much was expected from the grand designs of 1945–50 both by those who executed them and by those who were done to: what emerged were old problems in new cheapjack clothes. Macmillan, ever astute, sounded the warning in the now much quoted 'never had it so good' speech of 1957. The context of what he said was more warning than boast:

> Most of our people have never had it so good. Go around the country,

go to the industrial towns, go to the farms, and you'll see a state of prosperity such as we have never had in my lifetime—nor indeed ever in the history of this country. What is beginning to worry some of us is 'Is it too good to last?' For amidst all this prosperity, there is one problem that has troubled us, in one way or another, ever since the war. It is the problem of rising prices. Our constant concern is: Can prices be steadied while at the same time we maintain full employment in an expanding economy?

Yet the detailed recollections of politicians show little awareness that the forces of history and geography were combining to remove the brief period of power and glory experienced by those cities and regions where the industrial revolution had found its heartlands. Richard Crossman, epitomizing the patronizing omniscience of a political do-gooder, swanned happily between his country estate and his comfortable London flat intent on building up numbers of houses as electoral fodder. 'Urban policy' does not fill the pages of his Diaries nor those of other of our political masters who have expended so much energy in print (Crossman, 1975). It is not surprising therefore that, as the realization dawned that cities had problems and that these problems were getting worse rather than better, discussions amongst academics and policy-makers had an air of fantasy. Opinions and views glanced tangentially past each other since there was no consensus on the nature of the problem or on the perspective through which it could be interpreted.

The Coventry Community Development Project team produced an invaluable summary of the various competing perspectives through which the inner-city issues were severally interpreted (Fig. 3.1). The variety of models from which we start to interpret society produces different sets of problems, different goals, and therefore different solutions. Take, for example, the 'problem' of crime: seen as the product of social deviance, policy-makers would turn to intervention through education as a means of instilling communal responsibility; as the product of the inter-generational transmission of inadequacy, it would lead to arguments for the flooding of areas with social workers to intervene in the inadequacy of families; as the outcome of the ineffectiveness of the organs of the state to ensure order, it would lead to the creation of inter-agency

PERSPECTIVE	PERCEIVED PROBLEM	GOAL	MEANS
Culture of poverty	Pathology of deviant groups	Better social adjustment	Education
Cycle of deprivation	Individual inadequacy	Better families	Social work
Institutional malfunction	Planning failure	Rational planning	Corporate planning
Resource maldistribution	Inequitable distribution	Reallocation of resources	Positive discrimination
Structural conflict	Class divisions	Redistribution of power	Political change

FIG. 3.1. Varying perspectives on 'the urban problem'

Note: Different models of the world lead to the perception of different problems and to different goals and means for tackling them.

Source: Coventry CDP (1975).

linkages out of which corporate planning could emerge; as the result of inequitable distribution of resources within society, it would lead to forms of compensatory reallocation through positive discrimination; as an inevitable product of class conflict, it would lead to political reform. The interpretative spectacles that we choose to wear clearly act as prisms which produce views at variance one with another. They also affect the substantive issues which are stressed by different commentators or schools of thought. Solesbury, for example, uses the four metaphors suggested by Stretton (1978) to summarize this. The city can be seen as *machine* (with its infrastructure of roads, buildings, supply lines, and land, all of which raise technical issues of the physical factors of such provision), as *community* (with its groups of individuals whose separate and communal needs raise issues of government and governed), as *markets* (in which goods and services are traded, thereby raising issues of the price and availability of labour and other factors of production), and as *battlegrounds* (with vested interests and a stress on distributional questions of who gets what) (Solesbury, 1986).

Helpful though such tabulations of approaches and topics are, even they grossly simplify the multi-faceted nature of the inner-area issue. Over the past decade, however, a consensus view *has* emerged. It sees the problems as being fundamentally economic ones, that unemployment and its associated poverty have provided the seed-bed out of which dereliction, disinvestment, and the social malaise of cities have sprung. The great bulk of academic research has swung to look at the occupation-driven economic stimuli to life chances and to urban and regional change. Government is even more extreme in this since, partly at the prompting of the Community Development Project and largely by the impacts of recession, all of the changes to the Urban Programme especially since 1981 have been in the direction of switching the emphasis of policy to economic concerns. Social explanations have largely disappeared as prompts to the roots of urban malaise. This is both unfortunate and ill advised. Academic research tends to follow bandwagon lurches almost as much as do the views and fads of civil servants and government ministers. To ignore the social underpinnings of urban decay is to balance on a high wire without any head for heights. It was, after all, the loss of population and the social polarization which accompanied it which first betokened the collapse of cities; it has been the recurring social disturbances in cities which have prompted the intermittent flurries of concern by a government which, ironically and rightly or wrongly, has been at pains to deny the connections between unemployment and social disturbance. Unless we address the social malaise which gnaws at the heart of cities, all of the economic nostrums seem doomed to fail the long-term needs of the problems. Beyond the statistics of research and the analysis of computers there is a human dimension, idiosyncratic and unpredictable.

With that important caveat in mind, however, it is possible to tease out the economic arguments about the demise of cities and to discuss five distinct views about urban economic decline: economic restructuring; local industrial mix; factor costs; environmental perception; and locality-specific arguments. It would be unrealistic to think that any one in isolation provides an answer to why cities have suffered so greatly. As so often, elements of all need to be considered if we are to understand both the generality of the problem and the rich variety of the experiences of different places.

ECONOMIC RESTRUCTURING

In the face of recession, falling profits, and the downturn in the economy, firms have increasingly been forced to restructure their production so as to increase their efficiency and competitiveness. In the process of this restructuring, urban areas have suffered disproportionately, not because of anything intrinsic to cities but because of the nature of the employment and infrastructural base from which they started the recession. In theory, businesses could respond to economic change in a variety of ways. They could shed labour, alter working practices, introduce new production techniques or new products, seek new markets, or close down. For single-plant single-product firms the options have necessarily been limited. Strategies for large multi-plant multi-product enterprises have been more numerous. They have been better placed to alter the mix of their investments and thereby diversify or concentrate on a limited range of existing products or develop new ones, to use different plants to specialize in different parts of the production process, differentially to close or amalgamate different plants, and to internalize or put out parts of the production and its related services. Further, because their attachment to a specific labour market is less strong, the processes of closure or of job shedding have been less difficult for large corporate enterprises. It is significant in this respect that the percentage of net manufacturing output from the largest 100 companies in Britain has grown from 16 per cent in 1909 to 41 per cent in 1970 (Prais, 1976). The high degree of centralization of control in British industry has meant that restructuring has been able to take place in Britain to a correspondingly high degree.

It is from such processes that Massey's spatial division of labour has derived, emphasizing the split between large metropolitan areas and outlying rural regions and between the South East and the North and North West (Massey, 1984). The higher levels of policy and decision-making in headquarters have been severed from the routine manual processes of production to create a concentration of headquarters and research and development in the South East. The lower-level routinized production has been channelled to small towns and rural areas. In the urban North, old and inefficient premises and plant and established labour rigidities associated with trade-union activity and fragmented labour skills have been seen as presenting obstacles to maximizing the returns from the labour force. Where new investment in routine production has occurred, it has therefore gone to small towns and rural areas where such obstacles are not seen as standing in the way of maximizing returns. Such national division of labour is, of course, but a short step from the new international spatial division of labour in which production processes can as well be carried out by highly productive labour in Taiwan, Hong Kong, or other Third World countries as in areas within Britain or the developed world.

Examples of the spatial impact of restructuring are now numerous. In Clydeside, restructuring decisions led to the closure of the North British Locomotive Works in Springburn in north Glasgow and to the continuing uncertainty about the British Steel Corporation plant at Ravenscraig and the closure of Gartcosh (Lever and Moore, 1986, p. 151). Loss of employment in the vehicle industry in Clydeside—fragile ever since its initial establishment at the behest of regional policy—was one of the series of severe blows to the region in its economic contraction. This came to a head with the closure of the Peugeot-Talbot plant at Linwood with the loss of 4,500 jobs. The decision was a result of the overall national restructuring of the company. The Glasgow plant was originally etablished by Rootes in the 1960s, prompted by regional policy, and was transferred successively to General Motors-Chrysler and then to Peugeot-Talbot, with employment successively falling from its peak of 10,000. It was always expensive to operate because of the distances over which parts had to be carried and it had always run at a loss. The decision to close this, rather than some other part of the corporate company, was a result of contracting the least profitable plants and Linwood was the one which had tended to be most marginal and to have been allocated models late in their product life cycle.

Boddy provides a series of detailed studies of the way in which the Bristol economy has been affected by similar processes of corporate restructuring in the locally long-established sectors of tobacco, of paper, board, and packaging, of aerospace (which has been the motor of the local economy), of the relatively small electronics sector, and of the major growth sector of insurance. The example of the tobacco industry illustrates the process whereby restructuring creates winners and losers amongst the sets of localities involved (Boddy, Lovering, and Bassett, 1986, pp. 58–70). Imperial Tobacco Limited (ITL) is the tobacco division of the broader Imperial Group. Bristol had been the headquarters of Wills, Nottingham the headquarters of Players, and Liverpool that of Ogdens. Having been relatively autonomous, these branches were merged in 1983. Between 1980 and 1984 the pattern of employment amongst the various sites altered significantly as part of a process of corporate restructuring. In response to the slump in tobacco sales in the late 1970s, the Group as a whole first pursued a policy of diversification into its other interests in the hotel, brewing, foods, and leisure sectors and subsequently, in the face of continuing difficulties, it developed a recovery programme in its tobacco division which resulted in the following combination of streamlining: re-equipment with 'new generation machines' which enabled 3.3 employees to produce what it had previously taken 9.3 to produce; management restructuring to centralize and increase its efficiency; and the spatial reorganization of production to rationalize and relocate production. The latter entailed the closure of the site at Stirling, major contraction at Glasgow with the closure of one of the two plants in the city, and concentration of distribution from the three sites at Nottingham, Bristol, and Glasgow and the closure of distribution centres elsewhere. The changes, shown in Table 3.1, entailed the selection of Bristol rather than Nottingham as ITL's head office and hence an *increase* in salaried and managerial staff in Bristol, as against some particularly severe contraction elsewhere. The choice of Bristol was influenced by the fact of its having been the traditional centre of gravity for the Group as a whole, the availability of suitable premises as a result of earlier investment decisions, and the assumed residential attractiveness of the area for managerial and administrative staff. Restructuring therefore led to severe job losses in Nottingham, Glasgow, Liverpool, Ipswich. Bristol, like the other sites, may have emerged with fewer overall jobs, but it had a disproportionately

TABLE 3.1. *Imperial Tobacco Limited: employment change 1980–1984*

Production site	Numbers in 1980		% change to 1984		Total
	Production staff	Salaried & managerial	Production staff	Salaried & managerial	
Nottingham	4,200	1,392	−36	−25	−33
Stirling	0	24	—	−100	−100
Glasgow	2,800	232	−57	−35	−55
Newcastle	1,047	174	−31	−45	−33
Bristol	2,880	1,528	−37	+14	−19
Swindon	349	20	−30	−5	−29
Ipswich	933	52	−22	−15	−22
Liverpool	828	259	−26	−58	−34
TOTAL	13,037	3,681	−39	−13	−33

Source: Boddy, Lovering, Bassett (1986).

high share of higher-level staff: in 1984, whereas it had 32 per cent of the Division's total employment, it had 52 per cent of salaried and 67 per cent of managerial staff as a consequence of assuming a corporate headquarters function. The outcome of corporate restructuring in this, as in other of Boddy's sector case-studies, was to recompose the occupational mix as well as the size of the labour force in different parts of the country; and this process is one which occurs without regard to the urban or regional implications of such change.

The London case (Buck, Gordon, and Young, 1986) illustrates this tendency for headquarters and higher-level functions to concentrate and centralize within this process of restructuring. To this extent, London is clearly different from the large provincial cities of the North. Its job losses have been countercyclical. It lost jobs most rapidly in the 1960s, and its rate of job loss was *reduced* in the recessions of the mid-1970s and early 1980s. In the period 1961–78 London's differential job loss ran at 50,000–100,000 per year, but after 1978 this figure was reduced to some 30,000 per year. 'The long decline in London's share of national employment ceased in 1978–84' (Buck *et al.*, 1986, p. 66). This reverse trend was associated with the cyclical insensitivity of headquarters' operations and reflected the role that London has played as the centre of higher-level activities in production and services.

The position of the large old industrial cities in such reorganization has clearly been a very vulnerable one. Not only do they have long-established labour practices which are perceived as being resistant to changes aimed at increasing efficiency, but the buildings and machinery within them tend to be older and less modern than those elsewhere—they suffer, in other words, from the problem of older vintages of capital (Massey and Meegan, 1978). In this view it is less the fact that cities are inherently unattractive places, but that they suffer from having older plant and equipment and outdated labour relations and labour attitudes, that helps to explain the differential decline of employment in large cities. Such views, for example, accord well with the peculiar vulnerability of a city such as Liverpool, which had disproportionate numbers of large firms, with the labour militancy associated with size and conveyor-belt production, and with an unusually high proportion of branch plants and of external control of firms. The contrast between Manchester and Liverpool is interesting: whereas Manchester, in 1975, had 26 per cent of firms with less than 100 workers and 37 per cent with over 500, Liverpool had only 11 per cent and an abnormal 70 per cent respectively; and whereas Manchester had 48 per cent of locally headquartered firms, Liverpool had only 14 per cent (Lloyd and Dicken, 1982). Some of these arguments apply with similar force to other of the large provincial conurbations. Newcastle, for example, has 80 per cent of its employment in firms with headquarters outside the North East and hence many of the branch plants are particularly vulnerable to closure or contraction in a period of recession (Robinson, Wren, and Goddard, 1987; Townsend, 1983). Some part of this pattern is the result of regional policy in the 1960s, when it was predominantly branch plants which were attracted to the regions, thus in the long term leaving the regions more susceptible to contraction and failing to bring the benefits of higher-level and higher-paid staff and the research and development activities on which longer-term growth might better have been based.

It is the tendency of companies to establish London-based headquarters which has helped to maintain the relative economic ebullience of the South East in the last decade. It is the tendency for restructuring to favour small-town locations which has helped to ensure both the deepening of the divide between North and South and the collapsing fortunes of the large cities.

INDUSTRIAL MIX

The conventional wisdom on urban and regional change had been that it was largely a function of the inherited stock of activities found within an area which explained differential decline. In an overall economy which was changing its mix of activities—away from 'traditional' activities based on heavy industries such as ships, coal, steel, and heavy engineering, and on low-skill consumer goods such as textiles; and towards high-skill science-based industry and quaternary activities such as professional and technical services—those places with a predominance of the former would suffer a greater-than-average contraction simply as a function of having a high proportion of nationally rapidly contracting activities. Employment change greater or less than the expected nationally derived change could then be attributed to factors specific to the place itself. Shift-and-share analysis, which measures these elements of change, has generally shown that the industrial composition of cities in fact goes only a small way to 'explaining' their manufacturing contraction. Indeed, since many cities actually inherited a concentration of service-sector activities, the 'expected' employment change based on their composition should have been positive. Glasgow illustrates this (Table 3.2(*a*)). Shift-share measures three components. The national component shows the change in total employment which would have occurred in the area if total employment had grown at the same rate as the nation as a whole, and the Glasgow figures reflect the national change from a positive employment growth in 1971–8 of 1.9 per cent to a decline in 1978–81 of −2.3 per cent. The structural component is the change that would have occurred if each industry in the area changed employment at the same rate as that industry in the nation, excluding the national component. The structural component therefore measures the effects which are produced by an area's employment structure. For Glasgow, the structural figures show that the city itself should have produced *growth*

TABLE 3.2. *Shift-share analysis of employment trends, 1971–1978 and 1978–1981*

	Initial employment (000s)	Change in employment	National component	Structural component	Differential component
(a) Strathclyde					
1971–8					
Glasgow city	463	– 27.1 (– 5.8)	+ 12.9	+ 4.8 (1.0)	– 44.8 (– 9.7)
Outer conurbation	327	– 0.8 (– 0.2)	+ 9.1	– 9.0 (– 2.8)	– 0.9 (– 0.3)
1978–81					
Glasgow city	435	– 36.7 (– 8.4)	– 21.6	+ 3.1 (0.7)	– 18.2 (– 4.2)
Outer conurbation	326	– 39.4 (– 12.1)	– 16.2	– 8.4 (– 2.6)	– 14.8 (– 4.5)
(b) Metropolitan areas					
1971–8					
Bristol	411	17.4 (4.2)	11.2	2.0 (0.5)	4.2 (1.0)
Strathclyde	820	– 30.2 (– 3.7)	22.3	– 4.0 (– 0.5)	– 48.5 (– 5.9)
London	5,759	– 94.2 (– 1.6)	156.6	197.3 (3.4)	– 448.2 (– 7.8)
Newcastle	627	16.0 (2.6)	17.0	– 3.8 (– 0.6)	2.7 (0.4)
W. Midlands	1,338	– 10.6 (– 0.8)	36.4	– 24.4 (1.8)	– 22.6 (1.7)
1978–81					
Bristol	428	– 13.1 (– 3.1)	– 21.8	12.7 (3.0)	– 3.9 (– 0.9)
Strathclyde	790	– 77.7 (– 9.8)	– 40.3	– 5.1 (– 0.6)	– 32.3 (– 4.1)
London	5,665	– 142.7 (– 2.5)	– 289.1	170.1 (3.0)	– 23.7 (– 0.4)
Newcastle	643	– 76.1 (– 11.8)	– 32.8	– 1.8 (– 0.3)	– 41.6 (– 6.5)
W. Midlands	1,327	– 134.1 (– 10.1)	– 67.7	– 60.8 (– 4.5)	– 5.6 (– 0.4)

Note: Figures of jobs and job changes shown in thousands. Figures in brackets are percentage changes.

Sources: Lever and Moore (1986); Robinson, Wren, and Goddard (1987).

in employment during each of the two periods, reflecting its concentration of service-based activities; the outer part of the conurbation by comparison had a consistently negative structural component, showing its dependence on old declining heavy industries. The differential component is then the residual—the difference between 'expected' and actual employment change—and therefore provides an indicator of the competitiveness of the area. For the city of Glasgow, the differential has been consistently negative. Indeed, even though the service sector should have been a source of employment growth, the differential component for services has been as large as that for the non-service sector. The fact that the negative differential component for the city grew progressively smaller over time may indicate an improvement in the performance of those industries which remain, but is more likely to result simply from the deterioration in national employment change to levels closer to those of Glasgow.

The comparable shift-share figures for five urban areas are shown in Table 3.2(*b*). In each case, for the period 1978–81, the differential shift is negative. Only in the case of the West Midlands does the structural component contribute a larger percentage of the employment loss than does the differential component. There are clearly factors associated with the respective cities which have caused employment loss to be substantially higher than might have been expected on the basis of the industrial mix of the places concerned.

This is not to argue that the compositional effect of cities and northern regions is not important. The industrial structure of most large northern cities has clearly stood them at a grave disadvantage during a period of national restructuring of production. Despite their service employment (much of which of course is dependent on the performance of local manufacturing activities) most large cities have a base of traditional heavy industry and a mix of labour which has brought with it sets of inherited skills, of attitudes, of industrial scale, and of patterns of ownership which have not been helpful in enabling such city regions to make the transition to new types of production and activities nor to the attraction of new investment in high-tech. activities. Since the probability of generating new small firms is related to the prior size distribution of existing firms—

with potential entrepreneurs being drawn disproportionately from small firms—the inherited stock of firms is clearly of importance in affecting the ability or the probability of an area's being able to respond to new economic circumstances. Checkland's likening of Glasgow's industrial giants to the effect of a upas-tree—in whose shade all else withers—is a telling metaphor for the tendency of big firms to smother smaller enterprise within their area (Checkland, 1976). This image is of long standing in economic history. Jane Jacobs used it in her comparison of the strength and resilience which arose from the multiplicity of varied small-scale activities in nineteenth-century Birmingham by comparison with the inflexibility of the larger textile enterprises of Manchester (Jacobs, 1970). In the light of the recent collapse of the West Midlands, the comparison may now be greeted with some cynicism in Birmingham, but it is nevertheless telling. In the more recent post-war years the gigantism of the car industry in the West Midlands played for that region the role that textiles had in Manchester in the nineteenth century so that, as the car industry collapsed, it brought down with it many of the smaller component suppliers which had depended on it. The same argument applies to patterns of absenteeism of owners and managers. An area such as Tyneside and Wearside—which over its industrial history has experienced unusually high levels of absentee ownership amongst some of its principal activities, for example among coal-owners and shipyard owners—has inherited a pattern which is less likely to generate future entrepreneurial activities as a result of such an inheritance.

FACTOR COSTS

Labour

There are differential costs of production in urban and non-urban aras. The most extensive work on this is by Moore, Rhodes, and Tyler (1986), who used the 1982 Census of Production and data from the New Earnings Survey to suggest a profit gradient at successive distances away from London. For most of the industries which they studied, gross profits 100 miles from London along the M4 produced 20 per cent higher gross profits compared to inner London and at a distance of 200 miles profits rose by 30 per cent. Similar, but much smaller, values are suggested for some of the provincial metropolitan areas, with differences of 4 to 15 per cent as between the metropolitan area and the rural surroundings. Much of this differential comes from wage and salary costs together with local taxes and rents on factory premises. Such differences may, however, say little about the true relative competitiveness of urban and rural locations, since the salary differences could be as much a function of the mix of occupations in multi-plant firms (with more of the higher-paid salariat being found in headquarters within urban areas), and of the inherited higher levels of staffing in urban locations. This view is shared by Scott (1982), who, in explaining the decline of urban manufacturing, develops an argument of the dual nature of the location of production based on the labour-intensiveness of urban as against the capital-intensiveness of rural production. Traditionally, urban locations have acted as the incubators of new products—those which are early in the product life cycle—and while this incubator view may no longer be appropriate for new investment, its historical legacy helps explain the distribution of labour costs in urban and rural and small-town locations. Aggregate wage differentials may therefore say little about differential wage costs for comparable types of activity. Indeed Tyler and Rhodes (1986) show values for profitability and productivity between urban areas and their peripheries which suggest small and fluctuating differences. In any case the really significant gradient of overall wage costs is restricted to London, where wage and salary levels may be some 10–20 per cent above average (Buck, Gordon, and Young, 1986). However, since there is no suggestion that any of the differences are not of long standing, they go little of the way in explaining the scale of the loss of urban-based activity in the last decade.

On labour costs, therefore, the major urban and rural difference may not be financial (with the exception of the London allowance which adds significantly to the labour costs of a London location), since so high a proportion of jobs still operates under national pay agreements. Average wage costs in areas are therefore, by and large, a function of the mix of different grades of work found in local areas. This view is reinforced by government's increasing concern to argue that there should be higher regional differentials in wage settlements and by the upward drift of London and South East allowances (for example, *The Times* of 11 December 1987 reported that the National and Provincial Building Society now pays an inner London allowance of £3,450 and the main clearing banks have introduced a £3,000 allowance). Nevertheless, there *is* an important element to labour differentials. Rather than direct cost, it is the indirect element of the quality of labour which is a prime determinant of factor costs. For enterprises which wish to avoid the use of highly unionized labour, areas without a long history of work in the traditional unionized activities associated with heavy industry are likely to produce more malleable and flexible labour force. This is one of the attractions of rural locations, where workers are less likely to have been socialized into the culture of industrial confrontation, which is often associated with large enterprises with their conveyor-belt production, or of fragmented and rigid work practices associated with highly unionized skilled manual work. One of the reasons for the fact that, until recently, the female labour force has grown so rapidly—whether urban or rural—is that women tend or are believed to offer exactly this malleable, as well as a lower-paid, workforce. It is variation in these perceived qualitative differences between labour which provides the most significant element in the labour component factor of production and which has contributed to differences in the locational attraction of urban and rural sites.

Such arguments about the obstructiveness of a traditional unionized labour force are becoming less convincing with the apparent erosion of union power and the increasing number of firms and enterprises which are concluding 'modern' contracts with their workforce: most publicized of which are the agreements in South Wales and Tyneside involving Japanese companies. New work practices have been a growing feature of industrial change over the last decade. One of the elements of corporate restructuring during recession has been the attempt to create a more flexible workforce, which has led to an increasing polarization in the labour market so as to create a dual labour force (Fig. 3.2). In pursuit of flexibility, a core group of workers is created so as to form a primary labour market in

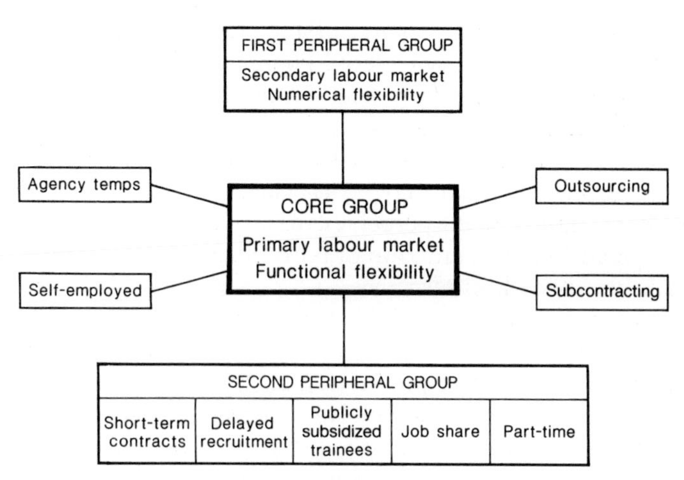

FIG. 3.2. The dual labour market: the search for flexibility
Source: Atkinson and Gregory (1986).

which individual workers are skilled, have good career prospects through internal mobility within the corporate context, and are encouraged to develop interchangeable skills, all of which is aimed to increase functional flexibility within the firm. Even where firms have not concluded formal agreements for 'quality circles', the more informal process of creating a dual internal labour market of stable skilled labour and unstable less-skilled workers has been widespread. Complementing this are peripheral labour markets which are aimed at numerical flexibility—at the ability of a firm to reduce or increase its effective labour force rapidly in response to changes in production demands which reflect the vagaries of the market. The increase in the variety of readily expendable labour provides a number of ways—job sharing, part-time workers, short-term contracts, the delaying of formal recruitment into the primary workforce, and the use of MSC trainees—in which corporations can maximize their ability to take on or to fire labour at short notice. The complementary development of externalized labour costs through greater subcontracting and out-sourcing, on the one hand, and the growth of self-employment and the use of labour from external agencies, on the other, has equally created numerical flexibility through externalizing labour costs outside the corporate context (Atkinson and Gregory, 1986). There is little evidence that urban workforces are intrinsically more resistant than are non-urban to such changes, as the experience of the Japanese firms in South Wales and the North-east suggests (Crowther and Garrahan, 1988). What may be at issue, however, is the degree to which management perceives urban labour as less likely to adjust readily to the creation of both functional and numerical flexibility of such kinds.

Land and premises

The second element of production costs is land and buildings. Urban land is still relatively expensive. The pattern of industrial rents shows a marked cost gradient outwards from London with minor peaks associated with large metropolitan centres elsewhere in the country (Fig. 3.3). Much of the continuing expense of urban land is a residue of historic cost, with owners unwilling to sell land at prices which reflect a 'true' estimate of its market capacity. Indeed it would be true to say that the land market has all but broken down in many large urban areas. There is, in addition, the extra cost of 'brownfield' sites associated with the need to make good the land on which redevelopment is to take place. Such making good often involves not only the clearance of prior construction but the removal or stabilizing of industrial waste and pollution and the need to fill cellars or foundations and to take account of existing utilities such as sewers and gas and electricity lines.

Adams, Baum, and MacGregor (1987) have explored some of the constraints which help to maintain the relatively high price of urban land, in a study of specific cases of land transactions in Manchester. They conclude that some part of the maintenance of high land prices is the result of the extensive use by valuers of *comparative* land valuation (by which values are assessed through comparison with actual transactions of 'similar' land) in preference to the use of *residual* valuation (by which the value of land is calculated as a residue, once returns from end uses are offset by the costs of the preparation, construction, and legal work involved). Comparative methods tend to be used by sellers, resulting in

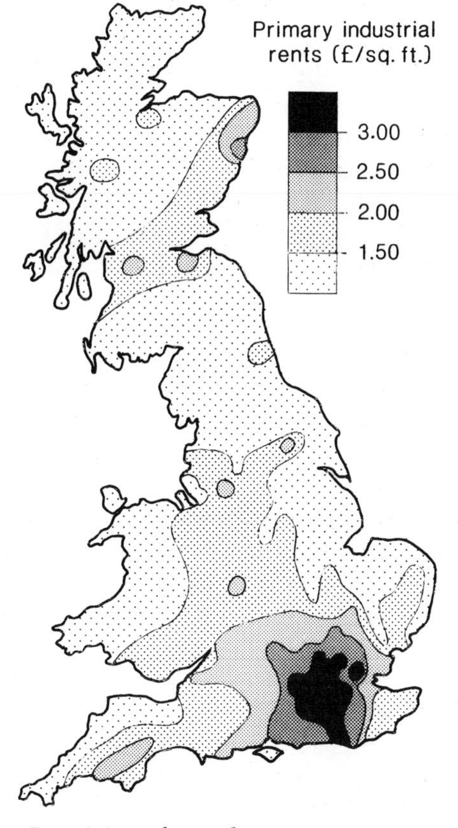

FIG. 3.3. Industrial rents in Britain.

high estimates of value, and residual methods by buyers, resulting in low estimates. The disparities help to freeze the operation of the urban land market. The comparative methods used by valuers suffer both from the small number of urban transactions, especially in a depressed urban land market, so that comparators are difficult to derive, and from the fact that comparisons tend to be with transactions which are historic and thereby place emphasis on the most favourable recent transaction. In a sluggish market and a declining economy, valuers' estimates based on comparative valuation are likely to boost asking prices to unrealistic levels. Potential developers, on the other hand, invariably use a residual method to calculate their expected returns. The disparity between asking and bidding price is likely to delay or block transactions. Further, the comparative method, while making some allowance for the conversion costs of brownfield sites, appears to underestimate the true cost of making land good. For example, of 11 transactions which Adams *et al.* study in detail, without taking account of the cost of making good the site difficulties, 7 cases showed that the actual land price was below the appropriate median cost for similar land uses, but that by adding in the eventual conversion costs the medians were exceeded in all but 2 cases; and exceeded by percentages varying from 8 to 86. The cost of making good can therefore make 'brownfield' sites uneconomic to redevelop.

An additional factor in maintaining urban land at unrealistically high values may be the role played by local authorities as major purchasers of urban land. Knowledge of the level of statutory compensation codes for compulsory purchase (while now not greatly used since the ending of large-scale redevelopment) may encourage local authorities to pay above the prices which the private sector would pay. Moreover, the pattern of local-authority finance often means that they have to spend monies within the deadline of a financial year. Both of these influences tend to increase the price levels at which local authorities will be prepared to buy land. Knowledge of this, and of the fact that local authorities act as buyers of last resort, may encourage owners to hold on to land at prices which are unrealistic.

There are numerous problems of redeveloping urban sites in addition to the unrealistic price levels sought by owners through the discrepancies between comparative and residual methods of valuation. First, difficulties can be caused by the small size of many plots and the unattractive environment of the immediate surroundings. If they are to build private housing in run-down urban areas, private developers consider it important that they are able to build on relatively large plots so that the development can create its own 'internal environment', often shielded or physically screened from surrounding areas of decayed industry or poorer housing. Only in such circumstances do they consider it likely that a market will be created, especially for medium or upper-income groups. Second, there are often problems in establishing legal title to urban land which is likely to have gone through complex ownership transactions over time or for parts of which leaseholds have been granted. Much of the land available for development in inner areas is in the sites of old clearance areas and compulsory purchase orders. While a local council may be in possession of the land, there may be outstanding claims under compulsory purchase orders which have not been settled within the three-year time limit originally laid down under the 1965 Compulsory Purchase Act, especially where absent owners are involved. In such cases the council may not be aware of constraints such as restrictive covenants on land. Where land is to be sold on via a developer to an eventual purchaser it is necessary to assemble good title to the land so that future disputes over compensation from absent owners will not present risks to a potential developer. The procedures to establish good title in such cases are usually time consuming and therefore discourage interest in possible development where the private sector is involved. Third is the cost of making good the land itself. Table 3.3 shows two examples from Salford to illustrate the impact of

TABLE 3.3. *Residual valuation of two vacant sites in Salford*

	Site 1 (1.29 hectares) (£)	Site 2 (1.12 hectares) (£)
Revenue	944,600 (40 houses)	1,071,500 (43 houses)
Construction costs	(728,000)	(770,000)
Sales & finance @ 7%	(66,080)	(75,005)
Overheads & profit @ 12%	(113,280)	(128,580)
Legal fees	(2,000)	(3,000)
TOTAL	(909,360)	(976,585)
Surplus for land	34,640	94,915
Abnormal making-good costs	500,000	
Less land surplus	34,640	
DEFICIT	465,360	

Source: House-builders Federation (1986).

such costs (House-builders Federation, 1986). The first site, two miles from the town centre and comprising 1.3 hectares of an old paintworks, is land which suffers from contamination of the ground through base metals, lead, and arsenic. The estimate for improving the ground conditions to allow housing is £500,000–£600,000 or, for a less demanding use such as open space, it would be £300,000. A plan for 40 semi-detached houses which would market for some £23,000–£25,000, given the prevailing market, produces an overall deficit of over £400,000. Some part of this could be offset by Derelict Land Grant were a builder to express interest, but none has been forthcoming. If the land is to be improved it will probably therefore be for open space. The second example is of 1.1 hectares on the site of a former mill which has now been demolished. The site has been prepared for development with hard-core filling of the old mill basement and the area itself is potentially attractive for residential development, having an existing mix of council and private houses. The present owner has put it on the market, with planning permission for 53 houses, at a price of £200,000. A private developer has prepared a plan for 43 houses which are estimated to market at between £20,000–£27,000. The residual calculation of land value, even ignoring any additional costs involved in making good abnormal ground conditions, is £95,000, which suggests that the asking price is twice that which the market would bear and that developer interest is unlikely to materialize unless the price is substantially reduced.

Land prices in cities are therefore revised downwards only slowly and with great reluctance in the face of lack of demand or excess supply. The consequence is not only a disincentive to new development in urban areas, but also the creation of increasing amounts of vacant land sterilized through unrealistically high asking prices and through the cost of land preparation. Part of the sterilization is also due to the reluctance of local authorities and other public bodies, which own so large a fraction of urban land, to release their land for development. It was this which prompted central government, as part of the Local Government Act of 1980, to force local authorities to compile and publish registers of land held in public ownership in the hope that this would encourage the market to develop unused land. Even additional ministerial directions for the disposal of sites have not led to any great overall change, partly because many of the vacant sites are of very small extent. By 1987, some 11,630 hectares of land were recorded in the registers for the seven English conurbations and, between 1984 and 1987, 2,230 hectares had been disposed of and a mere 881 had been brought into use (Chisholm and Kivell, 1987).

Most urban land is, of course, already built on and the age, quality, and context of those buildings can present further contraints on the attractiveness of urban sites for the expansion of existing premises or the investment of new resources. Fothergill and Gudgin (1982) have argued that the lack of available land on which urban premises can be expanded or rebuilt *in situ* is a major explanation of the decline of urban manufacturing. Fothergill, Monk, and Perry (1987) have explored the influence of the characteristics of industrial premises on economic growth and efficiency and on the location of firms and jobs. There have been substantial changes in the use that is made of industrial buildings and of space over recent years. There have been major falls in the land occupancy ratios (that is, the ratio of buildings to the land on which they sit) and a rise in the ratio of output to labour. The fact that the ratio of output to space has stayed surprisingly stable (partly because more space has been required for storage to accommodate increased output) has meant a dramatic increase in the amount of space per worker. Indeed, between 1964 and 1985, densities fell from 36 to 21 workers per thousand square metres of space. Where redevelopment of urban land takes place, this has considerable consequences for jobs. The redevelopment of a 10,000 square metre factory built on four floors and occupying the whole of its urban site would, for example, involve its replacement with a single-storey building covering 40 per cent of the site, and hence involve a contraction to 1,000 square metres—a reduction of 90 per cent in space and a consequent reduction of 95 per cent in terms of employment. The changes in jobs associated with such floorspace change for the period 1967–81 are shown in Figs. 3.4 and 3.5. Translated into industrial job changes, all areas suffered a similar decline in employment by some one-third through the lower density of workers per area (Fig. 3.4). In the metropolitan areas this

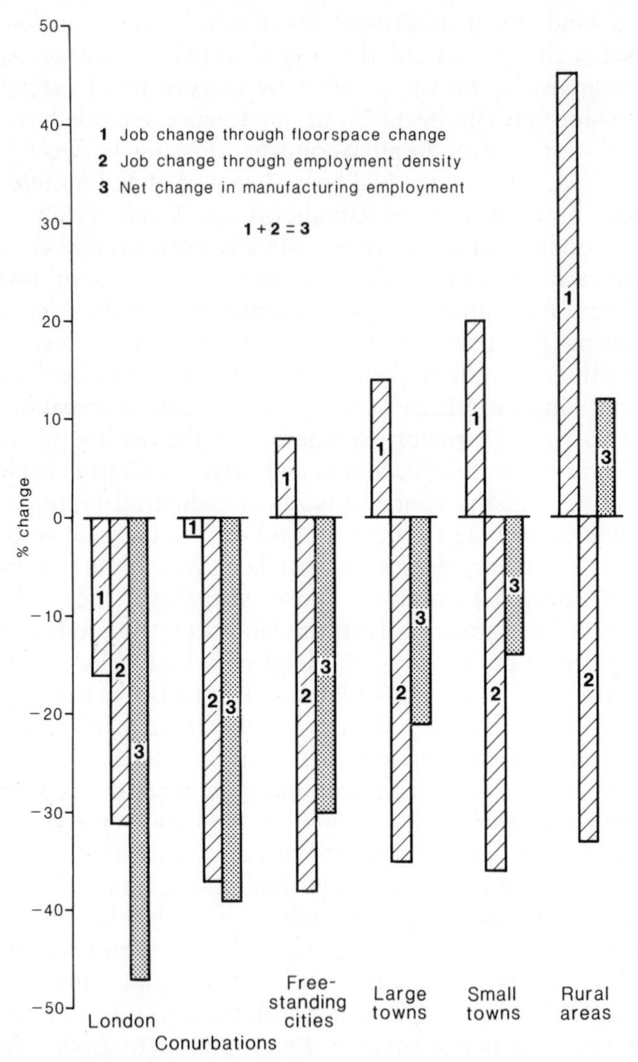

FIG. 3.4. Changes in manufacturing employment and industrial premises

Note: This shows the contribution of changes in industrial floorspace and of decreasing employment density.

Source: Fothergill, Monk, and Perry (1987).

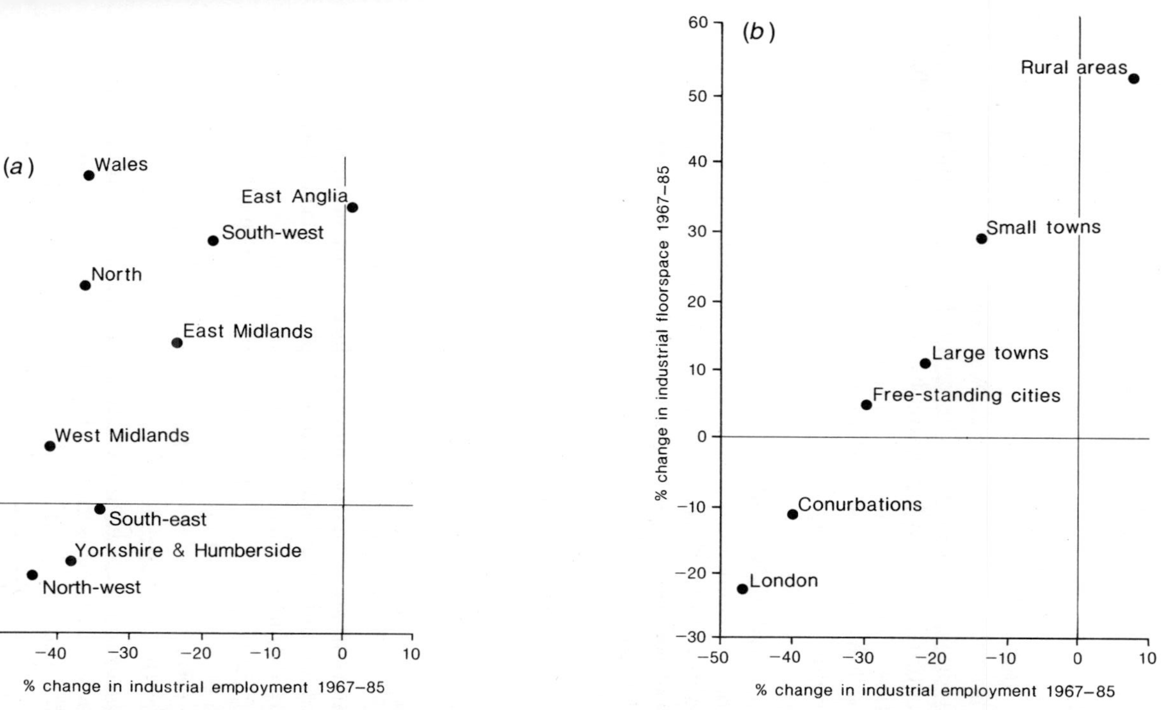

FIG. 3.5. Changes in manufacturing employment and industrial premises: (*a*) by regions; (*b*) by type of settlement

Source: Fothergill, Monk, and Perry (1987).

density reduction was added to by a loss of industrial floorspace, so as to produce very large falls in employment. Elsewhere, the reduction in density offset the increases in actual floorspace everywhere except for rural areas. The regional impact of these changes shows that only in East Anglia did manufacturing employment increase. In the South West an increase in floorspace was associated with a lower-than-average job loss. Elsewhere, the floorspace increase has been counteracted in job terms by the decrease in workplace densities. The most dramatic relationship is not the regional pattern but the urban/rural dimension, which suggests that settlement size is the most effective predictor of changes in industrial floorspace and industrial employment. The relationships are strikingly regular (Fig. 3.5). Only in the rural areas has there been a small net increase in industrial employment. This is attributable to a 50 per cent *increase* in floorspace in rural areas as against a 10 per cent loss of floorspace in the conurbations. Fothergill *et al.* develop a multiple regression using data for the East Midlands which show how employment change 1968–72 was associated with the age of buildings, the proportion of the site covered by those buildings, existing employment, and change in employment in Great Britain, but that there was no independent effect associated with whether an area was urban or rural. Thus, the contraction or the slow growth in urban manufacturing can be argued to reflect not any inherent disadvantages of urban location *per se*, but rather the fact that urban industry operated largely in premises which were older and on sites which were physically constrained. For new investment, urban areas were similarly disadvantaged by having fewer, more expensive, and lower-quality sites on which development could occur.

Even discounting the problems associated with urban land, the fact that there are lower overall quantities of available land for industrial development in cities in itself means that, whether or not industrialists favour urban or rural areas, there is a statistical probability that rural areas will attract a larger share of new investment. This is despite evidence that firms prefer urban locations—in 1982, London and the conurbations had 16 per cent of available land for industrial development, but received 28 per cent of new industrial floorspace (Fothergill,

Monk, and Perry, 1987). It is clear that constraints associated with the cost, quality, and availability of land and buildings in the large cities do present obstacles for new development or for redevelopment in urban areas.

Capital

A third factor which has worked against the economic fortunes of northern cities is access to capital for development. The lack of capital for loans and grants has been a recurring complaint of existing or potential businesses in the large cities of the North. This is less an urban than a regional phenomenon. It has two components. First is the fact that banks and public lending agencies invariably work to too short a time-scale in looking for returns on their investment. Small, often innovative, entrepreneurial enterprises are rarely able to achieve acceptable returns over a period of one or two years. By comparison with the United States, there are in Britain few sources of long-term credit which would enable entrepreneurs to avoid the temptation to aim merely for short-run profit. Long-term profitability means concentrating on building up more secure markets and more robust production and managerial structures. It would seem important to develop longer-term schemes which would meet reasonable expectations in terms of accountability for the use of public resources. Second is the difficulty faced by entrepreneurs in northern cities in raising small loans, since most financial sources are London orientated. More than half the funds raised for venture capital goes to London and the South East despite the fact that 70 per cent of registered businesses are located elsewhere in the country (*Financial Times*, 3 March 1987). The disparity reflects the fact that the overwhelming majority of venture capital is London based. Regionally sensitive firms such as Investment in Industry are very much the exception. Since venture capital is best invested on the basis of detailed knowledge of the potential of borrowers, the distance of regional businesses from the London-dominated headquarters of lending institutions works to the disadvantage especially of small entrepreneurs. Only 'big' deals in the provinces are worth the cost and trouble of investigative effort for London-based funds. 'Big' until recently was defined as some £250,000 and this figure may now have risen to £500,000. Since most intending new start-ups look for sums considerably less than this, it is not surprising that the current rejection rate for regional proposals is some 95 per cent. There would seem to be strong arguments for the establishment of regional investment agencies to fill the equity gap for sums of £20,000–£50,000.

ENVIRONMENTAL PERCEPTION

Residential preference

Views of the respective attractions of urban and rural locations as places in which to live and work are a further element in the investment changes which underlie urban decline. Just as with household movement, so it has been argued that production has moved away from cities because they offer an unattractive environment—one that is unappealing to the managerial, technical, and entrepreneurial personnel who have become an increasing key to production. Cities are seen as being bedevilled by high crime, they have few attractive houses of the right quality. If top staff look for appealing environments it is to areas such as the South West, East Anglia, the rolling chalklands and the clay vales of the Home Counties, or the royal country of the Cotswolds that they look. This view of industry having sought locations where the grass is greener (Keeble, 1976) is reinforced by the second-round effects on the location of services and manufacturing produced by the earlier outward movement of population, which was itself a reflection of environmentally determined relocation decisions. Little of the outward population movement was prompted by change of job, but once the centre of gravity of population had become more rural this led to second-round locational decisions on service and industrial activities. Much service activity is population-led. The growth of new shopping centres, new investment in schools, motorways, airports, and the like, are all developments which create both further rounds of population in-movement and further rounds of service and infrastructure investment and thereby create a self-reinforcing momentum to the switch away from large industrial cities.

Demographic trends

The second development which underpins this environmental view is the impact of demographic changes which have helped to provide a context for counter urbanization. The growth of owner-occupation from 29 per cent in 1951 to 63 per cent in 1985 has fuelled the outward movement of population. Since developers have found peripheral or small-town greenfield sites the most profitable and the easiest areas on which to build, this expanding market has accelerated the process of decentralization. Household formation in the post-war period has been rapid despite the slow overall rate of population growth. The new households were partly 'conventional' families, but increasingly were the product of the smaller average size of household which reflected the formation of young childless households, the falling birthrate, and the effects of the growing proportion of the elderly. From an average size of 3.09 in 1961, household size in Great Britain reduced to 2.56 by 1985. One-person households increased over that time from 12 to 24 per cent. The number of people aged 60 or over increased by 2.5 millions. These changes and the dramatic switchback of the fertility rate (with a total period fertility rate which grew from 2.16 in 1951 to 2.78 in 1961 and fell to 1.79 by 1981) have had profound impacts on the housing market and hence on the probabilities of population dispersal from cities. The fertility boom up to 1964 meant that over most of the inter-war years there was a consistent pressure for new family housing. In the 1950s and 1960s this was to house the swelling number of households created by the rising birth rate. In the late 1970s and the early 1980s, the 'echo' effect of the post-war baby boom should have provided a second upsurge in the market for family houses to cater for the new wave of marriages which were the product of the earlier boom. The equation has not worked out quite in this way since there has been a consistent fall in the marriage rate since the early 1970s. In 1971 there was a total of 459,000 marriages in the United Kingdom; by 1985 this had fallen to 393,000. Nevertheless, the demographic changes have meant that there has been increasing pressure on the housing market for family houses, which has fed the demand for suburban and non-urban expansion. Pressure from new families in the 1950s and 1960s meant that house-price inflation was fed in the post-war period with a wave of new housing investment after 1954. Once started, that growth has fed on itself through mobility associated with gearing-up in a housing market whose price inflation has consistently outstripped overall price changes. It has further been added to by the growing proportion and numbers of the elderly, for whom a virtually new market of bungalows and smaller retirement houses has emerged. This has had especial impact in a few retirement areas along the coastal strips, especially in the Sunshine Belts of the South, South West, and East Anglia and in selective resort towns elsewhere (Allon-Smith, 1982). The more popular of the south-coast towns now have over 40 per cent of people over retirement age and the growth in their relative concentration of elderly has been greater than the national increase, so that it is not too dramatic to talk of a costa geriatrica. Many of the retirees have been drawn from the large metropolitan areas: from London to the south coast and the South West, from Birmingham to North Wales, from Manchester to the Lake District, from Newcastle to the rather bleaker prospects of Northumberland.

Invariably, until the very recent development of sheltered housing, this bungalow culture has provided a significant addition to the stream of outward population movement. Contrary to this, however, has been the increasing market for smaller houses amongst the young single and young childless married, associated with new household formation, with affluence, and with the lower marriage and birth rates. In America, the growth of the yuppie and dinky populations—households of young upwardly mobile professionals and of double-income no kids yet—has helped to provide a considerable market for the gentrification of large numbers of inner urban areas across a range of cities (Gale, 1984). This range of cities includes places such as Philadelphia with its Society Hill, Boston with Beacon Hill and Back Bay, or Baltimore with its Harbour area. Even such unprepossessing cities as St Louis now have areas in which significant gentrification and revitalization have occurred. In Britain, by contrast, the effect has been much more partial, with only a very few cities—paramount amongst them being London—showing similar effects. Gentrification may have been marked in London, Bristol, and some of the smaller market towns, but is difficult to detect in the large industrial cities of the North, again reflecting the centralizing impact of London.

If British cities have not *generally* paralleled the American experience of inner-city apartment and loft development by the young and single, in the form of a 'back-to-the-city' movement, it could be that, for the future, a significant demographic development will be the era of the 'grumpies', those at the plateau of their careers and past the stage of child-bearing. By the end of the century people between the ages of 45 and retirement will have increased from 9.5 to 11 million and will comprise over one-fifth of the total population. This group *could* provide a more widespread market for urban residential locations through the potential new demand which they might offer for small properties, if they prove not to be seduced by the myths of landed estates in rural areas.

Undoubtedly, demographic changes in the population have created a very different kind of housing market. Currently the greatest need is for specialized housing investment—for flats or sheltered housing for the elderly, for small houses for the single, for large houses for some of the ethnic groups. There is ample stock of the three-bedroom housing which provided the standard accommodation of traditional families. Much of the new forms of specialized investment *could* appropriately go to urban locations. However, the momentum of earlier investment in new family housing in suburban areas has given an impetus to future outward moves of investment and population which will be difficult to deflect. So, even though the changes in age structure have had some beneficial effects on the property market of some British cities (and notably of London), overall they have been swamped in the general momentum created through the earlier outward movement associated with new suburban and ex-urban house construction.

Gigantism

The third element of the perception argument is the disincentives of gigantism within cities—the disillusionment with large bureaucracies and with large-scale developments, most evident in urban areas. The myth of the countryside has received great boost from the development of a more inhuman scale of organization and of building in urban areas. It is this which has been latched on to by the developers with their stress on the rural image of their developments—the Daffodil Dells and Woodley Copses of many new estate developments, whether they are located in cities, small towns, or genuinely village areas. In the 1930s, such images were translated into the Stockbroker Tudor of urban overspill in the ribbon developments at the edge and along the main arterials of large towns, especially in the London area. In the 1970s and 1980s response to this myth has taken more the form of a move to rural areas and to small towns outside the ambit of the metropolitan areas. The arguments about the soullessness of suburbia—of the sameness and facelessness associated with estate development rather than individual houses—was reflected later and to a lesser extent in Britain than in America. It has now received expression not so much in a distaste for suburbia *per se*, but in a distaste for large-scale building of identical housing in estate developments. The era of the instantly re-created village street with broken roof lines has been traded in for the cramped scale of the houses associated with such developments, and if that housing either is or appears to be in a rural setting, the trade-off appears even more acceptable.

All of such arguments take us back to the powerful myth of rurality which has sustained social attitudes for so long. They also invoke something of the strong streak of aggressive individualism which has long characterized the national spirit and which has provided a spur to individual mobility in a relatively hierarchical society. It may suggest that the scope for rescuing cities as places in which to live may immediately be restricted to those places which have dramatic environmental potential in which the creation of social scarcity can be translated into appealing residential environments—the quay-side developments of Bristol, Chatham, Hull, and the Thames or even the canal-side environment of Salford. Quays are one instance; striking vistas on waterfronts such as Liverpool can offer may be another. Water is a great lubricant to the pumping-up of property values in an environmentally conscious age in which the force of the image of rurality still prevails. The potential and the ability to create attractive environments is clearly an important component of the feasibility of rescuing at least parts of some of our large cities.

LOCALITY SPECIFIC ARGUMENTS

The variety of the experiences of different places cannot be doubted. There are a number of specific reasons to which some commentators have turned in explaining urban decline. First are the specific features of particular places. Liverpool, for example, has frequently been argued to have declined because it now faces the wrong way to attract the sea-borne trade on which it historically depended. As UK trade with the European Community increased from 18 per cent in 1965 to 45 per cent in 1983, so Liverpool's share of UK trade fell from 18.5 per cent to 2.8 per cent whereas that of Dover and of Felixstowe has grown from 5 per cent to 21.2 per cent. The changing geometry of trade has created a new map of peripherality within the country (Cheshire, 1987). Advantage has shifted to places in East Anglia and the east coast which had for long been historically decaying. The same could be said of Glasgow. But it would be difficult to fit such an argument to the Bristol case. The generality of decline, albeit with local variations in intensity, robs such specific arguments of much force.

Local politics

Arguments about political activity have been another strand in looking for more place-specific reasons for differential decline. The take-over of particular local administrations by especially virulent forms of hard-left council represents a form of locality-specific political influence. Liverpool and London are again hardy perennials. Committed council activity in support of the dependent population has been argued to drive business away both by the creation of an expensive operating environment through the level of local taxation and by the hostility and uncertainty resulting from a political environment which sees local business as something to milk for resources in support of social welfare and is hostile to the generation of profit.

The level of local rate tax is a recurring element in this. Much of the clamour which has unfairly castigated property-based taxes and has given rise to the proposals to replace rates with a per capita Community Charge has been prompted by arguments both about the unfairness of rates and about the disincentive to business represented by the high levels imposed by certain Labour-controlled authorities. The evidence of research on the impact of rates has not yet given much support to this view. The most recent study suggested that neither the level, nor the rate of change, of rates and rate poundages could be related to changes in employment in local authorities, with the possible exception of office employment (Crawford, Fothergill, and Monk, 1985). The Department of the Environment remains unpersuaded of the force of this view on the grounds that the study covered the period 1974–81 when the costs of the 1974 reorganization had already been incorporated and when rate rises were at a low level (Department of the Environment, 1987a). However, there is as yet no convincing evidence of the impact of rates even on household location, where one would most expect to find such evidence because existing owner-occupiers are unable to trade off between high rates and low values. Indeed, despite the clamour on rate levels, a study comparing the movement to identical new houses in adjacent high- and low-rated areas in Greater Manchester has suggested that it is hard to demonstrate that in practice households are influenced by rate levels in their choice of housing (Robson and Bradford, 1984). Part of the lack of impact is the result of many households' local taxes being met from public funds through rate rebates. Part is due to the capitalization of high rates in the value of land and hence the reduction in values and in rents charged for land in areas with higher rates. Part is due to the small marginal cost of local taxes for anything other than offices and shops. These arguments do not eliminate the importance of high rate levels and high rate rises. Non-residential land uses do not qualify for rate rebates. Most importantly, rate increases (as against existing levels) are not necessarily reflected in the short run by reductions in rent or in value. Moreover, for the owner-occupier of either business or housing, the increased outgoings cannot be offset against some other owner. There is an element of real disincentive and displacement through high increases in the level of rates, both for businesses operating on small margins and for more marginal owner-occupier households, and an opportunity effect on those firms or activities that might have located but decided not to locate in high-rate areas because of their perception of the relative operating costs of a high-rate and high rate-increase environment.

The most publicized of the left-wing authorities have consciously created bastions of state socialism in the areas which they control and, rightly or wrongly, have thereby created deeper divisions between central and local government, between owner-occupiers and council tenancy, between the private and public sectors, all of which are self-perpetuating and self-reinforcing. There are clear resource implications to such divisions. While Liverpool, for example, has received rather generous additional central-government provision, in most cases central/local hostility has reduced resources through the effects of the general reduction of central payments to local authorities and of specific instances of rate-capping legislation applied to a small number of key local authorities. Attitudes of adjoining authorities can create very different contexts for collaborative work between central and local government or in providing operating environments for potential private-sector investment. The worlds of a moderate Salford anxious to exploit such potential, and of a Manchester committed to opposition, are radically different environments. Left-wing control has generally denied additional resources through the local authorities' hostility to use of schemes such as those of the Manpower Services Commission, or to working with the Task Forces and exploiting the take-up of Urban Development Grants. It has reduced the probability of new private investment through overt hostility to the private sector. Indeed, even in the non-radicalized cities, one of the ironies of active local-authority initiatives in local economic-development schemes is that energetic public activity can diminish the likelihood of future private investment in an area. Success in building publicly provided advance factories reduces the probability of attracing private-sector investment since it removes the very market shortage which might otherwise have attraced such investment. Public-sector activity can therefore reinforce the conditions which deter the private sector. Many northern local authorities have had difficulty in developing in partnership with the private sector because of the lower market demand

(Fothergill, Monk, and Perry, 1987). In 1982, half of all active authorities had built some or all of their industrial units in partnership with the private sector (often through leaseback arrangements). In the South East this figure was over three-quarters, but in the North it was less than one-fifth. Private activity is guided by different principles from those of the public sector. The private sector looks for returns on capital and on accessibility; the public sector looks for access to labour markets.

NEW INVESTMENT AND SMALL FIRMS

These sets of arguments take us some way to understanding the context within which large industrial towns, and particularly those in the North, have suffered such dramatic reduction in their employment base. Cities have become increasingly unattractive locations in which to retain existing investments and the shake-out of activity over the recessions of the mid-1970s and 1980–1 have consequently hit hardest at the economic structure of the large old industrial cities. The obverse side of the coin is the question of where *new* investment is going.

Much of the new investment has been in small enterprises. There has been a striking growth of small firms in Britain—along with many other advanced industrial areas such as America and Europe. Having suffered a long secular decline in numbers from the 1930s, small manufacturing firms began to grow in numbers from the early or middle 1970s (Keeble, 1986). Frank, Miall, and Rees (1984) show that it was only the smallest UK manufacturing establishments which increased their total employment between 1975 and 1978: those employing 10–20 people growing by 7.5 per cent and those employing 20–50 by 3.1 per cent; as against those with 50–200 falling by 1.4 per cent, those with 200–500 falling by 4.7 per cent, and those of 500 and over falling by 7.3 per cent. Some have seen in this a panacea for employment decline, most notably Birch in the United States (Birch, 1980), and some part of the growth has reflected government encouragement to the small firm through a variety of schemes of financial help and advice. It has to be remembered, however, that the total employment contribution of such small firms is very small in aggregate. Most redundancies have come from large firms: for example in Manchester, of the total of 3,300 redundancies in 1984 no fewer than 1,800 were accounted for by only nine companies, each involving more than 100 workers. Over one hundred small firms would be needed to replace such losses. The sobering fact, too, is that the death rates of small firms are extremely high. Their births and deaths have been seen as an escalator progression; for every new small firm which joins the escalator through births, an older small firm is pushed off the top of the escalator and dies (Lloyd and Dicken, 1982). The analogy emphasizes a principal difficulty of the small firm; that of finding and expanding a market niche beyond the confines of its relatively protected immediate locality. The aptitudes out of which many small firms originate are essentially the technical skills of their founder; the transition from such skills to those needed for marketing, accountancy, and man-management—which would be essential prerequisites for subsequent growth—is one which few small firms are able to achieve.

Small firms can be seen as having grown on the basis either of recession-push or of technology-pull. Neither appears to offer great hope for the prospects of the declining cities of the North. The recession-push firms are those which have grown with the retrenchment of the large corporate sector, exploiting market niches left by the shrinkage of large enterprise or employing skilled labour released by the closure or contraction of large firms. Most do not aim at innovativeness and use only current technologies. They partly exist under the protective shelter of the subcontracting market provided by large firms, especially within local labour markets which are dominated by a few large firms, as with the car industry in the West Midlands or the engineering industry in the North West. The symbiotic relationship between the large corporate company and the small competitive firm means that it would be unrealistic to look for an autonomous revival in employment from such small firms alone.

The growth of small firms through technology-pull, on the other hand, has involved more genuine innovativeness and has drawn on science-based leading-edge technology. Here, the new locational impulses have equally offered little hope to the large urban areas. The great preponderance of such small high-technology firms have developed in southern and more rural areas—in East Anglia and the Home Counties to the west of London. It is along the so-called M4 Corridor and around the crescent to the west and and north of London that such firms have developed to form the high-tech. belt stretching from Cambridge west to Swindon, Reading, Cheltenham, and Bristol, and with a belt south to Southampton. Most of such firms (Storey, 1982; Lloyd and Mason, 1984) have been founded by entrepreneurs who themselves came from existing small or medium-sized companies rather than from large firms—and important in this respect is the role of existing research establishments. Since there is a clear relationship between such areas and the preponderance of managerial and professional workers, the location of such new enterprises, with the growth potential that they hold, seems predominantly to reinforce the disparities between urban and non-urban areas. This provides yet further grounds for considering the policy implications of the effect of the occupational composition of different areas and of public investment in facilities for research and development.

CONCLUSION

It is clear that aspects of each of these themes overlap and reinforce each other. The increasing concentration of high-level occupations in the South East is consistent both with ideas about restructuring and the new spatial division of labour and with views about the perceived residential attractiveness of areas within the South East. The impact of rates can equally be seen as consistent both with views about the locality-specific arguments on the decline of particular places and with arguments about factor costs. The decay of the environment, the characteristics of labour forces, and the age of the infrastructure of capital in cities are equally embodied in arguments about the restructuring of existing business and about the locational imperatives on new investment. To hope for a single consistent 'explanation' of patchwork Britain is chimerical. The instant analyses so favoured by politicians and pundits along with the equally facile responses have merely exacerbated a difficult situation. The intense and bitter politicization surrounding housing policy, investment, taxation, and the roles of every sector of government have added fuel to the fire.

Coherent, consensual policy—perhaps a figment of imagination in itself—needs to concentrate on four elements of the processes involved in urban change. First is the fact of industrial restructuring in pursuit of maximizing returns. This has involved centralization of control through a sequence of mergers and take-overs and a process of streamlining labour and skill inputs so as to achieve a more flexible labour force, a course of action which has worked to the disadvantage of cities because of the vintage of their capital and the rigidity of labour and managerial attitudes. Second are the factor constraints, amongst which perhaps the most important is the question of the availability of land and buildings. Third is the perceived or real unattractiveness of urban areas as a location for those who have freedom of choice in where they live and work. Within this, some of the principal elements which make cities unattractive are the squalor of the environment, the depersonalizing effect of the growth of large-scale bureaucracies, and the hostility to profit-making enterprises of local councils. Fourth is the social composition of local areas, with its implications both for the likelihood of generating self-sustaining business enterprise and for the creation of conditions of social unrest and political hostility which affect the buoyancy of local areas.

These processes of change have helped to create urban decline and to feed the downward spiral of social, economic, and environmental malaise in large cities. They are the elements which we need to consider both in evaluating the response of policy-makers to the fortunes of large cities and in considering ways in which such policy might best address the problems in the future. Much of the interest of the research which has evaluated the urban condition lies in its delineation of how lacking in coherence the response of policy has been. The adversarial nature of our parliamentary democracy coupled with the tunnel vision of our policy-makers has resulted in a frustrating mosaic of missed opportunities, of millions of pounds wasted, of embittered local communities, of deeper urban malaise—and of occasional success stories.

4

What has been Done? *There is no Health in us*

> We have left undone those things which we ought to have done; and we have done those things which we ought not to have done; and there is no health in us.
>
> *Book of Common Prayer*

Despite claims to the contrary, the resources which have been channelled to tackle urban problems have been quite generous. Unfortunately they have also been piecemeal, *ad hoc*, and subject to the law of one hand taking away what the other was giving. Since the start of the 'Urban Programme' in the late 1960s, the resources have grown progressively to a peak of over £300 million in the early 1980s (Fig. 4.1). In real terms, the Urban Programme grew substantially in the late 1970s to early 1980s and has seen rather less than level funding in the last few years. The major change was the development of the Enhanced Urban Programme from 1977/8 out of which were created the Partnership and Programme areas and through which specific new sums of resources were added. Under this enhanced programme, a growing range of specific policy instruments and kinds of public resource have become available under the aegis of the Department of the Environment over the years since 1977–8 (Fig. 4.2), with new schemes adding to the original Traditional Urban Programme to create a pot-pourri of programmes.

These, of course, are only one part of the public funds which have affected the fortunes of cities. Kenneth Clark, on his appointment as the government's co-ordinator of inner-city policy in 1987, suggested that the total annual expenditure on inner areas was £2 billion. Three months later, in March 1988 at the launch of *Action for Cities*, the Prime Minister suggested that £3 billion was being spent annually on inner-city programmes. Neither specified the items which might be

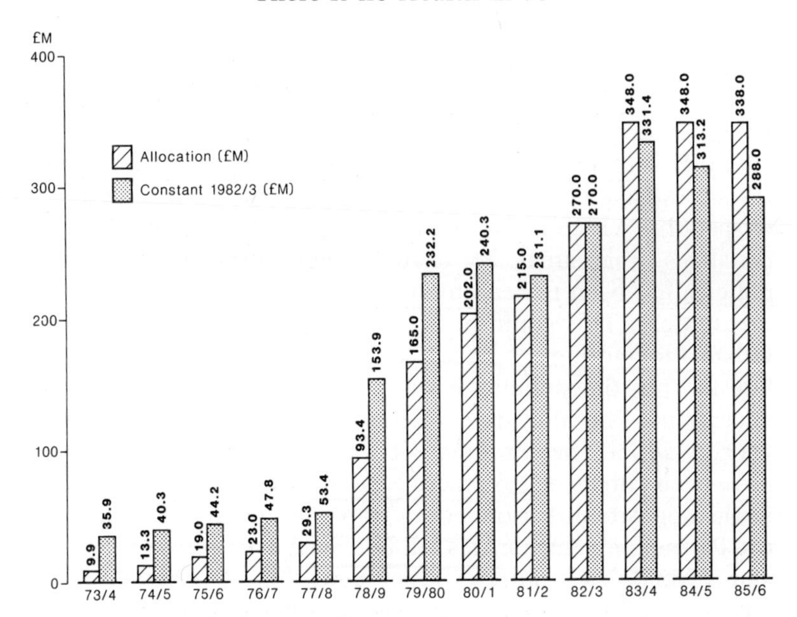

FIG. 4.1. Urban Programme resources, 1973/1974–1985/1986
Source: Department of the Environment.

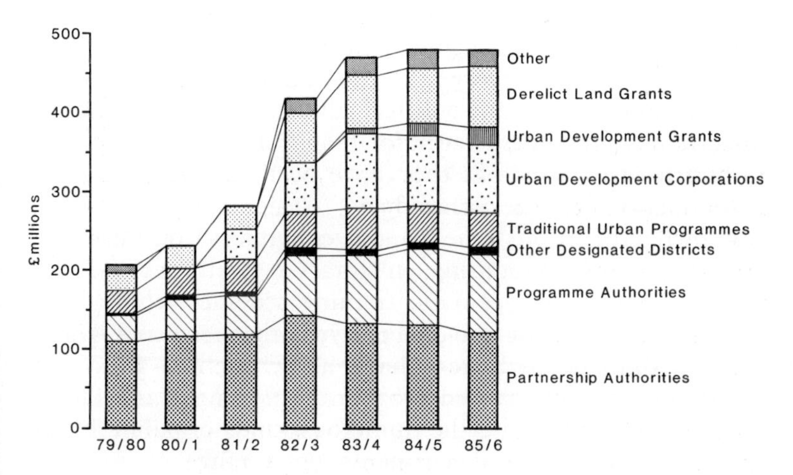

FIG. 4.2. Changes in expenditure for categories within the Urban Programme, 1979/1980–1985/1986

Source: Department of the Environment.

included in such overall estimates, but it is clear that there is a wide variety of measures which impinge on urban areas and can be considered as part of a wider urban programme. The bolder claims draw heavily on MSC expenditure (Hennessey, 1988). This makes it impossible to say with any certainty what resources have been devoted to cities since there is a plethora of spending which intentionally or unintentionally benefits or penalizes urban areas. For example, one of the aims of urban policies has been to bend mainstream spending so as to assist urban areas. This could have been a major way in which the Urban Programme resources could have been supplemented, but in this the policies have in practice not been notably successful. The allocation of Rate Support Grant is another way in which the resources of the urban programme could have been enhanced; in practice events have generally worked in the opposite direction. For example, Rate Support Grant for the Partnership Authorities fell by 25 per cent between 1980/1 and 1982/3, as against 13 per cent for all English local authorities (Buck, Gordon, and Young, 1986, p. 115). In London, boroughs designated under the Urban Programme received some £300 million between 1979/80 and 1983/4, but they 'lost' five times that amount (£1,530 million) through reduction in Rate Support Grant over the same period (Lever and Moore, 1986, p. 145). The rate-capping and rate limitation of the last few years has clearly worked to the financial disadvantage of urban areas (even if to the political advantage of their councils, since it has provided a lever for many of the affected local authorities to claim that they have been robbed by central government). On the other hand, a significant, although unknown, proportion of the Manpower Services Commission's resources—now amounting in total to well over £2,500 million—have been spent on training schemes which have disproportionately affected unemployed urban residents. Those cities within assisted areas have also benefited from the continuing, if much reduced, programme of regional assistance. Over and above this are the numerous kinds of public funds spent by government departments on a range of a-spatial programmes, some of which have beneficial or detrimental effect on large cities.

Formal allocation of Urban Programme resources has reflected many of the concerns identified in the last chapter. Not least it has responded to arguments about the primacy of the economic origin of urban problems. An 'Urban Programme' was started in 1968 under the auspices of the then Prime Minister Harold Wilson, and prompted by concern about social and ethnic problems (Lawless, 1986). Expenditure has undergone major changes in focus over the years since the Urban Programme began. In the early years of the late 1960s and early 1970s the focus was distinctly on social and community programmes (Edwards and Batley, 1978), reflecting the contemporary concern with ethnic issues and social deprivation out of which the programme began. Increasingly—in the face both of recession and job loss and of the growing consensus that the 'urban problem' was underlain by economic processes—the focus has moved to job creation and to economic issues. If resources are split crudely into economic, environmental, and social, it has been the economic and environmental which have grown or remained constant, at the expense of the social component (Table 4.1). Since 1981 resources have formally been bent towards economic aims: a DoE guideline of that year urged that there 'must be a presumption in favour of projects which have as their objective the stimulation of economic activity appropriate to the area'. Of the three principal aims in the guidelines which were issued—securing economic regeneration, improving the environment, and gearing services and amenities to the needs of local communities—it has been the economic which has had increasing primacy, not least through the

TABLE 4.1 *The changing balance of expenditure on economic, environmental, and social projects, 1979/1980–1984/1985*

Category of expenditure	Financial year					
	1979/80	1980/1	1981/2	1982/3	1983/4	1984/5
Economic	29	30	31	37	37	38
Environmental	19	18	25	27	25	20
Social	51	52	44	36	38	42

Source: Department of the Environment (1986).

priority given to expenditure on capital projects rather than revenue expenditure.

The aims of current policy are to tackle the impacts of long-term change in the economic structure of cities by restoring confidence, initiative, enterprise, and choice. In this there is an uneasy relationship between the two poles of attempting to enhance market viability and of offering assistance to disadvantaged individuals through policies of targeting at a local level. This is evident in the five official objectives which have been specified:

1. to enhance job prospects by providing increased job opportunities in inner urban areas, and improving the ability of residents to compete for them;
2. to bring land and buildings into use by reclaiming derelict land in inner urban areas and nationally, and by encouraging new private-sector development;
3. to encourage private investment in inner urban areas;
4. to improve housing conditions in inner urban areas by widening choice and reducing housing stress; and
5. to encourage self-help and improve the social fabric in urban areas.

The focus on economic aims and on encouragement to the private sector are unambiguous; the social aims are partly embedded in the first goal and more overtly, but very opaquely, specified in the fifth. The overall aim, of stimulating local economies, has involved either attracting new enterprise to distressed urban areas or helping to restructure existing old, and usually large, industries. In this process attention has been paid to both the supply and demand sides. Improving the commercial viability and attractiveness of areas as places in which to invest has been tackled through improvements to the local environment, through the provision of infrastructure and buildings for firms, or through the creation of an environment more receptive to and more ready to assist private enterprise through public/private partnerships. The need to improve the skills and aptitudes of local people has been recognized through the introduction of training programmes and incentives to enterprise. The social aim of assisting the disadvantaged has involved specific training of the unemployed and often the use of voluntary-sector bodies as means of reaching those most in need. There has been an obvious tension between these dual economic and social objectives and, underpinning this, there has been a more fundamental clash between the arguments of a national requirement for efficiency and competitiveness on the one hand and of the desire to meet the needs of deprived people and deprived areas on the other. The two goals have largely been seen as in conflict and, at the margin, national need has taken preference so that investment in 'attractive' areas has not been steered elsewhere on the grounds that, if obstacles were to be placed in the way of investment either from foreign- or national-based enterprise, this would run the risk of driving investment abroad.

In pursuit of these twin goals, we can identify three general sets of policy instrument which have consistently been used: spatial targeting to areas and to people; the encouragement of partnerships, first between different arms of the state and then between the public and private sectors; and the creation of new agencies. Within each of these there has been an ever-growing mix of specific policy measures and instruments developed over the last two decades.

SPATIAL TARGETING

Channelling benefits to defined spatial areas now has a long history in British public policy: longest in regional planning, where there has been the sequence of Special Areas, Development Areas, and Assisted Areas running from the 1930s; but also in the social field, with slum-clearance areas for housing and, after the late 1960s, the development of Educational Priority Areas and of housing-based priority areas in the form of General Improvement Areas and Housing Action Areas. The logic of spatial targeting has been vigorously debated ever since it was first introduced (Edwards and Batley, 1978). The arguments against any form of spatial targeting are that, where there is no overwhelming spatial concentration of physical or social problems, effort and resources will be wasted by being spent on areas which include only a small percentage of problem cases. As a result, in the processes of tackling such areas or people, public resources are given to many individuals and buildings which do not require assistance or could draw on their own private resources, thereby incurring opportunity costs for those people and areas in greater need. The second argument against such targeting relates to mobility and so applies to people rather than the environment. If people are mobile, is it not better to encourage them to move to areas of greater opportunity, not least because spatially targeted resources might merely draw in beneficiaries from elsewhere who are less in need than those living in deprived areas?

The logic of either form of targeting can be justified, however, on a number of counts. First they are justified if the identified problems are themselves sufficiently spatially concentrated so that, by defining areas on the ground, one effectively tackles a significant proportion of the cases at issue. Second, even if there is only some but no very marked pattern of spatial concentration of the problem, spatial targeting can still be justified on the grounds that there are additionality effects associated with tackling problems in a defined area: there can be spillover effects for the area as a whole and for areas immediately adjacent which will make investment more efficient, *or* there are efficiency effects associated with the administrative logic of concentrating action in a limited area rather than using 'pepper-pot' techniques scattered over a larger area. The case is nicely illustrated by the use of 'enveloping' in house improvement (by which whole areas rather than individual houses are rehabilitated), which was pioneered by Birmingham and subsequently taken up by some authorities such as Leicester. Even though some of the houses in enveloping schemes are less in need of rehabilitation and some of the residents are able to undertake repairs themselves, there are strong arguments based on externality effects and administrative efficiency for tackling whole terraces of houses in a concerted universal programme. Inevitably any form of spatial targeting must throw up some anomalies, as the Education Priority Areas showed only too clearly, but the balance of advantage suggests the value of tackling problems in a spatially concentrated fashion. Maclennan's study of the spillover effects of house improvement through housing associations within priority areas in Glasgow suggests the benefits that can accrue: private housing in blocks adjacent to the publicly funded improvement increased in value by 8 per cent over two years and building societies began to grant mortgages more readily to old houses in adjacent areas (Maclennan, 1987). The argument for spatial targeting of resources rests on the same firm bases of equity and efficiency which underscore the broader need for an urban policy.

Designated areas

The Urban Programme has used spatial targeting ever since its inception. Since the enhanced programme in 1977/8, however, the approach has been used to an increasing extent. The declaration of seven Parternship Authorities (in which central and local government were to work together to draw up agreed programmes of action), together with Programme Authorities and Other Designated Districts, each of which are invited to bid for additional resources from the Urban Programme, has spelled out a new form of geographical urban policy through which spatial targeting of public finance can operate (Fig. 4.3). Many of the related policy instruments have equally been targeted to these same sets of cities. Within each of the Programme Authorities this same spatial principle has been followed by designating defined areas demarcated as 'inner-city areas' which were allegedly defined on the basis of eight indicators of well-being: unemployment; overcrowded households; households lacking exclusive use of amenities; pensioners living alone; single-parent families; population in households with heads born in the New Commonwealth or Pakistan; population change; and standard mortality rates.

This declaration of defined sets of designated authorities to which additional aid has gone has created considerable opportunities for new projects within those areas, offering both local authorities and the voluntary-sector agencies within them the prospect of developing schemes to tackle economic, environmental, and social problems. It has been to the Partnership Authorities that the most generous funding of the Enhanced Urban Programme has gone, amounting, for example in 1987–8, to between £10m. and £25m. per annum (Table 4.2). The other authorities invited to submit bids for Inner Area resources have included both the Programme Authorities (which received considerably smaller sums) and Other Designated

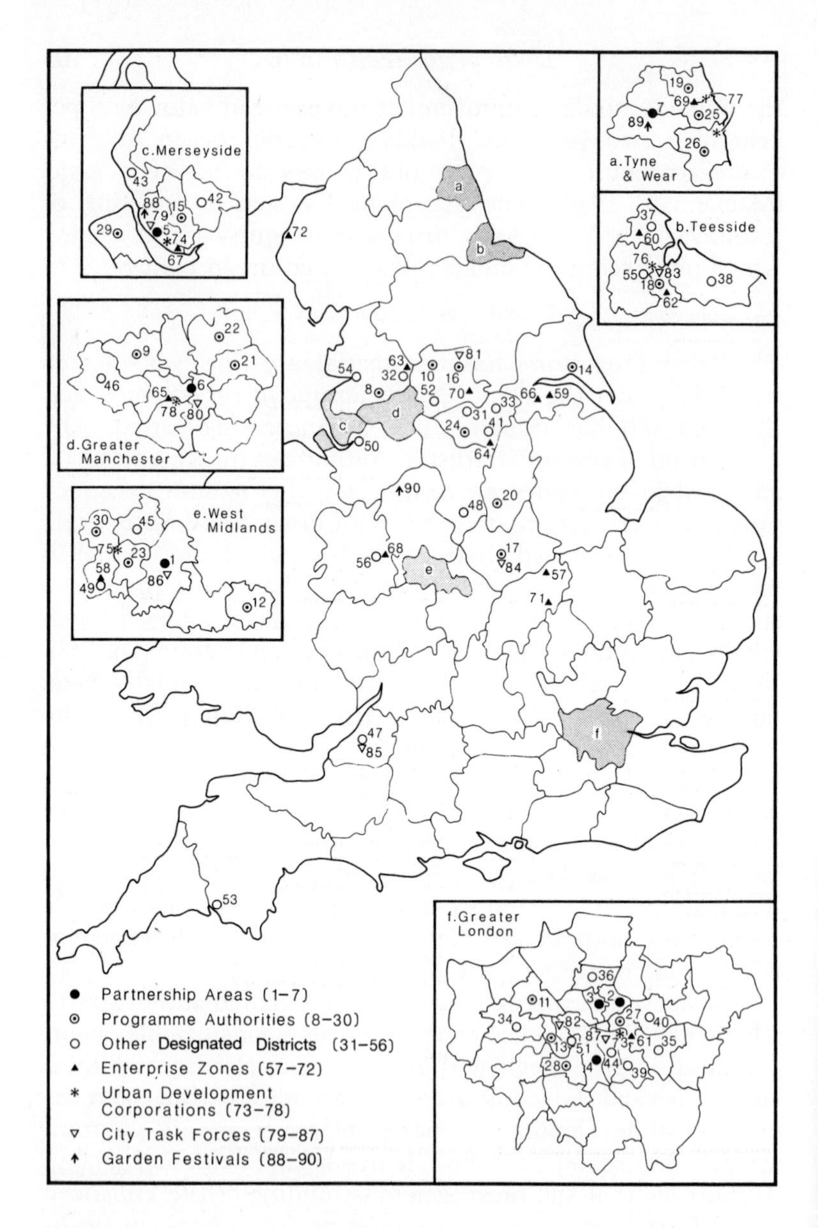

FIG. 4.3. Priority areas in the Urban Programme, England 1986

Note: To these area-based policy instruments must now be added the subsequent announcements of additional Task Forces and Urban Development Corporations. The names of the priority areas are listed in Table 4.2.

Source: Department of the Environment (1987).

TABLE 4.2 *Urban Programme allocations, 1987–1988 and 1988–1989*

	£ million			£ million	
	1987/8	1988/9		1987/8	1988/9
Partnership Authorities			*Other Designated Districts*		
1. Birmingham	25.0	24.7	31. Barnsley	1.5	1.5
2. Hackney	10.8	9.7	32. Burnley	1.0	1.8
3. Islington	10.0	9.7	33. Doncaster	1.8	1.8
4. Lambeth	12.8	11.8	34. Ealing	—	—
5. Liverpool	20.0	20.5	35. Greenwich	1.5	1.9
6. Manchester/Salford	23.8	22.2	36. Haringey	2.0	2.3
7. Newcastle/Gateshead	17.2	16.8	37. Hartlepool	1.8	1.8
			38. Langbaurgh	1.8	1.8
Programme Authorities			39. Lewisham	1.5	2.0
			40. Newham	1.8	2.3
8. Blackburn	4.0	4.0	41. Rotherham	1.8	1.8
9. Bolton	4.0	3.8	42. St Helens	1.5	1.7
10. Bradford	4.5	4.5	43. Sefton	1.5	1.5
11. Brent	4.0	3.9	44. Southwark	1.8	2.3
12. Coventry	5.0	4.8	45. Walsall	1.5	1.5
13. Hammersmith/Fulham	5.0	4.3	46. Wigan	1.5	2.2
14. Kingston-on-Hull	5.0	4.9			
15. Knowsley	4.0	3.9	*New Programme Authorities*		
16. Leeds	4.5	4.4			
17. Leicester	5.4	5.4	78. Bristol	1.5	1.5
18. Middlesborough	5.5	5.5	79. Derby	1.3	1.4
19. N. Tyneside	3.5	3.4	80. Dudley	1.3	1.3
20. Nottingham	5.5	5.5	81. Halton	1.3	1.4
21. Oldham	4.0	3.7	82. Kensington/Chelsea	1.3	1.9
22. Rochdale	4.0	3.6	83. Kirklees	0.8	0.8
23. Sandwell	5.0	4.9	84. Plymouth	0.4	1.0
24. Sheffield	5.5	5.5	85. Preston	1.3	2.0
25. S. Tyneside	4.5	4.4	86. Stockton	1.3	1.4
26. Sunderland	4.0	4.4	87. The Wrekin	0.4	0.6
27. Tower Hamlets	4.5	4.5			
28. Wandsworth	4.5	4.5			
29. Wirral	3.5	3.4			
30. Wolverhampton	5.5	5.4			

Note: Numbers refer to the references in Fig. 4.3. The 'New Programme Authorities' are those 'particularly needy' districts which were not designated under the Urban Areas Act 1978, but which were invited to submit programmes in 1987/8. In 1986/7, they and other districts had been invited to submit programmes, but this invitation was not extended in 1987/8 to the following: Calderdale, Camden, Corby, Derwentside, Ellesmere Port, Grimsby, Hyndburn, Lincoln, Luton, Pendle, Rossendale, Scunthorpe, Sedgefield, Stoke-on-Trent, Tameside, Trafford, Waltham Forest, Wear Valley, West Lancashire, and Westminster.

Source: Department of the Environment (1987).

Districts. In 1986–7 a range of authorities not designated under the original Inner Urban Areas Act of 1978 was invited to bid for Urban Programme resources in the final year of the 'Traditional Urban Programme'; however, the aim of avoiding too thin a spread of resources across numerous districts led the DoE both to exclude many of these areas for 1987–8 and to exclude Ealing on the grounds that its unemployment rate was well below the national average. The non-designated districts which *were* included in 1987–8 were determined on the basis of the scale and intensity of their deprivation and the concentration and persistence of their unemployment, using ward-based indicators from the 1981 Census (see Note to Table 4.2). The list of priority areas now numbers over fifty districts, each of which individually receives additional resources from the Urban Programme. It has been these sets of cities which have provided the backbone of the targeting of the resources of the Urban Programme.

Such targeting of Urban Programme resources has not always been complemented by the allocation of resources from other government programmes, many of which have not always worked in the same direction. This has been true of the spatial impacts of regional policy. Clydeside, for example, shows a marked disparity between the largely non-urban allocation of regional aid from DTI, which has gone to firms mainly in the peripheral areas, on the one hand, and on the other the Glasgow-based pattern of the distribution of Urban Programme monies from DoE. The disparity is a function of both the distribution of heavy industry in Clydeside—which largely lies outside the city of Glasgow itself—and the goal of regional planning under the Department of Trade and Industry, which looks for whatever areas appear most likely to offer returns on investment. Lever and Moore (1986, pp. 48–54) show that this tendency for regional resources to go to non-priority areas applies to most of the large regional programmes in Clydeside. Regional Development Grant in the four-year period 1979–83 was used to help in modernizing the old industrial base of the region, and was spent disproportionately outside Glasgow: 69 per cent of expenditure was incurred outside the city despite the fact that 55 per cent of employment was found within Glasgow. Regional Selective Assistance showed an even more extreme imbalance with only 22 per cent of resources going to Glasgow. By comparison, assistance to the service sector under the Office of Service Industries Scheme has gone overwhelmingly to establishments in and on the periphery of Glasgow's central business district. European development funds (European Regional Development Fund grants, European Investment Bank loans, and funds from the European Coal and Steel Community and the European Social Fund) for the six years 1978–83 have again shown a marked tendency to favour areas outside Glasgow—with only 22 per cent going to Glasgow and 78 per cent outside. By contrast, in the North East of England, regional assistance in the Newcastle metropolitan region *has* predominantly benefited the inner areas—reflecting the peculiar industrial geography of the region. The designated inner areas of Tyne and Wear (with 44 per cent of total employment and 52 per cent of manufacturing employment) received identical proportions of DTI regional funds as of DoE Urban Programme funds (at 65 per cent), reflecting the pattern of the area's industrial structure, in which some heavily aided industries—especially shipbuilding, engineering, and breweries—happen to be located in the inner area (Robinson *et al.*, 1987). Spatial targeting within the Urban Programme has in some instances therefore been counteracted by the different logic of non-Urban Programme resource allocation. As these examples suggest, whether the regional and the urban programmes work in the same or in conflicting spatial directions has depended on the happenstance of the industrial geography of different areas.

The kinds of activities for which the targeted Urban Programme resources have been used cover a very wide range of projects, culled both from local authorities themselves and from the voluntary sector. It is here that the switch from social to economic projects after 1981 can most clearly be seen. The pattern of spend for one area, Newcastle, shows this to good effect (Fig. 4.4), with the percentage of expenditure on social projects being halved from 60 per cent to 30 per cent and with economic projects more than doubling from less than one-quarter to 45 per cent. Under each heading, a wide variety of types of projects have been tackled. The typical range of economic projects has included the provision of sites and

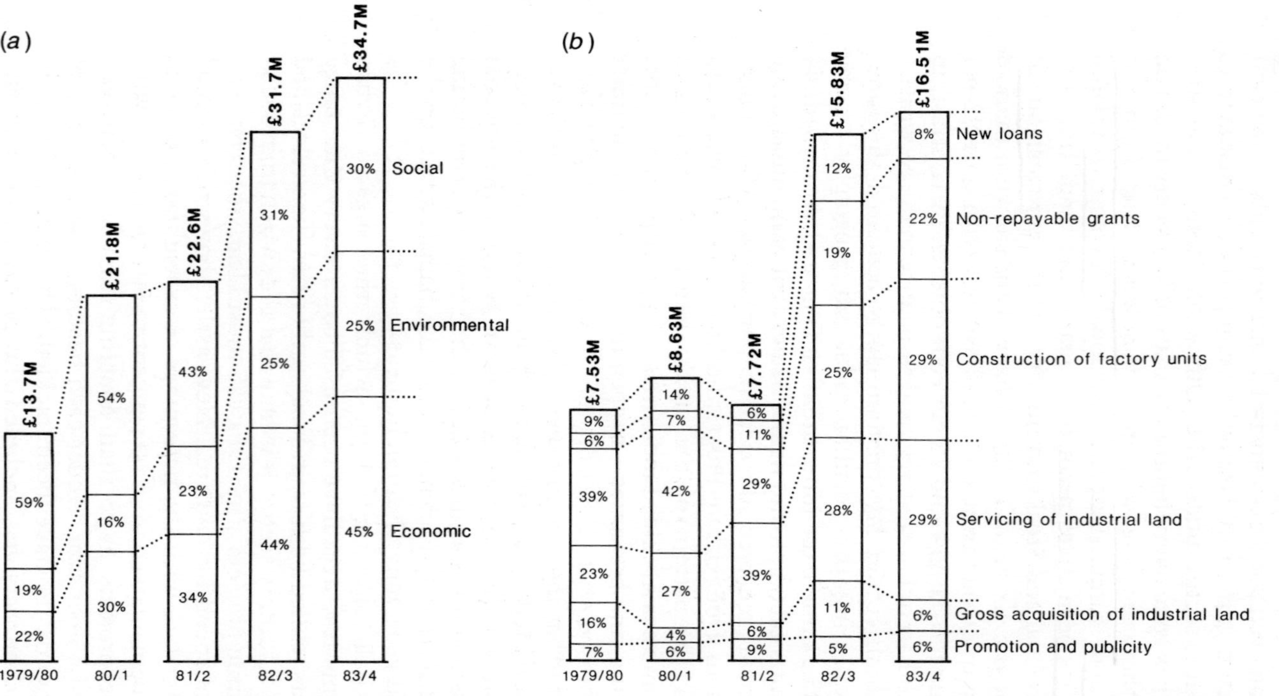

FIG. 4.4. Urban Programme expenditure by category in the Newcastle metropolitan area: (*a*) by category of overall expenditure; (*b*) by categories within expenditure on economic development

Source: Robinson *et al.* (1987).

premises to encourage employment, environmental improvements often linked to the attraction of new productive investment, and the payment of grants and loans. Again, the changes of emphasis over time are instructive, with a general tendency for rather less to be spent on physical planning in the form of construction and land assembly and much more emphasis on grants and loans.

In the social field, schemes have involved the provision of community facilities through advice centres, community centres, and play schemes and a range of community development initiatives, most of which have involved the appointment of new staff rather than the provision of capital amenities. Increasing difficulties have been experienced as resources have been switched from social to economic expenditure and from revenue to capital expenditure. This has particularly affected the voluntary sector—from which many of the most innovative projects have emanated in those local authorities which have allocated large proportions of social-sector money to voluntary agencies. There is a sense that the voluntary sector has increasingly been excluded from the Urban Programme, despite the early indications that the programme was seen as a way of releasing 'the energies of local communities' (DoE, 1977). The problem has been twofold. First is the silting-up of funds as the early projects have become 'time-expired'. This has presented local authorities with financial difficulties in being expected to take such projects on to mainstream funding. The more active an authority has been, the more difficult are these 'time-expiry' difficulties which they now face. In 1986–7, Bradford, which has long been generous in its support of the voluntary sector, had £700,000 of Urban Programme time-expired projects; Hackney had £1m., of which further DoE support will be offered to less than one-half; Manchester had £1.3m. of time-expired projects and has estimated that by 1990 it will face an additional expenditure of £6m. per year through time-expired projects. The Department of the Environment has developed a variety of tapering proposals for those time-expired projects to which it offers further resources, varying from one area to another. In Hackney, for example, it has proposed to pay 75 per cent of its previous grant in the first year of a time-expired project, 25 per cent in the second, and none in the third; in Nottingham, projects have been renewed for different lengths of time—some for a further three, some for two, and some for one year (National Council for Voluntary Organisations, 1986). In all cases, the piling-up of financial expectations to support the continuation of increasing numbers of highly worthwhile projects presents central government, local authorities, and the voluntary agencies themselves with very real difficulties. The second problem has been the switch from current to capital allocations within the programme so that projects looking for resources for new posts have found increasing difficulty in being funded. This contraction has been one of the forgone opportunities of the Urban Programme since, in the early years, the voluntary sector was able to develop a variety of novel and imaginative schemes, attuned in scale and sensitivity to the needs of local people and avoiding the bureaucratic cumbersomeness of many of the local-authority schemes. By comparison with many local-authority projects—some of which had the air of having been taken from the shelf of existing unfunded projects and dusted off as responses to the Urban Programme—much of the voluntary-sector response has involved genuine innovativeness and has developed schemes much better targeted to and much more accessible to those in need.

The principle of spatial targeting has equally been applied to many policy instruments in addition to the declaration of Partnership and Programme Authorities. Examples include Enterprise Zones; Garden Festivals; Simplified Planning Zones, in which certain types of development are permitted without the need to seek planning permission so as to attract new investment through the relaxation of controls; and Commercial and Industrial Improvement Grants, which have been widely used to clear up and improve the environment and infrastructure of small areas in the hope of attracting new businesses or manufacturing firms to inner areas. An example of the last, from Manchester, is the revitalization of the Smithfields Market through the general improvement of the environment of the area, into which have now been attracted a series of small retail workshops in a renewed market hall, small commercial establishments in adjoining streets, a garden centre, as well as newly built council housing. Oldham Street, much decayed as a shopping street in the CBD after the opening of a new Arndale Centre, has had Commercial Improvement Grant resources to improve shop premises, as have shops in Princess Road, the scene of the 1981 riots in Moss Side.

Garden Festivals

The Garden Festivals followed the example of Germany and were first introduced by Michael Heseltine in Liverpool in 1984. The Liverpool Garden Festival has had mixed fortunes. It made a £1m. operating profit in the five months of its running, subsequently the site turned into a white elephant, was taken over in 1986 by a leisure company which went out of business, and now the Merseyside Development Corporation is to sell sections of it for housing and will promote the rest as 45-acre regional 'theme park'. The Stoke Garden Festival in 1986 has had an almost mirror-image experience. It ended with a deficit after attracting less-than-expected custom, but is now being treated as one large development project which has attracted considerable commercial interest for the 180-acre site, suggesting the potential value of the initial investment in landscaping. A plan involving its development, with 70 acres for leisure, shopping, offices, and light industry, and the remainder as open space, is now being competed for by two developers. Glasgow, in 1988, will be the third such site—hoping to attract further tourist custom in addition to the trade generated by its recent exhibition hall, by the Burrell Collection in a new pupose-built gallery which has become a major tourist honeypot, and by a proposal to build a new concert hall in 1990 to mark Glasgow's designation as Europe's 'City of Culture'. After the Garden Festival, the site will be used by the volume house-builder, Laing Homes, which already owns it. Further such Festivals are planned for Gateshead in 1990 and South Wales in 1992.

Enterprise Zones

The most controversial example of spatial targeting has been the creation of Enterprise Zones, a package of measures which was announced in the 1980 Budget, with the first 9 areas in Great Britain being designated in 1981 and a further 13 in 1983 (Table 4.3). The package includes a variety of incentives aimed

TABLE 4.3. *Enterprise Zones in England, Wales, and Scotland*

	Designation date	Size (acres)	Existing employment at designation	Additional employment (to Sept. 1984)
Corby	June 1981	280	—	4,100
Dudley	July 1981	649	2,671	129
Glanford	Apr. 1984	124	41	159
Hartlepool	Oct. 1981	270	299	801
Isle of Dogs	Apr. 1982	362	641	1,859
Middlesbrough	Nov. 1983	190	1,356	− 656
NE Lancs.	Dec. 1983	282	740	560
NW Kent	Oct. 1983	370	752	1,548
Rotherham	Aug. 1983	260	531	569
Salford/Trafford	Aug. 1981	875	2,254	846
Scunthorpe	Sept. 1983	260		
Speke	Aug. 1981	340	565	235
Telford	Jan. 1984	279	—	600
Tyneside	Aug. 1981	1,120	10,363	2,137
Wakefield	July 1981	220	1,196	404
Wellingborough	July 1983	136	32	268
Workington	Oct. 1983	215	397	203
Delyn	July 1983	293	933	267
Milford Haven	Apr. 1984	362	1,200	0
Swansea	Jan. 1981	775	2,068	1,232
Clydebank	Aug. 1981	570	2,825	2,675
Invergordon	Oct. 1983	148	103	− 3
Tayside	Jan. 1983	260	546	654

Source: National Audit Office (1986)

at removing various tax burdens from firms within the specified areas and relaxing or speeding up certain statutory or administrative controls on firms within the area. Industrial and commercial firms, for example, were initially exempted from the now-abandoned Development Land Tax; most significantly, they are exempted from the payment of local rates on premises for a period of ten years. They have 100 per cent allowance for Corporation and Income Tax purposes for capital expenditure on buildings; they are exempted from industrial training levies and requirements to supply information to

Industrial Training Boards; applications for certain customs facilities are processed as a matter of priority; planning requirements are greatly simplified by allowing developments which conform to the general planning scheme for the area to proceed without detailed planning permission; and government departments reduce their requests for statistical information from firms operating in the areas.

Argument has surrounded the impact of the Zones since they were first mooted. The original concept was of a form of free-enterprise Hong Kong freeport with minimal control; a vision hardly borne out by the translation of the idea into another form of public subsidy to attract private investment to what in practice were very small areas. The areas designated as Enterprise Zones vary considerably in size: most covering 200–300 acres, but with Dudley, Trafford, Clydebank, and Swansea being significantly larger and Gateshead being over 1,000 acres. The demarcation of areas has given rise to occasional illogicalities through the drawing of detailed boundaries on the ground—in Trafford, for example, the tortuous boundary (shown in Fig. 4.5) was drawn so as to exclude most of the existing large firms but cut through the car park of one such firm, hence encouraging it to build premises on that area so as to qualify for the financial and administrative benefits of accidentally lying partly within the designated area. One criticism of the Zones has been that the changes simply represented a shift of value from the public purse (in the form of rates forgone or, strictly, paid by central government) to the private purse in the form of the capitalization of benefit through increased land values within the Zones. Erickson and Syms (1986), in the case of the Trafford/Salford Zone, suggest that pre-designation land values both in and outside the Zone stood at £1·09–£1·77 per square foot; by contrast, two years after designation, land within the Zone stood at £2·45 and land outside at £1·27–£1·30 per square foot. They suggest that 60 per cent of the financial benefit of the designation of the Zone has gone into the pockets of landlords. Kirwan (1986) provides similar comparisons both for the Trafford/Salford EZ and for Team Valley in Gateshead (Table 4.4), showing the contrasts in both rents and capital values in areas inside and outside the declared zones. The dual property market thereby created can be argued effectively to

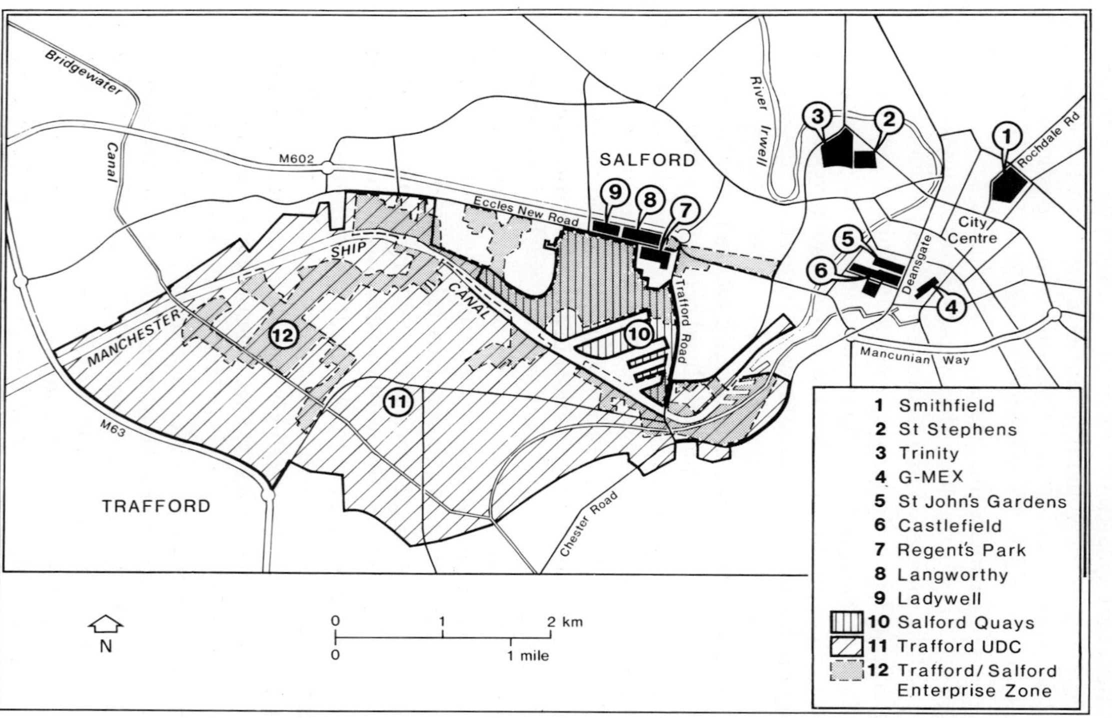

Fig. 4.5. Urban regeneration schemes in Manchester, Salford, and Trafford

Note: Details of schemes are given in the text.

TABLE 4.4. *Impacts of Enterprise Zones on rentals and capital values*

Area	Rents (£ per sq. ft)		Capital values (£ per acre)	
	Inside EZ	Outside EZ	Inside EZ	Outside EZ
Gateshead				
Team Valley	2.20–3.00	1.75–2.50	52,000	30,000
Greater Manchester				
Salford	2.75	1.75–2.00	70,000	30,000
Trafford	2.75–3.00	1.75–2.00	60,000–70,000	30,000–35,000

Source: Kirwan (1986).

cancel out the financial incentive of designation; contrariwise, it can equally be argued to have revived a property market in areas in which high land values and dereliction through firm closure had threatened to undermine the property market itself. A second set of criticisms about the Zones has focused on their claims to create jobs. It is argued that the jobs and enterprise created are spurious, representing either displacement —merely the short-distance moves of existing firms from within the locality—or the subsidizing of investment which would have happened without subsidy. The Tym study, for example, suggested that 85 per cent of Enterprise Zone firms would have been operating within the same region even in the absence of EZ designation (Tym, 1984). Furthermore, much investment in the Zones has been through the creation of warehousing activities which consume space but create few jobs. By 1986 the official estimate was that some 20,000 jobs had been created in the Enterprise Zones (raising the pre-designation employment from some 30,000 to some 50,000). Half of the new jobs have been in distribution, services, and transport. Trafford, for example, had 2,700 jobs by 1987, of which 1,300 were new; some 1,200 were in warehouse/distribution, 600 in manufacturing, and 900 in services. The largest beneficiaries have tended to be amongst the second wave of designated Zones, and in those located in the more buoyant parts of the country; the most dramatic example of which is Corby (Table 4.3, above).

The Enterprise Zones have in general proved to be a valuable mechanism for stimulating activity (some of it new, some merely transferred from adjacent districts) in areas which were in danger of suffering cumulative decline as large proportions of local firms succumbed to contraction or closure. In many cases, subsequent schemes (such as the Urban Development Corporations in Trafford and in London's Docklands and the Metro development in Gateshead) have been implemented on the back of the impetus provided by EZ designation. However, overall they appear to have had more impact on relocation than on new job creation. Moreover, what they have achieved has been at considerable public expense: exemption from rates represented some £180 million by 1984/5 and to that has to be added the direct costs of site preparation, land purchase, and service provision, which amounted to some £37 million.

PARTNERSHIP

Central–local partnership

The original concept of partnership was that between central and local government, best exemplified in the committees of the Partnership Authorities, in which officials from central-government departments such as DoE, DTI, and DE worked with officials from local government and the Regional Health Authorities, under the chairmanship of the DoE. The voluntary sector was given little or no formal role in this. Such partnerships were an attempt to overcome the cumbersome bureaucratic structure of multi-layered organizations at different spatial scales—reminiscent of the CDP views of managerial efficiency (suggested above in Fig. 3.1). In practice, the partnership arrangements in the seven authorities created their own highly complex structure of committees and subcommittees, with a welter of topic working parties and inner-city teams based in the local authorities. The size of the sums of additional resources involved hardly seemed to warrant so excessive a flowering of the spirit of bureaucracy and accountability. They did, however, provide a channel through which health authorities were encouraged to consider the inner-city dimension to health issues and, more especially for the DoE, a prompt for somewhat more direct ministerial and senior civil-servant involvement in areas outside Whitehall and Westminster. The drawing-up of proposals by Partnership Authorities rapidly became a routinized and bureaucratic process and, at least in the eyes of government, partnership with the local authorities concerned appeared merely to confirm the low esteem in which city government was held by central government. Partnership rapidly took on the very different flavour of developing a process of privatizing urban renewal through the encouragement of private-sector-led enterprise which increasingly marginalized the role of the local authorities themselves.

Public–private partnership

The later dimension of partnership which superseded the local authorities was the partnership between the public and private sectors. This has been the most significant shift in the direct of urban policy and one which has to be seen as only one strand of the government's wide policy of privatization 'in pursuit of the private city' (Boyle and Rich, 1984). The change reflects central government's concern to open the way for a renewed involvement of the private sector in the regeneration of cities by attracting private investement and an enterprise culture to areas in which the private sector had long showed a reluctance to develop interest. Such partnerships were early presaged in Michael Heseltine's creation of the Financial Investment Group in Merseyside, representing the worlds of finance, banking, insurance, and commerce, who were persuaded to second a group of middle-ranking managers to advise him on commercial initiatives in Liverpool, and the creation of the Merseyside Task Force under the umbrella of the DoE. The public–private partnerships which have emerged from this new focus have involved collaboration between, on one hand, the private sector with central and (some) local governments, especially through the use of Urban Development Grant and, more recently, the private sector alone with central government through the use of Urban Renewal Grant; and on the other hand, housing associations and local authorities with private developers through the use of Derelict Land Grant.

Urban Development Grant

Most joint schemes have involved the refurbishment of buildings and the environment and the provision of new or renewed housing. There have been some successes. The objective of the Urban Development Grant, introduced in 1982, has been to lever private resources on the back of relatively small sums of public monies. The public resources involved are split 75 : 25 between central and local government and schemes are expected to be ones which would not proceed in the absence of UDG. Again, the scheme has not been without its critics, who argue that the encouragement of private developers has given undue preference to commercially viable proposals at the expense of socially worthwhile projects. Nevertheless, there can be no denying the generative impact of many of the large schemes which have been set in train. By 1987, some £130m. of government funds had been allocated to well over 200 projects and these had attracted an additional £520m. of private-sector funds, thereby producing an overall gearing ratio of 1 : 4 (Table 4.5). It is significant that the variations in leverage show that the highest ratios have been for retail and office developments. The surprise has been the generally disappointing level of take-up of UDGs which has led to annual allocations being progressively cut back; from an initial £60m. to £40m. in 1985–6 (*Financial Times*, 6 October

TABLE 4.5. *Urban Development Grant gearing ratios*

	No. of projects	Grant (£m.)	Private investment (£m.)	Gearing ratio	Jobs created/ retained	Houses & flats built	Land reused (acres)
Industrial							
Factories/warehouses	70	22.6	82.0	3.6	7,942	15	247
Business expansion	27	9.0	33.8	3.8	3,391	0	67
Commercial							
Retail	35	31.4	158.1	5.0	6,632	46	182
Office	28	14.3	62.4	4.4	5,236	22	34
Tourism/leisure	21	18.4	65.8	3.6	2,083	15	54
Housing							
New build	46	20.8	83.7	4.0	185	4,086	371
Refurbishment	30	13.4	34.0	2.5	94	1,969	84

Note: the data show values for offers of grant up to Apr. 1987.

Source: Department of the Environment (1987).

1986). Even so, take-up has run well below these levels; with, for example, a take-up of only £28m. out of the £48m. allocated in 1984–5. Initially the invitation to submit bids in 1982 (made to the Partnership, Programme, and Designated Districts and to authorities with an Enterprise Zone) had attracted great interest, with over 300 applications involving all but one of the 61 authorities. However, many of these bids were rejected, either because of their ineligibility (since they were viable wihout grant or they were proposals virtually wholly to be funded from public sources) or because of the lack of financial or organizational commitment from the private sector. Many of the early bids sugest that some local authorities saw UDG as merely another source of extenal funds to supplement their land-use planning objectives, particularly in dealing with derelict or difficult sites. It is clear that achieving effective bedfellows of authorities and the private sector, where relations of mutual hostility and suspicion have long obtained, is neither easy nor likely to be achieved rapidly. Nevertheless, after this experience, the subsequent reluctance of authorities to submit bids means that the potential benefits of the scheme have not been as widely realized as they might be. This contrasts with the vigour which greeted the comparable Urban Development Action Grant scheme in America (from which UDG was derived). Some of the reluctance in Britain continues to derive from local authorities' political suspicion of associating with the private sector through joint activities, a view which had been true for example in Manchester until the 'new realism' following the outcome of the 1987 General Election; but some part is also due to the slow and cumbersome machinery with which bids are processed through the DoE.

Those authorities which *have* developed a strong political and administrative commitment to UDG—deploying staff resources, liaising with the regional DoE, and actively approaching the private sector—have both attracted funds and set in train valuable developments in the refurbishment of land and buildings and, less frequently, in business development. One example from a London authority is that of Wandsworth, who used a grant of £250,000 to help in the restructuring and re-equipping of a local firm, Price's Candles, when it was faced with the loss of 100 jobs. Of the large provincial cities,

Birmingham has been especially enterprising in submitting bids. For example, it attracted a £6m. grant towards a £22m. scheme for infrastructure improvements and the building of new industrial and warehouse units on the Imperial Metal Industries site (Spencer *et al.*, 1986, p. 182).

Urban Renewal Grant

The new Urban Renewal Grant, announced in 1987, will operate on a very different basis from UDG. The URGs will apply to larger areas—of between 20 and 100 acres—with some £20m. allocated for use in the first year. Evidence of appropriate leverage will also be required before URGs are granted. The most radical change, and one which illustrates the increasing hostility between central and local government, is the provision that developers will be able to apply directly to DoE for URG resources, without necessarily working through local authorities. The URG has provided a context out of which three sets of private consortia have recently been established to build homes, factories, offices, retail centres in a variety of large cities: in Manchester, Sheffield, Nottingham, Leicester, and the West Midlands. At least two consortia have applied for URG and started work at the end of 1987 with publicly provided pump-priming money. The consortia are: Phoenix (led by Sir Colin Corness, chairman of Redland); PROBE (Partnership Renewal of the Built Environment) associated with the construction firm Y. J. Lovell; and The Group of Eleven which is based on a set of large construction companies including Wimpey and Mowlem. Phoenix, whose chief executive has been seconded from Shell, will act as honest broker to mobilize interested parties to tackle the renewal of vacant land. Its major Manchester project (over which some doubt was subsequently cast by the declaration of its area of operation as a 'mini-UDC' in 1987—a development from which it is difficult not to draw inferences about government's view of the governance of Manchester) was aimed to develop a large area on the edge of the commercial district near the new G-Mex exhibition hall, together with a 20-acre site of a nearby gas works and the Refuge Building left vacant by the move of Refuge Assurance to a new suburban site. The Salford Phoenix is currently developing schemes for the refurbishment of housing and buildings in Ordsall and in the centre of Salford. It has declared its intention, alongside its commercial development, of creating a network of local community involvement in drawing up plans within the city.

In its most recent statement (Cabinet Office, 1988), the government has announced its intention of replacing the UDGs and URGs with a single City Grant which will 'bridge the gap between costs and value' and 'simplify procedures with quicker decisions direct from the Department of the Environment'. Its intent seems closer to that of URG than to UDG.

Private housing and privatizing housing

Housing development has been the second principal field in which the private sector has been drawn into the inner cities. The involvement of private developers in taking over council housing estates and in building new housing in urban areas has succeeded in reversing the long-run trend for the private sector to steer clear of brownfield urban sites for new housing development. Derelict Land Grant has made it attractive for the private sector to tackle sites whose construction problems have deterred previous private-sector interest. By effectively reducing the price of land—which, as Chapter 3 suggested, can be kept artificially high in urban areas where the housing market is not buoyant—many cities have now experienced private house-building in inner areas for the first time in decades. Since 1979/80, some 25,000 acres of land have been reclaimed through DLG in England and redevelopment has created over 12,000 new homes and over 5,000 jobs in new businesses.

Glasgow provides the most dramatic example of the use of public money to lever private-sector interests in the housing field. Between the mid-1970s and the mid-1980s, unusually generous annual sums of £100m. of public funds spent on housing refurbishment within the city have generated investment of some £175m. per year from private developers in what would until recently have seemed an unlikely venue for such activity (Maclennan, 1987). The generous resources devoted to public-sector rehabilitation within the city have helped to attract private investment, especially in areas adjacent to completed Housing Action Areas. Since 1980 new private housing has begun to be offered in the price range £17,000–35,000. The volume of private houses rose from 200–800 per year in the mid- to late 1970s, to 1,200 per year since 1982. Between 1976 and 1984 no fewer than 8,000 new private houses have been completed within the city. Within this total, the proportion of houses built on 'brownfield' sites has increased from 10 per cent in 1980 to 80 per cent in 1984.

Even the combination of public resources and the effect of subsidy through the use of Derelict Land Grant, however, cannot hide the difficulties of the lack of a buoyant private housing market in most of the large northern cities. Salford is one such area. It provides an example of a local authority which has been unusually ready to collaborate with the private housing sector in an attempt to stem the population decline in the city. It has encouraged private investment through the disposal of council estates to private house-builders for improvement and sale, through identifying new land for housing, and through the promotion of the Salford Quays redevelopment project in conjunction with DoE and the private sector. Amongst the housing developments that have come on stream through this collaboration are: some 170 flats in Regent's Park, an inter-war walk-up block rehabilitated by Barratt Urban Renewal (Northern); a similar scheme of rehabilitation of some 100 dwellings in St Stephen's redeveloped by Barratt; a number of small clearance sites and of sites bought from private owners on which 75 private houses and flats and 200 housing-association houses and flats have been built. It has in addition a major scheme in Salford Quays which will ultimately provide over 500 new houses, together with three further major council-estate rehabilitation schemes involving a mix of private developers: Langworthy, an inter-war deck-access estate from which Regalian will produce 450 units over three years; Ladywell, a 1948 estate of flats and maisonettes which will produce a total of 144 private houses and a further 150 for rent through a housing association; and Trinity, a post-war estate of terraces and high-rise housing which will produce 212 new dwellings of over five years. The sites of all of these privatization schemes are shown above in Fig. 4.5. While there is local demand for low-cost housing in the £15,000–£20,000 range, this stream of new and refurbished units coming on to the market begins to raise questions about the saturation of that low-price market and about whether there is better-quality land and a market for medium- and high-price housing in an area of predominantly low-income households. The hope is that the Glasgow experience will be replicated.

The taking over of council estates by the private sector has again been highly controversial. At the extreme, there are now cases where private developers have not merely taken over properties, at bargain prices, but have also assumed responsibility for tenants as well—as in the case of one estate in Rochdale. On the other hand, most of the council estates concerned were problem 'sink' estates used by the local authorities as housing in which to accommodate the poorest of families. They both presented significant maintenance expenditure for the authorities and offered minimal accommodation for the tenants. In areas without an extreme general shortage of family housing (and Salford would undoubtedly qualify on this count), the loss of such properties cannot be bemoaned in the way that criticisms can be levelled, within areas of greater housing pressure, at the selective loss of the better-quality houses through the operation of the Right-to-Buy legislation. Furthermore, evidence that most of the previous tenants have been rehoused throughout the wide spread of better council properties across the whole of Salford suggests that the privatization of such estates and blocks of flats has worked to the individual net benefit of the rehoused tenants (Robson and Bradford, 1988).

Such schemes have clearly introduced a valuable new social mix to inner areas which had become virtually the terrain of a solely state-dependent population. The benefits, through the greater influence and the spending potential of that more mixed population and the tax potential that it brings, must outweigh the ideological complaints against the losses of public-housing stock incurred by local authorities as housing managers. Furthermore, it increases rather than diminishes the argument for the need for greater public resources in housing for those unable to enter the ranks of the property-owning democracy; the 'creaming-off' of those able to enter the private market should reinforce the case of the homeless and of those households 'left behind' that they need resources both through local authorities and housing associations and through schemes to encourage private rental. It is the withdrawal of general public resources for housing which has weakened the stated concern of government that its housing policy aims to increase choice. Even though programmes of specific grants given for refurbishing of selected council estates through the Estates Action programme spent some £50 million on 130 estates in 1986/7, this cannot in itself counteract the impact of the withdrawal of general housing funds. Privatization, allied with an alertness to the social needs of the excluded, should not be an unattainable balance.

NEW AGENCIES

The partnership with the private sector represents a major change in the management and functioning of inner areas, since it has eroded the increasing hegemony which local authorities had established as agents of physical planning, of housing management, and of social control through their role in education and social welfare. This change has been furthered by the development of new agencies at the behest of central government, many of which have usurped some of the traditional roles of the local authorities in large cities.

Urban Development Corporations

The most dramatic of these new agencies are the Urban Development Corporations, first established for the Docklands in London and Liverpool in 1981 and extended in 1987 on a smaller scale to areas in eight new English cities, four of them having now been formally established in the West Midlands, Trafford/Salford, Teesside, and Tyneside. The same principle was applied at the very end of 1987 in the declaration of even smaller 'mini-UDCs' in Bristol, Leeds, and Manchester and, in 1988, in the declaration of a UDC in the Lower Don Valley in Sheffield and the doubling in size of the Merseyside UDC.

The role that all of these agencies play within the context of large cities is somewhat akin to that which development corporations played in the establishment of the New Towns from the 1940s. While they are not, for example, housing or transport authorities, the Development Corporations are essentially agencies which assemble and regenerate land and plan and co-ordinate its subsequent use. They therefore represent a direct assault on some of the traditional duties and the sensibilities of local authorities in whose area they fall. Such conflict has been especially apparent in the case of the London Docklands Development Corporation (LDDC) which covers a large area of 5,100 acres, with over 50 miles of waterside frontage from London Bridge to Woolwich. The area included large numbers of council tenants; with some 15,000 existing dwellings, 95 per cent of which were council property, within the three boroughs of Tower Hamlets, Newham, and Southwark, within whose area LDDC was established. Development in London's Docklands has been dramatic. Over 5,000 private houses have been built and large numbers of businesses have been attracted to the area, including a large proportion of Fleet Street. Generous sums of public money have been involved; over £300m. since 1981, which has levered some £1,600m. from private sources. The vast acreage of Docklands has been partially converted in a short space of time to a thriving private housing market with rapidly escalating house prices now measured in hundreds of thousands of pounds, a considerable development of industry and commerce, and the opening of a new light railway to open up access to an area which had long been isolated from central London (Ward, 1987). The Canary Wharf consortium's scheme has proposed an office city which promises 7,000 construction and almost 50,000 subsequent service and office jobs.

It could be said that it would be surprising were the developments not to have been so commercially successful since here we have an area lying cheek by jowl with one of the world's three major financial centres. Deregulation of the finance market in the City of London has further boosted the demand for office space in the development boom in London and the South East. The spillover potential of that location clearly seems calculated to have offered vast potential for the redevelopment of the area. Yet events might not have warranted such expectation. The 'miracle' of the Docklands is miraculous only because it has taken so long to materialize. After the effective closure of the Docks to commercial traffic, the area stood undeveloped for a decade while the respective local authorities disagreed about the planning framework within which development might occur. After the rejection of earlier plans, the Docklands Joint Committee was set up in 1974 by five boroughs (including Lewisham and Greenwich as well as the three ultimately involved in the LDDC area). Its eventual plan gave high priority to housing, of which up to half was to be council property. It was this plan which was overtaken by the declaration of the UDC. Central government's view that local authorities are too slow, too lacking in commercial sensibility, and too trammelled with the dictates of local democracy, and too preoccupied with maintaining a dependent tenancy could hardly be better exemplified. Yet there have clearly been considerable costs associated with the success of the development of the LDDC area. Relations with some of the boroughs have been strained—to the point of severance for example in the case of Southwark (Buck *et al.*, 1986, p. 117). Existing residents have voiced their objections vociferously through bodies such as the Docklands Forum and the Joint Docklands Action Group. Local residents have both failed to benefit from the jobs which have moved into the area and undoubtedly been priced out of the market created by private housing. Since the UDC is not a housing authority and can only act as an articulator of housing development and since the local authorities were faced with the prospect of buying back 'their' land were they to build houses, the mix of housing development has overwhelmingly favoured private construction. As against the intention of creating a 50:25:25 split between private, shared equity, and council housing, the total of 7,000 new houses have overwhelmingly been private with a split of 77:17:8. Some of the estates of private housing development have been offered to local residents at 'affordable' prices of less than £40,000 on a first-refusal basis. However, the rapid escalation of house prices in the area meant that such affordable properties proved more realistic in the early than in the later years of development; for example, some 14 per cent of the properties in the first phase of a Barratt's development in Becton did go to local residents, but this figure fell to 4 per cent for the second phase, and to zero for the third. For every taxi-driver who has succeeded in buying in to the local housing market, there remain large numbers of local residents for whom the prospect of purchase is illusory and who remain trapped in inadequate council housing. For them, the burgeoning development activity in an area of long-standing disadvantage merely represents yet further evidence of their deprivation.

Such overt conflict has been only somewhat less in the case of the Merseyside Development Corporation (MDC). Not only is the dockland area of Liverpool and Birkenhead much smaller—some 865 acres—but it contained no resident population. This has not stopped the local council from expressing consistent hostility to what it perceives as the parachuting-in of an outpost of central government (Parkinson, 1986). The developments in Merseyside have differed dramatically from London both in scale and in kind, reflecting its very dissimilar commercial potential as perceived by the private sector. As against the leverage of 1:6 in London, Merseyside has attracted a leverage estimated at 1:0.5. Virtually all the expenditure on regeneration—amounting to some £80 million between 1981 and 1986—has come from the public purse. The course of development has therefore been very different; rather than commercial renewal, it has been the development of leisure and recreational facilities which has been the keynote. After the impact of the Liverpool Garden Festival in 1984—a legacy of Michael Heseltine and one which earned a grudging and slow appreciation from the local Liverpudlians—MDC has exploited the leisure and tourist potential of the sequence of Docks along the shores of the Mersey. They have offered a site for large-scale renewal which now represents one of the most striking of any in Britain, capitalizing on the density of grade-one listed buildings around the docks. The Albert Dock has been converted into a marina and the 1840s' warehouses to a shopping development and maritime museum, with a centre for Granada Television in the previously derelict Dock Traffic Office building. The northern Tate Art Gallery is planned to be opened in 1988 and additional warehouse conversions are now in train. As job creation, the sums of money spent have generated little for a chronically jobless city (Wray, 1987). A possibly ominous portent for the future is the cash-flow problems faced by many of the small businesses at the prospect of a steep rise in the service charges of the shopping development. Nevertheless, the Albert Dock attracted some two million visitors in 1986 and its prospects as a focus for future development and as a node about which to turn around the perception of the city represents a beacon of hope for a bealeaguered city.

The critics of UDCs argue that similar developments have been achieved elsewhere without the imposition by central government of so unaccountable a body as a development corporation—as for example in the Docklands in Bristol—but there the existing commercial ebullience of the city presented very different options from those in Liverpool, nor did it suffer from the delays associated with attempting to achieve a consensus between a number of districts as in London. Examples more comparable with Liverpool *have* begun to develop outside the ambit of direct central-government intervention. To a large extent they have been prompted as reactions to the formal declaration of UDCs elsewhere. In each case they represent attempts by the local authorities to develop their own versions of urban development corporations, but without the direct intervention of central government. The approach adopted has strongly reflected the political style of the city concerned and what is now emerging is a continuum of varying approaches: Sheffield (with its well-articulated version of local state socialism) adopting a strongly public-led approach in the Lower Don Valley; Salford (with its long-established pattern of moderate Labour paternalism) maintaining a council framework within which joint public–private enterprise has been developed; and Birmingham (with its history of pragmatic politics, allied with frequent change of political control, and its closer relationship with the private sector) exploring a more explicitly private-sector-led model. Sheffield's plans have now been overtaken by the declaration, in March 1988, of a UDC in the Lower Don Valley, capitalizing on the city's own intentions for the 2,000 acres of derelict industrial land and offering a budget of £50 million over seven years (Cabinet Office, 1988). However, the Birmingham and Salford proposals are of particular note, since they have now progressed some way and represent alternative models based on the concept of a development corporation but with the blessing and the involvement or co-operation of the local authorities concerned. Both are in local authorities which are under moderate Labour control and which have consistently shown their readiness to work with central government and the private sector.

In Birmingham the city council has now effectively transferred its traditional planning remit, within a 2,000-acre zone in the eastern part of the city, to a company jointly run by the city and the private sector. Birmingham Heartlands Ltd. is a joint venture between the council and the Chamber of Industry and Commerce and its board of directors is comprised primarily of private developers and industrialists with only two councillors. The Chamber of Industry and Commerce will take the lead in deliberations with central government in looking for public funds. Currently it has commissioned studies of the area, which is an old industrial zone, but one with no fewer than 60,000 existing residents. Plans for its renewal will ultimately be drawn up by the agency and the particular interest will be not only its success in generating private capital, but its ability to avoid outright conflict with the interests of established residents; a conflict which may be lessened by the continuing role played by the council itself. This Birmingham development was an attempt by the council to create an alternative to a centrally imposed UDC. The second example, in Salford, is one in which the authority has directly taken the lead in drawing up a plan for Salford Quays which is in process of being implemented in association with private developers: notably through a partnership with the private developer Urban Waterside through which the development of Pier 6 has been achieved; and with Paul Sykes Ltd., a Leeds-based developer; and, in the northern part of the area, with the Manchester Ship Canal Company, which still owns part of the land in that area (Law, 1987). Co-ordination of the various developments has remained effectively in the hands of the city council. The site is at the head of the Manchester Ship Canal, whose trade in the upper reaches of the canal in Manchester Docks declined sharply from two million tonnes in 1972 to virtually none by 1982. In 1981 the city purchased much of the former docks from the Manchester Ship Canal Company (MSCC), began the clearing of the site, and commissioned a redevelopment plan, submitted in 1985, which has formed the basis of subsequent rapid developments (Fig. 4.6, see also Fig. 4.5). A £25 million

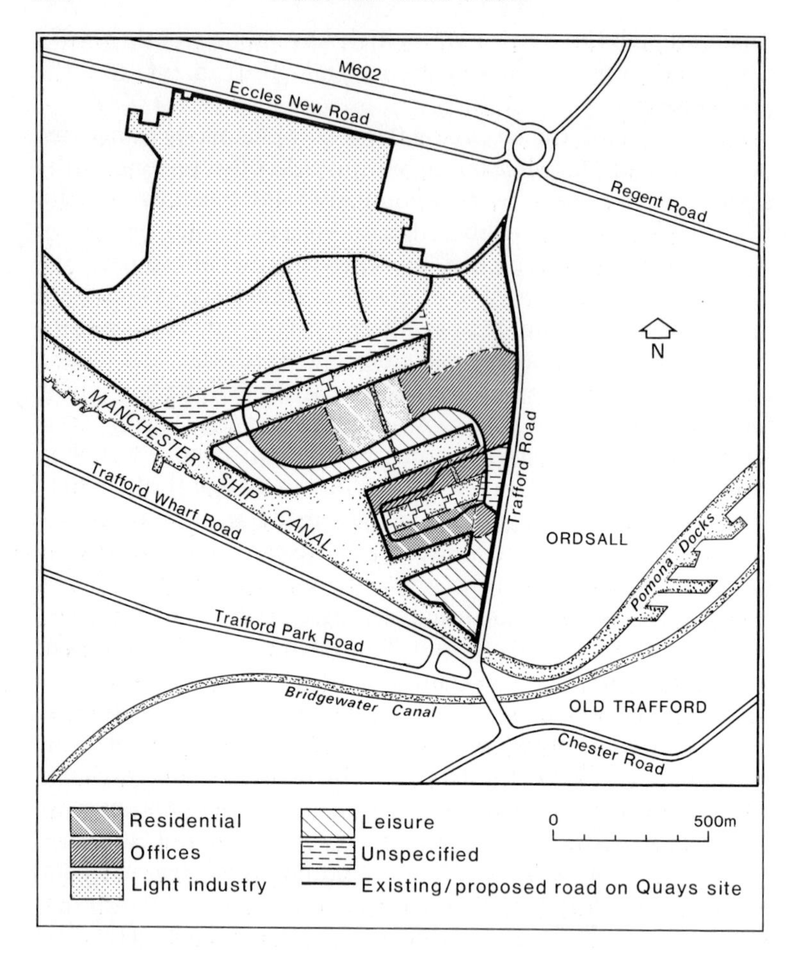

FIG. 4.6. Salford Quays: developments and future plans

Note: Developments are largely complete in the southern part of the area.
Source: Law (1987).

rolling programme of funding from the DoE was agreed in 1985 with funds from Derelict Land Grant and the Urban Programme, MSCC has itself contributed £1m. for site preparation, and the city itself expects to contribute up to £1 million per year. By 1987 some £15 million of public money had been spent and this had attracted some £90 million of private finance to give a leverage ratio of 6. In a short space of time, a £3.5 million multi-screen cinema by Paul Sykes for EMI, an £8.5 million hotel development by Urban Waterside for Copthorne Hotels, an industrial business park Waterfront 2000 by the local firm Fearnley, a public house/eating house for Toby Inns, an office park by the local firm of Snape, and new private housing by the Bristol firm of Spencer Homes and Lovell Urban Renewal have been completed or started (Salford City Council, 1986). Further plans include a shopping and leisure centre. The residential developments will ultimately produce over 300 houses, the first of which have now been completed and sold for prices up to £70,000, and sales for the earliest of the main phases have been committed before construction has been completed. Out of the completed plan, some 2,000 additional jobs should be created. To date, social conflict over the plans has been minimal, reflecting not merely the welcome accorded to any development in an area of extreme deprivation and dereliction, but also the involvement which the city council has effectively maintained from conception to execution. The expected completion of the development by 1991 will represent a substantial and rapid achievement. Whether the circumstances in Salford are repeatable elsewhere must be a moot point, but the development in what must originally have appeared a less-than-promising site demonstrates what can be accomplished in circumstances in which the three cogs of central government, local council, and private sector are meshed smoothly together.

The principle under which such development have occurred is similar to the UDC, but without the formal creation of a separate quango over and above the local authority. The critical difference, however, is the attitude of the local authority concerned. Salford is political light years removed from Liverpool or from Southwark. It seems unlikely that, without the intervention of the UDCs in the London and Liverpool cases, and the stimulus which they offered, what has been achieved in the London and Mersey docklands would have been realized.

Of the newly announced UDCs, the size of the areas involved is strikingly different. All encompass now-decayed industrial areas, partly abandoned by shipbuilding or heavy industry (Fig. 4.7). Like London, Liverpool, and Salford, three of

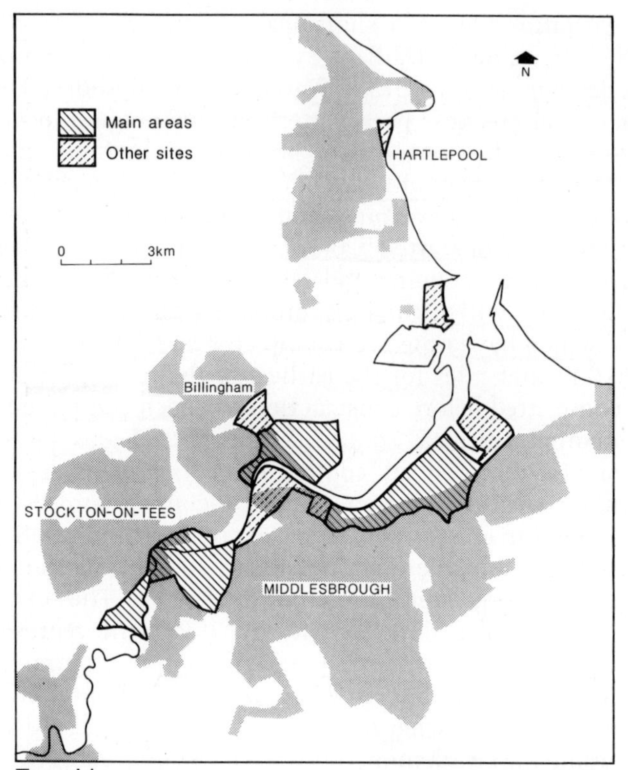

Teesside

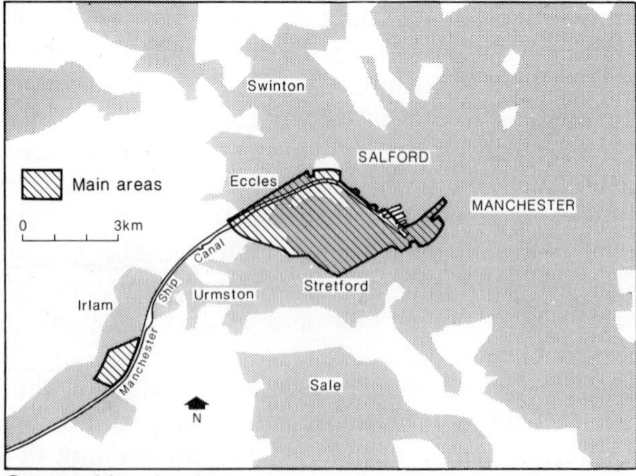

Greater Manchester

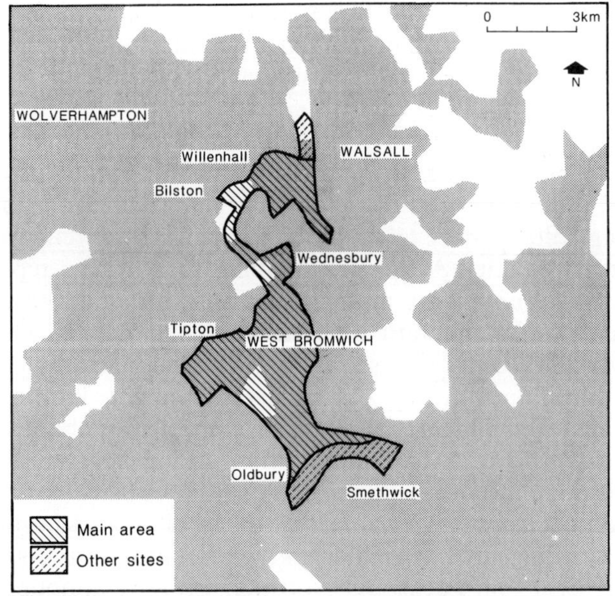

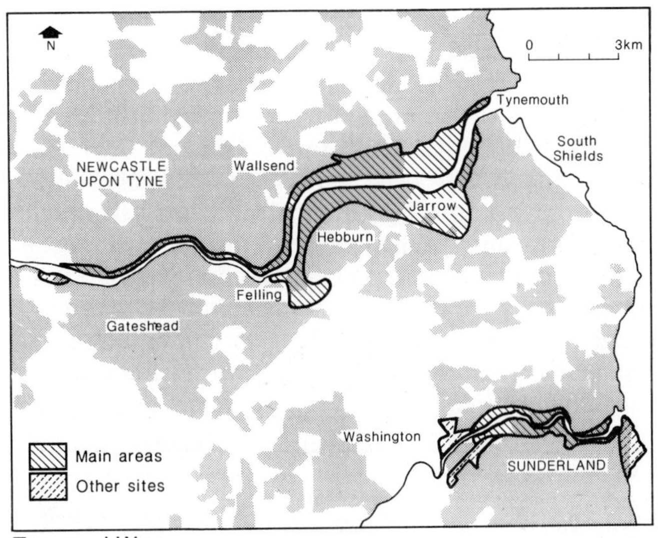

FIG 4.7. Recently declared Urban Development Corporations in West Midlands, Greater Manchester, Teesside, and Tyneside.

the sites are focused on river frontages or dockland areas and hence offer something of the same potential for a mixture of housing, recreational, and commercial development.

City Action Teams and Task Forces CATS

The second kind of new central-government agency has been the co-ordinating bodies set up by central departments to develop collaborative effort to tackle problems of renewal and job creation. City Action Teams and Task Forces represent central-government attempts to create new corporate structures to overcome bureaucratic fragmentation and overlap. The five City Action Teams, for example, were established in 1985 in the Partnership Authorities of London, Newcastle, Birmingham, Manchester, and Liverpool. They are comprised of the Regional Directors of DoE, DTI, DE, and MSC and operate within the Partnership Authorities to provide departmental co-ordination and the development of priorities for local areas, to establish joint working arrangements, and to monitor outputs. Two further CATs, in Leeds and Nottingham, were announced in 1988.

The Task Forces were established with a more local focus and, not unlike the UDCs, have been seen as attempts to parachute central-government activity directly into local authorities. Eight were originally established in 1986 in North Kensington and North Peckham in London, Chapeltown in Leeds, Highfields in Leicester, Moss Side in Manchester, St Paul's in Bristol, North Central Middlesborough, and Handsworth in Birmingham; with a further eight declared in 1987 in Spitalfields in London, and in Preston, Rochdale, Wolverhapton, Coventry, Doncaster, Hartlepool, and Nottingham. They aim to provide jobs for local people, to encourage local enterprise through training and financial and managerial help, to improve the employment prospects of local people through skill training, and to support environmental improvement initiatives. To this end they have tried to create networks to draw in government, the private sector, and local communities. Both their power, as relatively free-floating bodies, and their scale are too small to have allowed them to create much impact. They do, however, provide a potential arena sensitive to local conditions. Some part of their limited impact has again reflected the frequent unwillingness of local authorities to co-operate with them, but the suspicion that they are cosmetic is hard to dispel. They have raised expectations amongst the local, often predominantly black, communities and there is a clear need for them to deliver effective projects if they are to avoid merely adding to the frustration of those communities. As an example, the Task Force in Moss Side, Manchester, is typical. Like the other Task Forces, it has very limited funding—some £1m. over a two-year period—but in practice (and not least in the face of a considerable underspend in its first year) it can be argued that it is not primarily concerned with spending money. Its greatest potential innovation is as a local facilitating body through which to create networks between central government, the local council, the private sector, and the local community and thereby to encourage the development of training and the generation of local enterprise. In the absence of local employers, the Moss Side Task Force has developed small-scale local projects: a workshop to convert buses for community use; a training scheme in construction industry involving a local housing association; funding for an outreach worker for Project Fullemploy. Unlike the other areas, it is the only Task Force which has operated with a locally elected steering group which, while slowing the process of developing projects, has helped to provide a valuable integration of the views of the local community. Such local involvement is reflected both in the allocation of funds of £500,000 jointly from the Task Force and the Urban Programme for the establishment of a West Indian cultural centre, the Nia Centre, in a refurbished building and in the establishment of a £100,000 scheme (funded jointly from Barclays Bank and the Task Force) for small business loans administered by the black Agency for Economic Development. The reactions of the local Manchester council have been represented unambiguously in a report of March 1987 from the city's Economic Development Officer:

> There can be no doubt that the operations of the Task Force and City Action Team in Hulme/Moss Side are undemocratic and much of the current spending and proposals would not be acceptable by the City Council. It is hoped that the new structure for the Economic Development Department will provide staff and resources *for the City*

to take control, once again, of economic planning in Hulme/Moss Side. [Emphasis added.]

The balancing of the interests of the local community and the attraction of private-sector interest in a run-down area clearly become problematical in so charged a political atmosphere. Such attitudes, even in the more doctrinaire authorities like Manchester, have been softened somewhat in the wake of the 1987 General Election and the realization that Labour local authorities cannot hope for immediate relief from a change of national government. The 'new realism' has led many of those local authorities which had been implacably opposed both to working with central government and to collaboration with much of the private sector to recognize the short-term damage to which such opposition can lead and to adopt a more conciliatory stance whereby they can benefit from some of the fruits of partnership.

Local authority economic development activity

While such bodies as the UDCs and Task Forces represent the direct imposition by central government of bodies which have commandeered some of the traditional roles of local authorities, many of the new agencies have been established by local authorities themselves. It is clear that the traditional roles of local authorities have altered drastically in the face of sustained and deep levels of unemployment. Traditionally the local authorities played no, or only a small, role in economic development. More recently, to complement their role in consumption activities—through the provision of housing, schools, social services, transport, and other public goods and services—many local authorities, especially in the large cities and particularly amongst the Labour-controlled bodies, have begun to play a more interventionist role in production. Much of this has gone little beyond the provision of premises and of environmental improvements to increase the attractiveness or improve the operating environment of establishments. But an increasing number of authorities now either give grants directly to firms for job creation or job retention or have established new agencies funded through local authorities as enterprise trusts to fund production.

A progression of approaches can therefore be recognized. The older pattern of local-authority involvement in the economic sector was almost exclusively one of property-led local-authority aid and this was underlain by an *assumption* that this brought employment benefit. Since the late 1970s there has been an increasing stress on financial assistance to firms through either direct or indirect subsidy. Since the early 1980s this has moved further to an emphasis on what Mills and Young (1986) call a people-orientated rather than firm-orientated approach. The progression has been from premises-planning to manpower-planning: from initiatives concerned with land and buildings, to those focused on firms and to those concerned with employment; a concern, in other words, with the planned beneficiaries of public assistance, taking the form of increased training and targeted aid which aims to help the most disadvantaged. Such changes need to be put into perspective. As the Mills and Young surveys show, in practice it is still land-led initiatives which predominate in local-authority economic expenditure. Relatively few authorities spend significant amounts on local economic initiatives: only 5 per cent of the authorities they surveyed had expenditure of over £2m., 9 per cent spent £1–2m., and no fewer than 31 per cent had very marginal expenditure levels of less than £100,000. Nevertheless, amongst the leading edge of local authorities (of whom Sheffield, the ex-Greater London Council, and the ex-West Midlands have been prime examples), researched and often innovative schemes have clearly been developed.

The political complexion of authorities has been an important element in determining the degrees and kinds of activity in which they have taken a lead on economic-related infrastructure planning, local economic initiatives, manpower planning, and the like. Not surprisingly, the most interventionist have been strong Labour authorities, partly as a reflection of local need and partly reflecting ideology. Local authorities such as Sheffield, the now defunct West Midlands, Leeds, and the ex-Greater London Council have argued that local government is not powerless to influence the course of local economic development: local authorities can mobilize local skills, they can have impact on the local labour market through their own role as employers, and they can work with the private sector.

Most positively, of course, local authorities can be much more alive to the specific needs of their own local area. Among the examples of more politically informed economic development activity is the work of the Sheffield Employment Department, which has developed a well-articulated view of the interventionist role of the public sector. The Council controls no less than 17 per cent of total employment within the city and its capital and revenue spending in construction have been calculated to represent some three-quarters of all investment in the local construction industry. Such local leverage has provided a strong base for the city to begin to develop an economic and employment policy aimed to maximize jobs, to influence the skills composition of those jobs, and to target benefits to specific disadvantaged groups, including women and ethnic minorities. Amongst its aims has been that of introducing a form of contract compliance whereby contracts are placed only with suppliers who pursue approved employment practices such as the provision of training, health and safety, equal opportunities, and access to trade unions; an approach pioneered in Britain by the ex-GLC, which was able to use its £500m. of purchasing power as leverage (Mawson and Miller, 1986).

A further example is provided by Kirklees (an authority which includes the much-decayed textile towns of Huddersfield and Dewsbury), strongly influenced by a new head of the Policy Unit who had previously worked in Sheffield. Its emerging strategy is based on developing a rolling programme of projects and schemes of renewal and of industrial diversification of both existing and new enterprises, and the key to such a programme lies in creating a partnership based on networks forged between the city, the local Polytechnic, the regional office of the DoE, and the private sector, which includes the Chamber of Commerce, Huddersfield 2000 (a broadly based private-sector organization with strong industrial representation), and Enterprise Dewsbury (with community representation and members from the retail sector). A key element in the approach is to incorporate Kirklees in the capital programmes of the private sector rather than concentrating more narrowly on the resources of the local authority and central government.

Local authorities have also established new development agencies specifically to enable them to work with the private sector through giving loans and grants to existing or new companies within their areas. The Greater London Enterprise Board (GLEB), established in 1983 and with Section 137 funds of some £20m. per year, has developed a broad-ranging brief, providing support for new and existing enterprises, developing new technology networks, and pursuing investment packages which are aimed at economic and social objectives broader than commercial rates of return from those companies which it supports. The West Midlands Enterprise Board, established in 1982, has a somewhat narrower industrial investment brief. Other such agencies founded under the aegis of local authorities are the West Yorkshire Enterprise Board, Lancashire Enterprises Limited, and Merseyside Enterprise Board. They have in common the aim of acting more rapidly than traditional local authorities, of mobilizing private funds, of focusing public-sector skills in the field of economic development, and of bypassing the legal restraints which deprive existing local authorities of the right to take majority shares in private companies. A 1984 survey of the five boards suggests they made investments of some £24m. with leverage of between 1:1 and 1:4 and a cost per job of £2,500–£4,500 (Mawson and Miller, 1986, p. 170). As yet, and despite the adverse media publicity given in particular to the commercial failure of some of the firms supported by GLEB, such agencies have hardly been in operation for sufficiently long to provide solid evidence one way or another of the success of their investment strategies. Mawson, writing as a participant in the development of such strategies, has concluded:

> The interventionist authorities have . . . widened the agenda of this policy field in local government; they have stressed that the economic domain is not simply about infrastructure, investment and unemployment matters, but is also concerned with distributional questions, access to opportunities, income levels etc. They have challenged . . . the often artificial distinction between economic and social policy issues in local economic development. (Mawson and Miller, 1986, p. 194.)

Funds for such local authority activity have come from a variety of sources; from MSC, from the Urban Programme itself, from Derelict Land Grant, and from European funds in the form of the European Regional Development Fund and the European Social Fund. Funds for manpower-related schemes have presented considerable difficulties because local authorities have no statutory responsibility in this area. This has resulted in the more interventionist authorities using a variety of devices to circumvent the legal niceties. The case of the Greater London Training Board, which had a small expenditure of over £7m. in 1984 (but one that was relatively large compared with other local authorities), illustrates this to good effect. Having initially pursued powers under Section 45 of the Miscellaneous Powers Act, which allows authorities to use expenditure to assist MSC schemes, a government decision that such expenditure would be deducted from MSC's training budget forced GLTB to use resources from Section 137 of the Local Government Act 1972, which permits authorities to incur expenditure up to the value of a 2p rate product for expenditure which is in the general interests of an authority's residents. Section 137 has been used by a great many authorities for a variety of local schemes and there is consequently great pressure on such resources. GLTB has therefore been forced to look within the same Act at another section, Section 142, which permits authorities to incur expenditure on information to the local community. This provision enabled GLTB to use resources to finance the provision of information about access to training opportunities and to pay the salaries of advice and outreach workers (McArthur and McGregor, 1987, p. 133). It is clear that the lack of statutory powers can constrain the implementation of often innovative programmes by local authorities; at the least, the ambiguous position of councils can strain their inventiveness in spending time and resources to discover new ways of circumventing the intent of legislation.

The voluntary sector

Thought vol sector suffered due to social → ec/env switch.

The growth of local economic activity under the aegis of local authorities has also provided opportunities for the voluntary sector to expand its role in local economic projects. Some of the most dramatic local activities have involved the growth of community-based enterprises. Worker co-operatives, for example, grew in number from 90 in 1980 to over 1,000 in 1985. Community businesses have begun to appear on the basis of locally controlled non-profit-making activities. Both are more relevant to poor local areas than are conventional funds, which tend to do less to benefit local people. Like local authorities, the voluntary sector has made considerable use of MSC resources. The voluntary sector, for example, has one-half of all Community Programme placements and many schemes are again targeted to specific groups such as women and ethnic groups. Many of the voluntary-sector schemes such as Intowork and Project Fullemploy have been very successful in terms both of subsequent placements of trainees and, in so far as can be measured, cost per job. They have also been very flexible and accessible as regards their client populations. The use of outreach workers, taking training to the unemployed in their own communities or recruiting trainees through information networks and contact within those communities, has been an important element in their success in targeting the more needy, and one for which the voluntary sector is clearly best suited. For an unemployed population of disillusioned and suspicious young people, or for the older worker who has lost hope of finding work, it is vital that the frequent reluctance to make use of formal office-based agencies or the lack of belief in the value of using such agencies should be broken down; and this is one of the greatest strengths of many of the community-based voluntary-sector schemes. Questions remain as to whether voluntary-sector schemes are merely still creaming off the more suitable and promising of the unemployed and whether their undoubted innovativeness could therefore be extended to wider ranges and larger numbers of the disadvantaged.

The major switch in the focus of urban policies has clearly been the drive to involve the private sector in urban renewal. The political hostility from many local authorities and the diminution in resources both to authorities and to the voluntary sector which this has entailed are the principal costs associated with this changed emphasis. Had more resources been committed to urban policies overall, some part of these costs might have been defrayed. Nevertheless, the new focus of policy is a valuable corrective to what had become a growing schism between 'enterprise areas' and areas of 'local state socialism'. Without private-sector involvement, long-term regeneration of decayed urban areas would seem a fragile hope. If the jolt of new central-government agencies leads more local authorities to develop new dialogue with the private sector and if the seduction of the private-sector investment into deprived areas proves to be more than their short-term response to recession, then genuine partnerships of private sector, central, and local government could emerge out of the mutual recriminations and suspicions which have generally obtained up till now. If a more balanced three-legged stool of private sector, central government, and local authorities is not developed, what is most at risk is the role of the multi-purpose bodies which local authorities represent. Single-purpose agencies such as UDCs or development agencies are always likely to perform better at the single task to which they are committed, but that is largely a result of their more limited brief. Much of what is at issue in urban development requires the negotiation and resolution of the interests of innumerable voices in the community. These are precisely the tasks which multi-purpose agencies can best achieve. A hopeful pointer is that, even among the more hostile of the local authorities, there are signs of an increasing willingness to work with the private sector. In this, the post-1987 'new realism' has played no small a part, but some of the change has also come as part of the learning process on both sides, prompted by the climate created by the principle of private/public partnership within the Urban Programme. To this extent, the catalytic effect of UDCs and the new agencies has been successful. The importance now is that the short-term impact of the imposition of new agencies should be translated into a longer-term partnership between central and local government, which presupposes that there has been a genuine sea-change in attitudes on both sides. The question remains of how best to achieve and maintain a balance between public and private funding so that the rigour and speed of commercial discipline can be made consistent with the need for a humane and caring society.

5
With what Success? *Like the Curate's Egg*

Oh no, my Lord, I assure you. Parts of it are excellent!

Punch

In the motley pot-pourri of these diverse sets of policies there have indeed been some successes. We can look at the achievements of policy on the environmental, employment, and social fronts, to add a rather more systematic discussion to the evaluations of the previous chapter. One of the conclusions of any study of outcomes must be that there is a bewildering variety from one city to another. Some places appear to have 'succeeded' and others to have 'failed' in their attempts to adapt to change. The local chemistry which helps us to understand these variations is exceedingly complex; a mixture of local skills and attitudes, of politics, of the vitality of local leadership, of the regional economic context, of the inherited social and economic structures derived from the employment history and the local cultures. All of these elements comprise the mosaic of localities out of which geographical variation emerges and is re-created over time (Cooke, 1988; Massey, 1987). Given this, to draw on the experience of any individual cities must inevitably do less than justice to the rich variety of outcomes across the country. Nevertheless, the evaluation will draw on the specific experiences of a few selected cities and in particular on those of Greater Manchester.

THE GREATER MANCHESTER EXPERIENCE

Inevitably the easiest and most visible achievements have been the improvements to the physical environment and the provision of new and improved facilities within inner areas. Greater Manchester can serve as an example (the locations of most of the schemes which are noted being shown above in Fig.

4.5). Parts of its central commercial area have been transformed by a sequence of large-scale projects. At its core, the abandoned railway complex of the Central Station, which had stood empty since 1969, has been converted into G-Mex, an exhibition hall which opened in 1986 and has since attracted a continuous and growing flow of trade. This £24m. scheme was a collaborative one between the now-defunct GMC and the private insurance company Commercial Union. As a flagship venture, its psychological boost to the city has been considerable. It has also raised the commercial viability of the surrounding area, which is adjacent to the central business district. The potential of adjoining buildings has already begun to be exploited. The adjacent Midland Hotel has been refurbished in a £14m. scheme by its new owners Holiday Inns. A second nearby hotel has been extensively refurbished with private money, thereby adding to a significant growth of hotel accommodation throughout the central area, since some half-dozen major new hotels or major refurbishments have been completed in the last three years or are currently in the pipeline. Plans are mooted to rehabilitate a large nearby railway goods warehouse. The Phoenix proposal (noted in the previous chapter as having been challenged by a new mini-UDC) had drawn up plans for a £70 million scheme of renewal through a major refurbishment of commercial buildings in the vicinity of G-Mex. The knock-on effect of this sequence of developments on a large—and commercial, and visually significant—part of the central city has been considerable.

A second major scheme, involving both the city and the old GMC, is the conversion of the area of the Roman fort into a heritage area, Castlefield, with a complex of museums which now includes, in addition to the excavated and partly reconstructed Roman fort, a major Science and Industry Museum housed in the shell of the world's first passenger railway station at Liverpool Road, an air and space museum, and an urban heritage centre, which organizes urban trails and displays of historical features within the conurbation (Fig. 5.1). The latest phase in this £9m. project is to open an exhibition centre in disused railway sheds dating from 1831; funding has been through the ex-GMC, English Heritage, and EEC resources. This area has now begun to attract a significant tourist traffic

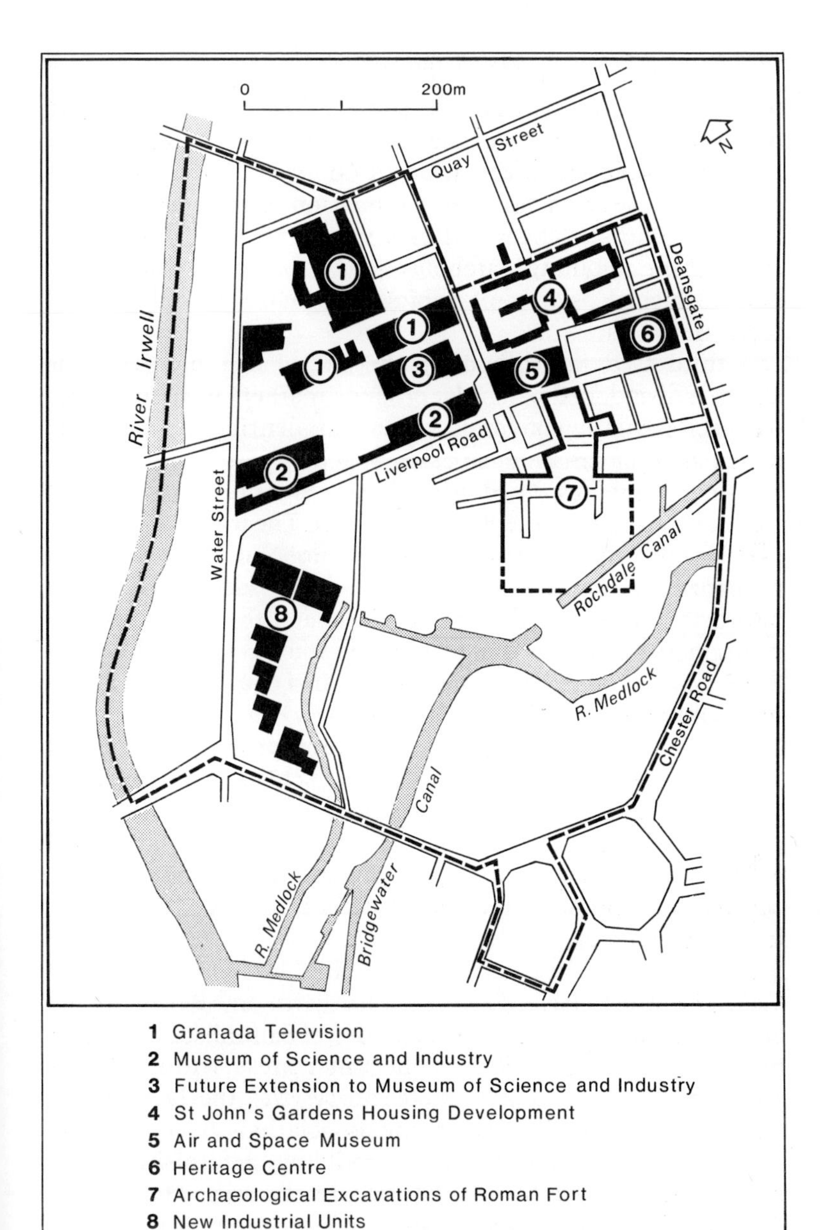

FIG. 5.1. Castlefield, Manchester: an urban heritage site

Note: The area includes a variety of buildings of industrial and historical interest, many of which have been converted for tourist and leisure activity. The complex of canals offers a rich variety of townscape and many of the warehouses flanking waterfronts are in process of refurbishment.

to the city centre; for example, some 300,000 visitors a year to the Museum of Science and Industry. This is likely to be further boosted when the adjacent Granada TV Centre opens some of its sets, such as the Coronation Street set, to public viewing. The site incorporates a variety of canal basins and many of the adjoining warehouses and industrial fixtures are to be refurbished as part of a broader scheme for leisure and recreational uses.

A third area, Smithfield, on the site of fish and vegetable markets abandoned when the produce markets were relocated, has been partially converted into a craft centre, garden centre, and a mix of small businesses together with new council housing. There has, in addition, been a significant investment in local theatres: to the Royal Exchange Theatre, dramatically and inventively constructed on the floor of the old cotton exchange in the 1970s, have now been added two newly refurbished theatres, the Opera House and the Palace, and an experimental theatre in old railway arches, together with a film and arts centre, the Cornerhouse, in a conversion of an old furniture shop.

Private-sector housing has begun to appear in the central and inner areas. One joint public–private scheme, involving the volume builder Wimpey, has produced new maisonette blocks in St John's Gardens at the heart of the commercial district of Manchester. Other joint schemes in Salford have involved the rehabilitation of problem council estates of walk-up blocks built in the 1930s and 1950s. Three such areas, Regent's Park, St Stephen's, and Langworthy, involving building companies such as Barratt Urban Renewal (Northern) and Regalian, and each in the moderate Labour authority of Salford, have brought private ownership back into the inner areas within two or three miles of the centre. Increasingly over the last decade, small-scale locally based housing associations have begun to play a more active role in the building, refurbishing, and subsequent management of housing in the area. The current contribution of housing-association houses is a minute proportion of the total stock (some 3.9 per cent in 1981), but as a proportion of new activity they are highly significant (having contributed 25 per cent of the total new build between 1981/2 and 1985/6). Amongst their rehabilitation work has been the conversion into flats of a textile office and warehouse close to the city centre.

A vigorous campaign to promote the regional shopping centre for the peak Christmas period has helped to ensure that the central area has increased its share of retail trade during that season over four consecutive years, even though the region is now faced with no fewer than eight proposals for mega-centre shopping complexes on open sites in the Dockland and peripheral suburban areas. Three of the proposals have net retail floorspace of over 1.5 million square feet; and, together with the existing 'soft' proposals in the pipeline, the set of proposals represents over 80 per cent of the existing retail provision in the twenty-three shopping centres within the conurbation. Were any combination of the proposals to be given planning approval by the current DoE inquiry, this would deal a severe blow to the prospects of central areas.

On the purely environmental front, major reclamation schemes have made some inroads into the vast acreages of despoiled land within the conurbation. Groundwork Trust, based in St Helens and now extended to other districts within the region, has reclaimed land with strong emphasis on involvement by the local community. Under the ex-GMC, a sequence of major river-valley schemes have been undertaken, capitalizing on the number of rivers which push fingers of potentially open land into the very heart of the conurbation. The ex-GMC undertook major reclamation of some larger tracts on the periphery of the old county area, such as Higher Folds in Leigh, a 470-acre site contaminated with waste from three collieries, with polluted lagoons, flashes, and waterlogging through ground subsidence and through slack heaps which regularly caught fire. Now, with nearly £2m. spent on the site, it has been converted into land for agriculture, public open space, and woodlands. GMC also began a programme of country parks at the fringe of the built-up area, such as the creation of the Moses Gate Country Park in Farnworth, which was reclaimed from a 124-acre site formerly occupied by a derelict paper mill and reservoirs. Much of this work is being continued on an inter-authority basis in the post-abolition period. Within the heart of the industrial zones—and especially in the massively derelict area of East Manchester where a major local-authority-led scheme has been implemented—trees have begun to sprout where factories have closed in small areas where, inexplicably, during the resource-rich years of the 1950s and 1960s empty abandoned sites had lain idle and offered an invitation to fly-tipping.

Such schemes of environmental improvement are typical of all of the large cities throughout the country. It is easy to pour scorn on tree planting and the sprouting of signboards proclaiming improvements under the Urban Programme, but it would be idle to deny that successful environmental improvement has important impacts both in terms of restoring an element of confidence to an area and its residents and in terms of improving the image of areas and thereby undermining the prejudices of potential investors from outside. Greening the city—either in terms of multitudes of such schemes or of Heseltine-inspired Garden Festivals—cannot be dismissed as mere palliative. The fact is, however, that the scale even of such environmental improvement has not been large enough in most areas to hold at bay the new derelict land coming on stream through continuing closures of firms. Again to quote the Greater Manchester case, the DoE surveys of derelict land showed that 3,405 hectares of derelict land existed in the county in 1974 and that some districts had over 10 per cent of their land lying derelict. Yet, despite their having reclaimed 1,727 hectares between 1974 and 1982, by the latter date the amount of derelict land had increased to 4,035 hectares, thanks to the growth of disused railway land the closure of factories, power stations, docks, and canals (see above Table 1.5). The scale of urban environmental dereliction has meant that such schemes have as yet merely scratched the surface. Continuing resources are needed if sufficient impression is to be made on the problem to achieve the necessary momentum.

Equally as depressing environmentally are the increasing numbers of boarded-up houses and flats on inter-war and post-war council estates which have suffered from underinvestment. Particularly in areas where there is no overall shortage of family housing, houses have been prone to the vandalism associated with long-term vacancy and to the temporary boarding-up of properties awaiting repair and refurbishment by local councils. The reduction of public resources for housing and the frequent inefficiency of council repair procedures have combined to ensure a downward environmental spiral of depressing proportions in most large cities. Such problems are of horrendous proportions in the industrialized buildings of the high-rise and walk-up flats of the 1960s and 1970s; as for example in the Hulme Crescents in Manchester (Manchester City Council, 1986). Yet they are by no means restricted to such areas. Even many of the recently built traditional houses have begun to show similar evidence of decay and abuse in inner areas; for reasons which are social and are connected to sheer bloody-mindedness or poverty rather than because of the structural or design inadequacy of the buildings concerned.

All of the recent schemes of improvements to the central areas of Manchester are visible evidence of the impact of both local-government and central-government spending and of the increasing involvement of the private sector in ideas and in areas in which it had previously shown great reluctance to become involved. There is a sense—at least in the more commercially attractive areas—that years of decline have begun to be reversed within the central city itself. It is of course significant that much of this improvement has been in central areas where the market-led potential for renewal is considerably greater. Improvement is much harder to discern in the collar of areas outside the central city or in the more peripheral council estates which are found in most large cities. As renewal has been increasingly led by the private sector, so the suspicion lurks that it is only the areas with commercial potential which have benefited from public subsidy. A test of the broader success of renewal still lies in its ability to address the needs of the less commercially attractive areas whose economic and social problems remain.

If the most evident signs of improvement are to the environment and within the commercially attractive central areas, this is not to belittle the general benefits which have flowed from them. However, it leaves many questions about the overall assessment of the impacts of policy on the improvement of local economies and employment in inner areas and of the community-based responses within inner-city areas.

ASSESSING THE EMPLOYMENT IMPACTS

On the employment front, success is more difficult to chart. The complex array of new job and training agencies and projects have involved both local and central government and the voluntary sector. Most are concerned with sustaining or creating small firms and providing training facilities. In the mean time, however, the loss of large-scale employers and job contraction in large enterprises continues unrelentingly. The awesomeness of the equation of the number of small firms needed even to achieve a numerical replacement for (let alone the skill and pay characteristics of) the jobs lost in such contraction makes it difficult to be optimistic about the net impacts of employment creation in conurbations and, indeed, in their surrounding regions. It would take 260 Nissan factories, 500 Commodores, or 26,000 small firms to replace the jobs lost from the West Midlands' traditional metal manufacturing in the years between 1979 and 1984; it would take 100 years of small-firm policy to replace the jobs currently provided by British Leyland in the West Midlands (Mawson and Miller, 1986, p. 154). That is not to deny the value of those jobs which *have* been created or sustained; but it puts in perspective the scale of the continuing endeavour that would be needed to make a significant dent in the unemployment experienced in the last decade.

Given the number and variety of employment initiatives, it is important to evaluate the incidence and the degree of benefit that may accrue from them. How many new jobs have been created; how much public money has been spent in creating them; who has gained from the incidence of such expenditure? Such questions are the obvious ones to pose. They are less easily answered than might at first appear. Any such evaluation of the employment impact of financial assistance is faced with a variety of complex and ultimately intractable calculations. Lever summarizes them under the head of five 'Ds': deadweight, displacement, duration, duplication, and distribution. Each of these complicates any calculation of the 'real' employment benefits which may accrue from public expenditure (Lever and Moore, 1986). *Deadweight* is the extent to which assistance goes to developments which would have happened even in the absence of financial or other intervention; for example the Manpower Services Commission (1984) estimated that 72 per cent of start-ups assisted through the Enterprise Allowance Scheme would have begun regardless of assistance, thereby implying that the real cost per job should be four times more than any simple division of jobs by cost might suggest. It was noted in the previous chapter that deadweight affected many of the claims made for job creation in the Enterprise Zones. By its nature, deadweight is difficult to measure since there are vested interests either in claiming that projects are wholly dependent on assistance so as to justify financial support or, conversely, in claiming that it was wholly the enterprise of the individual or organization receiving benefits that generated new employment. There is a natural tendency either to understate or to exaggerate the level of deadweight. *Displacement* arises as the negative side-effect of assistance, since any help—through premises, finance, or advice—can make the recipient more competitive and thereby displace competitors from within the same local area, leading to their closure or a reduction in their manpower. An alternative form of displacement is the tendency—again seen in the Enterprise Zones—for business merely to be moved from one area to another so as to benefit from more generous public assistance in its new location. *Duration* is a measure of the longevity of benefit. Jobs which survive for many years clearly represent a different order of success from those which terminate after a short time. If large and small firms have different rates of probable survival —for example with the latter having high rates of closure—new jobs created in firms of different size may have different levels of net achieved benefit. While the implication of measures of net employment benefit is that new long-term jobs are created, this is an assumption which ideally needs to be tested and hence incorporated into more sensitive measurements of effectiveness. *Duplication* raises the issue of the multiplicity of sources from which establishments receive benefit. In calculations of cost per job it is usually assumed that whatever agency provides assistance is the *only* source of aid, but particularly in assisted regions there may be a multitude of programmes, initiatives, and agencies offering assistance. Any true evaluation of cost per job should therefore take account of the sum total of assistance received from all the sources concerned. This requires the calculation of comprehensive and exhaustive data for all assistance channelled to a study area. Each of these first four elements is concerned with the overall economic benefits which may accrue from assistance. The fifth and final—*distribution*—is a measure of the social incidence of benefit: who gains from employment and, if targeting benefit to the disadvantaged is a goal of employment creation, to what extent the intended recipients of benefit do actually gain. It is the difficulty of taking account of all such aspects that makes the claims of crude cost per job especially suspect.

There is, of course, the converse side to the coin since there are equal potential imponderables on the benefit side of any evaluation of the impact of assistance. Two, in particular, should be considered even though they also produce methodological conundrums for evaluation. First is leverage, the degree to which additional private resources are raised through public expenditure, so as to increase the net benefit of public spending for economic regeneration (even though increasing the real cost-per-job measure). Second—and yet more difficult to calculate—are the positive spillover effects of public expenditure—both in retaining jobs which might otherwise have disappeared and in generating additional jobs through the multiplier effects associated with new activities generated through such financial outlay.

It is clear that calculations of net benefit are difficult. Yet evaluation is of critical importance in the development of any public policy; an importance which has increasingly been recognized both generally, with attempts to develop forms of impact assessment, and specifically within the Department of the Environment in, for example, its Urban Programme Management initiative, which started in 1985. Unless the relative impacts of different policy instruments are known, policy development will remain a seat-of-the-pants art and the tendency to lurch in a damagingly short-term and unpredictable fashion from one seemingly bright idea to the next will persist. At present, monitoring of the range of initiatives is ill developed: indeed, even disaggregated statistics are difficult to assemble (not least in terms of the spatial incidence of public expenditure). This is an area to which attention needs to be paid if intelligent critiques are to inform policy.

The case of Tyne and Wear

The most authoritative study of the employment benefits flowing to an area through financial assistance is the work of the Centre for Urban and Regional Development Studies (CURDS) in looking at the Newcastle metropolitan area (covering Tyne and Wear and parts of southern Northumberland and northern Durham), an English area in which urban policy has been supplemented by regional assistance. It represents the closest and most robust approach to a comprehensive evaluation and it is therefore worth quoting some of its findings in detail (Robinson, Wren, and Goddard, 1987).

The Newcastle region suffers many of the classic problems of urban and regional decay. Historically it depended heavily on traditional manufacturing industry, especially coal, shipbuilding, and heavy manufacturing; it has a high proportion of branch plants whose control is vested outside the area and which therefore lack high-level management functions and R. & D. and in which routine production of mature products predominates, thereby reducing the linkages to other activities within the region and reducing the probability of self-sustaining growth within the region as a whole; the small-business sector is less well developed than elsewhere, self-employment is lower than in any other region, and the failure rate of small businesses is high—over 30 per cent to trade within three years of start-up—all of which suggests the lower likelihood of indigenous generation of innovation within the region; there is a low presence of producer services, especially in the critical sector of insurance, banking, and finance, partly because of external control of firms which means that many services are provided from headquarters elsewhere; and there is a high proportion of employment in the public sector, where again decisions are taken on national financial grounds, rather than with any explicit regional-planning dimension, and hence beyond direct local influence from within the region. The area has long been the recipient of the whole range of regional and urban policy programmes. To assess their effects the CURDS team collected comprehensive data on financial assistance from the great majority of sources of aid: from the Department of Trade and Industry, with its three main programmes of Regional Development Grant (RDG), Regional Selective Assistance (RSA), and National Selective Assistance (NSA); from the Department of the Environment in the form of Urban Programme resources, Urban Development Grant, and the rate relief associated with Tyneside's Enterprise Zone, all of which are operated through the region's local authorities (UP); from English Estates (EE), largely in the form of rent relief to tenants of EE factories; from the British Technology Group (BTG), in the form of equity investments; from Washington Development Corporation (WDC), through rent relief to factory tenants; and from the British Steel Corporation (Industry) Ltd. in the form of grants and loans (BSC). This body of data for the period 1974–84 provides a relatively comprehensive tabulation of the flows of financial assistance to the area.

Of the total assistance of £370m. during the decade 1974–84, DTI resources were overwhelmingly dominant, comprising some 88 per cent, with 62 per cent through RDG and 23 per cent through RSA. Urban Programme resources for economic development, channelled through UP activities, represented a much smaller, although a growing, proportion (Table 5.1). The differences in the aims of each form of aid can be seen in the nature of the recipients. Many of the DTI payments were made to subsidize major investment projects, hence the size distribution of its payments has emphasized large grants, with almost half being in individual payments of over £100,000. Likewise with RSA, which is paid as grants or loans to support the retention or the creation of jobs, 22 out of the 483 payments were of over £500,000 and these represented 69 per cent of the total expenditure. By contrast, UP expenditure under the Urban Programme was spread quite widely on assistance to firms and to industry in Improvement Areas. Over 66 per cent of UP expenditure involved sums of less than £5,000 and only 12 cases were of over £100,000. Such differences are also evident in the size distribution of firms which received assistance from these different sources (Fig. 5.2). The great bulk of this overall expenditure clearly went to the traditional manufacturing sector, thereby achieving little by way of diversification of the metropolitan economy. RDG

TABLE 5.1. *Financial assistance for economic development, Newcastle area, 1974–1984*

Agency	Total expenditure (£'000s)	No. of cases	Average expenditure (£'000s)
Dept. Trade & Industry	326,150	2,434	134
RDG	(228,361)	(1,606)	(142)
RSA	(86,301)	(483)	(179)
NSA	(11,488)	(345)	(33)
Urban Programme	14,876	1,909	8
Urban Development Grant	6,374	381	17
English Estates	5,615	26	216
British Technology Group	2,416	249	10
Washington Dev. Corp.	1,446	130	11
British Steel (Ind.) Ltd.	5,800	12	483
Enterprise Zone	7,253	NK	NK

Source: Robinson, Wren, and Goddard (1987).

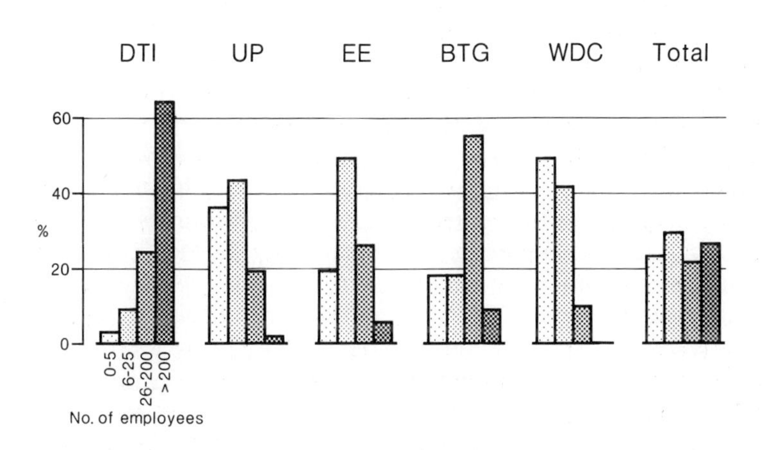

FIG. 5.2. Size of assisted establishments by source of public funding in the Newcastle area

Source: Robinson *et al.* (1987).

went predominantly on capital-intensive industries within the manufacturing sector (although the data predate the 1984 revisions to regional aid which extended eligibility to some service-sector activities). RSA included some payments to the service sector to encourage relocation, but 88 per cent went to manufacturing, notably shipbuilding and mechanical engineering. UP expenditure, like its size distribution, was somewhat different, with a larger proportion of aid having gone to firms in the service sector (especially to small firms starting up in this sector), but even so nearly 75 per cent of UP aid went to manufacturing industry. Overall, only 5 per cent of total aid went to the service sector even though that sector represented 62 per cent of employment. Such strengthening of the established manufacturing base could be argued to have done little for the long-term prospects of the area. It reflects the largely reactive, rather than pro-active, nature of the way in which the bulk of policy has operated. Nevertheless, by strengthening the traditional economy it can be argued that such investments could lead to the development of new products and processes on which greater diversification could occur in the future.

In studying the employment impacts of this investment the researchers were able to use both their comprehensive data base of financial assistance and a survey of managers and employees at assisted firms so as to examine the incidence of displacement, duplication, and deadweight. Their data also enabled them to assess the overall effect of leverage. They found a leverage ratio of 1:2.31 overall (in other words that every £1 of public resource generated an additional £2.31 of private funding, thus adding to the overall resources available for assistance in supporting and restructuring the local economy). There was a somewhat higher level of leverage for RDG at 2.7 and lower for RSA/NSA and for UP expenditure at 1.9. On deadweight, despite the difficulties of confidently interpreting the expressed views of recipients of resources, they were able to conclude that there is a high level of deadweight associated with RDG grants: some 53 per cent of assisted projects would have gone ahead regardless of aid (20 per cent of enterprises would have used finance from the firm itself, 19 per cent from other sources, and 13 per cent of projects would have gone ahead in a different form). For RSA the deadweight figure was

23 per cent and for UPs it was 58 per cent. There is a suggestion that projects involving new start-up have higher levels of deadweight. For UP expenditure the high level of deadweight is probably associated with the fact that much of the aid was in the form of rate or rent relief and, since the objective may have been to rent a factory unit owned by the local authority, the high level of deadweight may not have been considered important by the local authority itself.

Displacement measures are especially difficult. Of the total of 254 projects, 69 reported that they had taken business from their competitors in the study area. The overall degree of displacement, measured by the percentage of all projects which had increased their market share at the expense of local competitors, suggests a figure of 27 per cent. Such a finding is encouraging in that it shows that resources have increased the competitiveness, efficiency, and profitability of firms through the implementation of many of the projects and yet done this without too great a damage to existing firms in the area.

On duplication, the researchers looked at the extent of multiple assistance from more than one source and found it to be surprisingly low. Of the 412 establishments that received RDG aid, 251 received *only* RDG, 105 received aid from one other source over the ten-year period, and 54 had aid from two or more others. Of the total of 2,457 establishments receiving assistance from any of the sources, 84 per cent only had aid from a single source. In the case of multiple aid, this often reflected putting together 'packages', for example, the assembling of aid from DTI, English Estates, and BSC.

They also attempted the fraught task of calculating costs per job and in this their technique allowed them to take account of deadweight and duplication, but not of displacement (or of the converse multiplier effect of positive spillover to the regional economy as a whole). RDG is shown to be relatively expensive: for example, looking at only additional jobs created through single-funded projects, each RDG-assisted job cost £17,650; each RSA/NSA-assisted job cost £7,200; and each UP-assisted job cost £8,700 (Table 5.2). Such comparisons cannot simply be read as implying that RDG is not cost effective. By its nature RDG has tended to support large capital-intensive establishments and, while this may not have been the cheapest way of

TABLE 5.2. *'Cost per job' from public assistance in the Newcastle area, 1985*

Source	Total assistance from source (£'000s)	No. of 'new' jobs	Crude cost per job (£)	No. of 'new' jobs excluding deadweight	Refined cost per job (£)
RDG	5,421	593	9,150	307	17,650
RSA/NSA	2,278	522	4,350	317	7,200
Local authority	1,366	567	2,400	157	8,700

Note: Figures based on a survey of 201 establishments.

Source: Robinson, Wren, and Goddard (1987)

creating new jobs, it can lead both to the retention of existing jobs and also to the underpinning of some of the mainstays of the local economy and hence indirectly to the creation of jobs in firms which are linked as contractors (in other words, to positive spillover effects). Nevertheless, the cost-per-job figures suggest the value of selective assistance and of linking aid to employment creation. This adds support to the post-1984 change in DTI policy which made the provision of RDG more dependent on job creation. It also offers support to the government's recent decision to abandon automatic RDG resources (Department of Trade and Industry, 1988). So long as the government's undertaking not to reduce the overall level of spending on regional industrial measures is honoured, the evidence lends weight to the extension of the principle of selectivity in assistance.

As far as firms were concerned, the benefits in terms of productivity, profitability, innovation, and sales were considerable. Three-quarters of projects had resulted in greater productivity, 73 per cent in increased output, 64 per cent in greater profitability. Many projects also helped the assisted firms to produce a greater market share (which was true of 62 per cent of firms), to introduce new processes (54 per cent), or new products (49 per cent). However, not many reported greater research activity (25 per cent) or increased exports (20 per cent); findings which must bode ill for an area in which lack of entrepreneurial talent and indigenous research and development have played a significant part in explaining poor economic performance.

It is in the light of such analysis that it was possible to assess the size and incidence of overall employment benefits and thereby to evaluate the effectiveness of the use of resources. Some 137 (54 per cent) of the selected 254 projects reported an increase in employment, 37 helped to retain jobs, 58 had no employment effect, and only 2 led to job reductions. Of the extra 1,118 jobs created, 71 per cent were filled by those previously unemployment. However, these benefits arising from the specific projects need to be set against the overall losses of jobs in the companies themselves: of the 195 establishments which provided employment data, 100 had been in operation throughout the ten-year period and their total employment had decreased from 7,400 to 6,400.

These results demonstrate that the policies of assistance have produced valuable benefit for the metropolitan area, but that the overall employment effects are nevertheless disappointingly small. For the three-year period 1981–4, just after the worst of the effects of recession, £137m. was spent from the three main sources of RDG, RSA/NSA, and UP expenditure. Taking account of duplication, displacement, and deadweight, this expenditure gave rise to approximately 5,000 'real' additional jobs. This has to be set against the loss to Tyne and Wear of 38,000 jobs in the same period. Even in an area where there is 'full-on' policy with both regional and urban assistance, this suggests the limited impact on employment *per se*.

Judged from the Tyne and Wear case, it seems clear that the overall impacts on employment have been slight, but that many of the individual schemes and the assistance which they entail have had the kinds of stimulative effect at which policy has aimed. The achievement of creating a net total of 5,000 jobs may appear minute in terms of the scale of unemployment and of job loss within the area, but is no mean feat in view of the scale of the recession of 1980–1 and within an area with seemingly few prospects for economic growth. It is hardly grounds for shouting about achievements, but it is more than merely being seen to be doing something.

SOCIAL FRUSTRATIONS

The failure of such economic measures to have a major and demonstrable effect on the prospects of the unemployed and deprived has produced increasing social frustration. Politicization of this disappointment, especially amongst the young, has meant that some initiatives, such as the YTS, have not had much support in those areas most in need. The voluntary sector has experienced increasing difficulty in starting new schemes on the community front and has been bedevilled by the problem of the piling-up of time-expired schemes; housing conditions have become more polarized through the massive reduction in public-sector starts and the lack of success of attempts to encourage private tenancy schemes such as assured tenancy. Worsening employment and housing conditions have produced nastier tensions between ethnic groups and the 'host' community, emphasizing the deep but hidden racism in British society. The last-hired-first-fired mentality so well known to earlier immigrant groups such as the Jews and the Irish has been further heightened by the innate but unadmitted colour prejudice which permeates so much British thinking. The higher rates of unemployment experienced by those, more particularly young, people whose families originated from the New Commonwealth or Pakistan have aggravated and intensified other causes of social unease and unrest.

Inextricably interwoven in these tensions are both the increasing awareness and experience of crime and, in some urban areas, the almost total breakdown of confidence in the police. One of the most distressing outcomes of the concentration on economic regeneration has been the failure to tackle this very real cancer at the heart of most cities. New training programmes for the police coupled with greater expenditure in the form of good salaries and modern weaponry have not really gone much of the way to implementing the sensible recommendations of the Scarman Report. Still missing is a viable and genuinely independent Police Complaints Procedure as well as universal small-scale community liaison panels, while better forms of accountability seem even more remote since the abolition of the metropolitan country authorities in 1984. In the vacuum created by this policy failure have poured the vanguard of a political motivated army. Some are genuinely well-meaning, but a powerful section are intent solely on destabilization. Their influence is out of all proportion to their numbers since they have so much ammunition to hand. At every opportunity they utilize the ethnic minorities' well-founded fear and mistrust of the police to turn attention away from other possibly more easily curable ills, into creating an even greater gulf.

A tragic and poignant example was provided in Manchester in September 1986 when a 13-year-old Bangladeshi boy was stabbed to death in the playground of an all-boys' comprehensive school. A white pupil was subsequently found guilty of murder and a number of violent incidents continued to occur both within and without the school. Every action and statement by the police was adroitly used to suggest that it was the police who were to blame for the tragedy. That the police were guilty of some incomprehensible statements about the absence of racial motives to the murder cannot be denied, but this served to turn attention away from the responsibility of a local education authority which had earlier received a report from one of their own inspectorate about the lack of discipline and extreme violence at the school and from the school's politically controlled governing body which had agreed to destroy a damaging report on the state of the school. It also side-stepped the part played by the local council's vociferous policies on equal opportunities which succeeded in setting up an unpleasant backlash against those suffering discrimination. In this too Scarman had emphasized the need for a *national* policy (Home Office, 1981, p. 132):

> I suggest that there is a lack of a sufficiently well co-ordinated and directed programme for combating the problem of racial disadvantage. It is clear from the evidence of ethnic minority deprivation I have received that if the balance of racial disadvantage is to be redressed, positive action is required.

Unfortunately the past six years have seen a failure to heed his later clarion call (p. 135):

> on the social front . . . the attack on racial disadvantage must be more direct than it has been. *It must be co-ordinated by central government* who with local authorities must ensure that the funds made available

> are directed to specific areas of racial disadvantage. I have in mind particularly education and employment. [Emphasis added.]

Instead of such co-ordination, the ethnic minorities have found themselves part of a shopping list of groups which the political masters of cities deem disadvantaged. In Manchester, a spontaneous and well-organized Ethnic Minorities Consultative Committee, comprising representatives of communities not necessarily always willing to work together—such as Pakistanis, Afro-Caribbeans, Africans, Indians, and Bangladeshi—fought bitterly and to some extent successfully to try to divorce their needs and aspirations from others such as homosexual groups. In the final analysis, however, despite managing to gain the establishment of a separate race subcommittee and a separate race-relations unit, it made no difference to the council's political determination to implement their equal opportunities policy as a blanket across a very broad range of groups suffering real or imagined discrimination. As a result the ethnic minorities not only lagged behind other groups in levels of support, but also found themselves made more unpopular in the public mind by their association with those seen as the undeserved or undeserving favourites of the council. Out of this, and out of the keen competition for jobs which is especially prevalent on inner-city council estates, racial harassment has grown progressively worse. The well-documented failure of the police to offer a coherent, positive approach to this problem has added fuel to the fire of already bad police/ethnic-minority relations. This, in turn, is augmented by vicious propaganda from some of the more scurrilous representatives of the Press who take delight in implying that all increased crime should be laid at the door of the ethnic-minority populations. None of this makes for a better quality of life in those inner-city areas shown to be most disadvantaged and all of it works against a more positive outcome from either current economic or social policies. In the early years of the Urban Programme few ethnic groups played much part in bidding for inner-city resources. Increasingly, more of the inner-city schemes have consciously incorporated an ethnic dimension (not least in the work of the Task Forces, two of which are headed by blacks, and in specific schemes such as the Ethnic Minority Business Initiative announced by the Home Secretary in 1985). Ironically, just when more ethnic groups are readier to collaborate in projects and to bid for resources, they find themselves caught in the trap of the increasingly angry and acrimonious division between central and local government.

Those at the bottom of the urban underclass could be forgiven for thinking that to most of their political masters, whether central or local, they are so much cannon fodder to be thrown into the political battle. Their one classic route of escape through the educational system, much used in the past by other similarly disadvantaged groups, no longer offers much hope. Bedevilled by falling rolls, constantly changing educational theories, ill-trained and dissatisfied teachers, some of whom are themselves highly politicized, caught in a national school system which cannot make up its mind whether it wants to retain elements of 'sponsored mobility' or to pursue a more single-minded approach of 'contest mobility', and thereby failing at both, education offers far too little hope and to far too few pupils. Nobody who has talked to members of the ethnic minorities and especially to those who originated from the West Indies can escape the feeling of desolation at the sense of waste and despondency which emerges. The impression of frustration, resignation, and embitterment has been graphically reinforced by Dervla Murphy's anguished writings from her participant observations in Handsworth (Murphy, 1987). A number of those fortunate enough to be in employment, no matter how poorly paid, admit that they are sacrificing holidays, cars, clothes, and household amenities in order to send their children out of the state sector into private education. One such father tackled by a fellow member of the Labour party retorted indignantly that he was not prepared to see *his* children sacrified on the altar of political ideology. Another from the Bangladeshi community has expressed dismay that his children are not being encouraged to become fluent in English. He is even less pleased that, in the muddle of multi-cultural policy and pleas for mother-language teaching, one of his daughters is now being forced to learn Urdu. A local Manchester woman complains that in her children's school they are more fluent in Punjabi than in English. In 1981, Scarman endorsed the call of the Home Affairs Committee for a reform of Section 11 of the 1966 Local Government Act, a section so often misused by local authorities and astute headteachers. Efforts at reform by the Home Office in 1985 appear merely to have opened up fresh avenues of distortion as councils like Brent have used Section 11 grant to develop a cohort of supposed anti-racism specialists. Manchester City Council, despite pleas from the communities that Section 11 marginalizes them, has leapt eagerly on the bandwagon of more money from central government. Increasingly there have been calls from the ethnic-minority groups that money gained by the council from the Home Office through Section 11 should not be pooled but be specifically assigned to a strengthened Race Unit for the employment of more blacks within the education and social-services fields, thereby avoiding political appointments in fields such as immigration. The large number of Section 11 appointments, ranging from several hundred in Education to smaller numbers in Housing and Social Services, seems designed merely to suggest that 'something is being done'. What, nobody is quite sure.

THE SUCCESSES AND LIMITATIONS OF POLICY

The five policy objectives noted in Chapter 4 (above, p. 100) provide one framework for summarizing these achievements and failures. Job opportunities have not been greatly enhanced and the ability of local residents to compete for what new jobs have been created has only fitfully been addressed. Derelict land and buildings have commanded a major effort and much has been achieved through public and private activity, although insufficient to keep pace with the rate of new dereliction created at the height of recession. The private sector has certainly been enticed into the kinds of inner area from which private investment had long been withdrawn, although the concentration on more central areas has meant an opportunity cost for the less commercially attractive areas. Local authorities have been relegated to the sidelines in the drive to privatize the cities and in the political clash of wills between central and local government. Housing choice has been widened through the growth of private housing, but the massive withdrawal of mainstream housing resources has meant that specific schemes of improvement have made little headway against the continuing housing stress of the poor. Finally, the encouragement of self-help and 'the improvement of the social fabric'—the least well specified of government's aims—has proved the most obvious Achilles' heel of policy, with all of the threat of disruption, disillusionment, and hostility which this has entailed.

Some part of the social tension is undoubtedly the result of frustrated expectations. The advent of new schemes under the umbrella of the Urban Programme and related activities inevitably begins with the fanfare of sales pitches which promise new levels of co-operation, new tiers of job creation, new opportunities for people to control their own destinies and their own environments. Some of these may come, but their realization is inevitably longer than the time span of aroused expectations. Frustration, disbelief, and disillusionment are all too often followed by outright hostility. The more imaginative instruments of policy like the Urban Development Grants have succeeded in levering private resources and have helped to bring to fruition some renewal schemes that would otherwise not have occurred. The lesson, so effectively illustrated by the Birmingham case, is of the importance of political will on the part of local authorities, and of the importance of creating the climate, the mechanisms, or the development agencies through which private-sector incredulity and reluctance can be overcome. The Urban Development Corporations have brought more new activity and regeneration than their critics would allow. Many of the local-authority-led job-creation schemes undertaken through enterprise trusts have brought new jobs and at costs per job which are highly efficient by comparison with the costs per new job which resulted from regional assistance through DTI. The additional resources through the Urban Programme have created opportunities for some imaginative schemes of undoubted benefit to local communities. The whole focus on the inner areas has opened up opportunities for local groups to develop political skills in lobbying, in analysing their needs, and in managing subsequent developments. It has also raised the profile of the debate about the social and economic needs of inner areas. It has equally changed perceptions about the respective roles of central and local government, on the one hand, and the private sector and the voluntary sector on the other.

Much of what has been done has entailed notable achievement. But it is not mere academic carping to argue that the successes have been muted and that some fundamental limitations to these approaches to urban policy have blunted the impact of what has been achieved. Set against the successes, there have been some recurring failures which have surfaced throughout this discussion:

- not many new net jobs have been created from all of the activity;
- very few of those jobs which have been created have gone to the most deprived because of the leakage of benefit through open labour markets;
- where success has been achieved it has invariably been on the back of considerable sums of public expenditure so any assumption that private investment can *replace* public must look suspect;
- little account has been taken of whether local agents in the public sector are trained to implement policies of local eonomic development;
- there has been a continuing difficulty in developing coherence amongst sets of policies in different fields and across different government departments and there has therefore been a conflict between policy outcomes;
- the emphasis on economic development has been at the expense of a more balanced concern for community development and this has been exacerbated by the increasing dependence on the private sector.
- and the clash between the ideologies of central and local government has created a context of perpetual warfare which has limited the effectiveness of many of the most imaginative schemes.

Some of these themes are worth developing at greater length.

Consistency

The variety of programmes and measures which have been implemented to assist urban economies are no substitute for a consistent long-term urban policy. If one says to civil servants that the policies of different government departments are inconsistent, they will usually reach for their hats if not their guns. They have a point. It would be idealistic to expect an urban dimension to be a universal dominant across all government departments since other objectives—of national economic growth, of national security, of rural development, of encouragement of competitiveness—which may not coincide with an urban policy, are inevitably going to compete with the goal of underpinning the vitality of cities. However, if a declared intention of having an urban policy is to be taken seriously, one could reasonably look not merely for more resources but for a higher priority to be given to the urban dimension of other policies and hence an overall coherence which would support the distressed urban areas.

There are innumerable instances of policy conflicts between the different arms of government. At the least there is considerable jostling between the many central-government departments involved in urban policy: Environment, Employment, Trade and Industry, Home Office, Health and Social Security, Education, and, above them all, the Treasury. Each department has to be consulted and its responses considered in a snowstorm of paper. The DoE has long been the lead department for the Urban Programme itself and has the lion's share of the resource expenditure, but as the focus has crystallized on economic issues so its overall paramountcy has been challenged. The CATs and the Task Forces are now both led by the Department of Trade and Industry and in 1987 Kenneth Clarke, from that Deparment, was appointed official co-ordinator as Minister for the Inner Cities. The lack of automatic consonance between the views of the two departments was neatly encapsulated by the conflict between Nicholas Ridley at Environment and Kenneth Clarke, then at Employment, over the question of whether or not to make use of affirmative action in employment recruitment in the West Midlands; a conflict in which the positive views of the Department of Employment eventually won the day. The spatial pattern of regional assistance from the Department of Trade and Industry, on one hand, and the urban focus of the Department of the Environment, on the other, is one of the most evident instances of directly conflicting approaches.

Attention was drawn in Chapter 4 (above, pp. 106–7) to the contrasting cases of Clydeside and Tyneside, which showed that urban and regional policy can work either to reinforce each other (as in Tyneside) or to counteract each other (as in Clydeside). The principle of investing either in areas of economic potential or in areas of need is a dilemma which faces development agencies with particular poignancy in a period of recession and, as the impacts of recession have spread beyond cities to their containing regions, so the dilemma becomes more profound. At the least, it requires some form of planning framework within which priorities might better be agreed. To this extent, the demise of strategic planning (both in the abolition of regional economic planning councils and in the more recent abolition of metropolitan counties) has removed one of the forums through which such frameworks could be developed.

Such limitations are true, for example, of the multiplicity of training schemes and economic development schemes within local areas. In Newcastle, despite the numerous agencies offering resources for economic development (DTI through RDG, RSA, and NSA; 13 out of the 14 local authorities in the region with forms of financial assistance; English Estates; Washington Development Corporation; Enterprise Zone; Urban Development Grants; and the Manpower Services Commission), there was relatively little duplication, less chaos than might have been supposed in the agencies which offer aid (Robinson, Wren and Goddard, 1987). Nevertheless, even though the system seems to operate in a relatively orderly way, with different agencies serving different 'markets' in terms of size and location, the authors could still argue the need for a clearer strategic framework. Only in such a way could trade-offs in development programmes be agreed in the face of inevitably limited resources. Such networking of activities would be of even greater benefit in the case of training programmes. The potential beneficiaries of training are faced with a bewildering array of schemes and agencies. Inconsistencies are inevitable, given the number of initiatives which exist. For example, workers on Community Project schemes cannot currently move on to receive Enterprise Allowance assistance which might offer them an opportunity to develop acquired skills in new businesses; workers in community businesses are defined as employees rather than as entrepreneurs and so do not qualify for assistance from the Enterprise Allowance Scheme (McArthur and McGregor, 1987, p. 147). A recent study of Moss Side, done by the Manchester Polytechnic for the City's Economic Development Department, showed that most of the 'underclass' in the area did not know which agencies might offer them help in training. At the least, a better signposting of opportunities would be helpful; at the best, it could be argued that what is needed is a more formal articulated framework within which the agencies might operate. The announcement of the Inner Cities Initiative in 1986 (Department of the Environment/Department of Employment, 1987) and the establishment of the CATs and of the Task Forces were a tacit recognition by central government of this need for greater coherence. So too was the setting-up after the 1987 Election of a Cabinet committee chaired by the Prime Minister and the subsequent appointment of a co-ordinator of inner city policy —although, even here, the relationship of co-ordinator and Cabinet committee remains ambiguous. Many of the individual programmes clearly need to be more effectively dovetailed together to make more intelligible sense, not only to deprived residents but also to businessmen faced with the alphabet soup of acronyms of the innumerable schemes and programmes operated by central and local government and the voluntary sector.

One view of such clashes and inconsistencies suggests that all is chaos and inefficiency. Another, however, suggests that the lack of co-ordination offers potential for those groups and individuals able to exploit the possibility of stitching together resources from a variety of different policy instruments. In support of the latter view, there is increasing evidence that some local projects have grown out of being able to identify such opportunities to assemble resources from a variety of sources so as to develop large projects, for example by combining Urban Programme and Enterprise Allowance. The benefit of negotiated integration between different agencies is well illustrated by a Medway initiative through which the local DHSS has agreed that, despite the rules on benefit disregard, unemployed young people can work on local schemes and earn money which is held for them on trust so that the cash may eventually be used to finance the start-up of a small business or co-operative. There is a need for such flexibility so that the schemes of different departments do not directly conflict. The almost inevitable confusion associated with the multiplicity of schemes *can* be turned to advantage by the more astute and alert groups who have successfully found their way around the maze of initiatives. Nevertheless, it has to be seen as a costly and sub-optimal way of generating initiative. At the least, there would be benefit were government and voluntary-sector bodies such as the National Council of Voluntary Organisations to help such enterprise by developing more widespread publication and dissemination of manuals of 'best practice' from around the country.

The government has clearly shown an increasing awareness of the need for greater co-ordination amongst the variety of programmes from within the range of central departments involved. This was one of the potential strengths of the new emphasis proclaimed in its *Action for Cities* which was launched in March 1988 (Cabinet Office, 1988). At the launch, the Prime Minister was joined by six Cabinet Ministers: Douglas Hurd (Home Office), Nicholas Ridley (Environment), Kenneth Baker (Education), Norman Fowler (Employment), Paul Channon (Transport), and Kenneth Clarke (Trade and Industry and with responsibility for co-ordinating inner-city policies). In what turned out to be not the long-promised White Paper but a brief and glossy pamphlet, the policies which were highlighted reflected the interests and the existing policy instruments of each of these central ministries. Indeed, the Prime Minister responded to a question by stressing: 'I don't think there is a single new policy here.' The implication must be that co-ordination of existing initiatives will be sufficient to build the 'new vitality in our inner cities'. New initiatives were nevetheless introduced and they included many of undoubted value: an extension of the Five Towns programme to tackle crime in an extra 20 cities; the extension of the Compact scheme to link schools and local employers in 12 inner cities; the provision of additional managed workshops through English Estates; the declaration of the Sheffield UDC and the extension of the Merseyside UDC by an extra 800 acres; two new CATs; the merging of UDGs and URGs into a City Grant to support private-sector developments in inner cities; six new offices for the Small Firms Service and an 85 per cent guarantee on bank loans to firms in Task Force areas; improved access to information about public land on the national land registers and streamlined procedures for requiring the public sector to sell sites. These new initiatives need to be read alongside the earlier and related announcement from the DTI (Department of Trade and Industry, 1988), with its emphasis on consultancy advice and aid to small businesses. The thrust of *Action for Cities*—the redemption of the pledge that something must be done for those inner cities—seems clear. The message is unambiguously addressed to private business. It is they and government who must lead any regeneration of the cities. Indeed, it is not without significance that the launch coincided with three private-sector announcements: a campaign by Business in the Community to establish new teams of business leaders to promote involvement in education, training, and investment in inner cities; a programme in which the eleven largest British civil-engineering and construction companies will seek inner-city development sites with a £55 million fund; and an expansion of the venture-capital fund from Investors in Industry to encourage new inner-city investment. The booklet itself includes a guide to action which gives 'companies and businessmen practical advice about how they can help the drive to make inner cities more prosperous'. In the launch the Prime Minister said, 'The new initiatives being taken by the Government and announced by the private sector show that we all [*sic*] mean business'. This is privatization of the city with a vengeance. There is no mention of the role of local authorities and no reference to the part which might be played by the voluntary sector. Indeed the financial data in the booklet suggest that, between 1983/4 and 1988/9, spending to assist private investment has increased by £121 million while spending on social and community projects has gone down by £20 million.

While the encouragement to private business to develop a responsibility for inner cities cannot be other than welcome, there is a need both for a fiscal framework to encourage business to invest in the non-profitable social infrastructure of cities and for a broader and more realistic concept of partnership which offers a place for local governance and for local citizens. The government's own attempt to co-ordinate action across the relevant departments is a welcome intent. The cynic might suspect that co-ordination is easy to suggest around the table at a Press launch, but, given that central departments have their own organizational imperatives and their own priorities, might be more difficult to achieve in practice. This is particularly so in the absence either of a central mechanism to resolve the kinds of inter-departmental conflicts discussed earlier or of competent local multi-purpose agencies which can identify the contradictions and illogicalities in localities and can develop local strategies to achieve more effective and efficient co-ordination on the ground.

The broader impacts of unintended conflicts

Such inconsistencies are embedded within urban policy itself. Overarching this is a variety of broader impacts of policy inconsistencies. One of the most telling examples of inconsistency in major policy arenas is the unintended effect that many decisions on the allocation of public resources have on the spatial patterns of economic and social well-being. The Bristol illustration of this draws on the procurement and investment decisions made by the Ministry of Defence (Boddy, Lovering, and Bassett, 1986). Contracts for defence equipment—not least the funding pattern of the aerospace industry, which has provided so strong a prop to the regional economy of Bristol and the South West—have largely gone to areas which do not qualify for regional assistance. Calculated as a proportion of total manufacturing expenditure, the procurement expenditure from the Ministry of Defence dwarfs the assistance given to needy urban regions such as South Wales and the North (Table 5.3). This represents, in Boddy's words, a hidden regional policy which works directly at variance with overt regional policy (Boddy, 1987). The same kinds of argument apply to the concentration of R. & D. expenditure through public investment in the government research establishment in the Thames Valley and to the public infrastructure investment, such as in Heathrow and the M4, M11, and M25 motorways; all of which have played some part in encouraging the development of

TABLE 5.3 *Defence procurement and regional assistance, 1974/1975–1977/1978*

Standard region	Regional assistance (£m.)	Defence procurement (£m.)	% of regional net manufacturing output	
			Regional assistance	Defence procurement
Wales	239	112	3.2	1.5
Scotland	424	549	3.0	3.9
North	476	573	4.5	5.5
North West	250	949	1.1	4.0
Yorks./Humberside	89	245	0.6	1.6
West Midlands	2	599	0.0	2.9
East Midlands	10	744	0.1	6.2
East Anglia	0	264	0.0	5.7
South West	26	889	0.3	9.8
South East	0	3,674	0.0	7.9
Great Britain	1,516	8,598	0.9	5.2

Source: Boddy (1987).

economic activity in the Cambridge to Bristol belt. The step from highbrow to high-tech. has been liberally larded with indirect government aid.

Other examples of the indirect effects of non-urban policies would include the urban impacts of the cutbacks in public expenditure on housing and on benefit payments. Both have had differential effects on large cities since it is in the large cities that there is a greater reliance on public-sector jobs and that both council housing and the poor are overwhelmingly concentrated. The greater the squeeze on public expenditure, the greater is the negative impact on cities. Likewise, the intention to replace the property-based tax of local rates with the regressive per-capita tax of the Community Charge or Poll Tax will work to the overall disbenefit of large cities. This is so both for the domestic and the non-domestic elements of the proposed tax. The domestic charge will hit the large poor urban family, will doubly penalize households in the multi-occupied houses in the private rental sector whose rent bills are unlikely to be reduced to reflect the withdrawal of rates, will lead to high levels of non-collection in the areas of high turnover typically found in large cities, and will not address the problem of cities providing services enjoyed by those living outside and not contributing to the local tax base. The uniform business rate element will lead to significant reductions in the local taxes paid by commerce and industry in towns which have traditionally had high rateable values. This may appear to offer new locational attractions for inward movement of firms. However, if industry and commerce have not been attracted to relocate in northern areas in the face of existing differentials of land costs it seems unlikely that uniform costs through a Community Charge will impel them to change to new urban locations. More seriously, the per-capita redistribution of this centrally collected business tax will mean that large cities will lose the benefit of the considerable financial resources on which they have long been able to draw by taxing their concentrations of shops, commerce, and industry. Calculations of the expected incidence of benefits and disbenefits of both elements of the Charge show that the large cities would be major net losers (CIPFA, 1987).

At the least, if there is to be a commitment to assist the most needy areas, it seems vital that there be a presumption that policies and programmes in other fields which conflict with the aim of urban assistance should be examined to see if new emphases could be given to them so as to support the defence of urban interests without deflecting the principal goals of the policies themselves. Support for the Channel fixed link is an example. The defenders of the interests of northern cities recognize the profound damage to their long-term economic prospects that could ensue from the further diversion of activity towards the south coast and the London region. None would argue that a Channel tunnel should be extended to emerge at Birmingham or Liverpool. Yet the interests of the northern cities might at least be met in the short term by developing a conscious strategy of placing contracts with northern firms, other things being equal. Further, in the longer run, a policy of fixing freight charges uniformly throughout the country and of developing container ports in one or two northern centres could go some way to allaying the justified fears of those who feel penalized by geographic factors beyond their control. The additional capital and operating costs of either move would appear not to undermine the overall objective of the fixed link itself.

Such bending of policy presupposes that there is a national will to support urban areas. The existing scale of the resources devoted to urban programmes—and to policy areas, such as housing, which have direct impact on the fortunes of cities—suggests that there is less genuine commitment to the reversal of urban decline than the rhetoric might lead one to suppose. Plainly, too, if the evidence of people voting with their feet to leave large cities is to be believed, there is little popular support for cities as places in which to live. Yet no little part of such movement is the product of myth and of the financial context which has determined where new housing has been and is being built. Government itself is a powerful propagator of national sentiment and much could be done to counter some of the wilder myths of the city to establish a platform for a forceful consensus for a genuine urban policy. It has been one of the major achievements of the Prince of Wales that the interest which he has shown in the inner cities has helped to focus the attention of government, of private business, of the media, and of the nation more broadly on the condition and the needs of inner areas and their residents.

The ineffectiveness of targeting

The open nature of labour markets has meant that jobs created in deprived areas have not necessarily benefited those who live there. All of the evidence suggests that there is a high degree of leakage to the more prosperous outer and suburban areas. Nationally, almost 40 per cent of jobs in inner-city areas are filled by commuters from outside the cities. Recent research has shown how great is the degree of leakage of employment benefit from the inner areas. For example, in the Newcastle area, the beneficiaries of the jobs created in the inner area were studied by comparing the location of *all* employees with those recruited after the inner-area establishments had undertaken a project supported by assistance. For all employees of inner-area establishments, no fewer than 66 per cent commuted from outside the inner area. Thus, even though the inner area itself is relatively self-contained (with 60 per cent of inner-area employed residents working in inner-area establishments) large numbers of inner-area jobs are filled from outside. The pattern of post-project employment was almost identical to this; the jobs newly created in inner-area establishments through public assistance recruited only 37 per cent of inner-area residents. There was not even any specific benefit to the disadvantaged: only one-sixth of the 'new' jobs were semi- and unskilled posts—a lower proportion than for the broader region as a whole—and hence they tended to include fewer people previously unemployed. As the authors conclude; 'Overall, assisting inner area firms does not, by itself, appear to be a particularly efficient way of providing job opportunities for disadvantaged inner area residents' (Robinson *et al.*, 1987). Similar findings have been reported for Birmingham (Spencer *et al.*, 1986). Help to inner-area firms has, therefore, conferred some benefit on local inner-city residents, but only in line with existing labour-market patterns. The leakage typically associated with open labour markets means that spatial targeting is not equivalent to people targeting.

If it is considered important that deprived people benefit, ways need to be explored to ensure a closer match between the spatial and social focuses of policy. There is here, of course, a latent conflict between the economic and social aims of policy. This is the broader and more fundamental ambiguity in the aim of policy. Is the effectiveness of policy to be measured in terms of the creation of enterprise, the number of genuinely new jobs which are created, the net addition to the productive output of the country as a whole through the creation of greater competitiveness, on the one hand; or is the aim the distributional one of spreading opportunity and involvement to those at the back of the queues of access for jobs, housing, and the range of public and private amenities in what is regarded as normal civilized life? The whole thrust of policy has been to focus on the former and to see the latter as merely an additional beneficial extra if it so happens that the deprived gain some benefit. Given the relatively small numbers of real jobs which public assistance can create, it may be that the emphasis is misplaced. In reality these two poles cannot in the long term be dissociated; long-term economic effectiveness can only fundamentally be achieved if the whole of the population derive some benefit from it. There is a point at which inequality and frustrated ambitions in an open society lead to serious levels of disruption, disillusionment, and rebelliousness. That must impinge on the plausibility and the cost of economic performance. We should not have to wait for yet more riots for that relationship to be apparent. Even if we leave the moral arguments about equity to one side, and are unpersuaded by the blackmail inherent in the potential threat to effectiveness posed by social disturbance, we are still faced with the arguments about the efficiency of the nation's economic performance. House-price differentials of a factor of three; idle and underused land and resources in large areas of our cities; strong hands lying idle; these are not the underpinnings of a maximally efficient economy.

The fact that leakage through labour markets has meant that benefit has not accrued to the most needy is therefore a major current limitation to which future policy must address itself further and in more concerted ways.

The assumption of development capacity

Policy has clearly marginalized the role of local government. Agencies such as UDCs have been 'imposed' on cities, direct central-government involvement has grown, and the focus of development has been narrowed to a partnership between central government and the private sector. Yet, if regeneration is to carry long-term conviction and avoid the kinds of conflict which have been so apparent in the London Docklands, it continues to be important that local governance should command popular legitimacy and play a secure role in the implementation of policy at local level. It remains an important third side of the triangle of implementation. If local-government officials are to be involved in implementation, there is now sufficient evidence to suggest both that most local-authority officials have little feel for or experience of economic development in a commercial market and that they are hedged around with too many limitations on their fiscal ability to implement policies. The last decade has seen profound changes in what is expected of officials in the most innovative authorities, yet there is urgent need for more specific training of local officials in the business of local economic development. Most of the officers who have been charged with the development of local economic policies within local authorities have been drawn from planning departments (Mills and Young, 1986). It appears that they work largely on a seat-of-the-pants approach. Certainly, the finding that only 2 per cent of those without planning qualifications regretted that fact suggests that different forms of training are needed if informed decisions in the field of economic development are to be taken at local level. This is not to condemn the efforts of all local authorities; some like Sheffield have shown praiseworthy developmental capacity. Others have sunk deeper into a mire of their own making. Furthermore there is a need to consider ways in which to develop appropriate long-term frameworks for fiscal planning through which local authorities can most effectively use resources to achieve the goals of local economic packages, instead of the hole-and-corner creative accountancy through which currently many authorities attempt to bypass the restrictions placed on them by central government. It is beyond doubt that the ambiguity of the role of local authorities needs to be resolved. If they are to play the locally sensitive role which clearly they are best placed to fulfil, their capacity to develop innovative economic development needs to be strengthened.

The same argument is likely to apply with increasing force in future to other local agents, of which housing asociations are a prime example. The new roles which they are assumed to play under forthcoming housing legislation will dramatically change the scale of operation of housing associations and the environment in which they will operate. Questions must be raised about how well placed they are to respond to the opportunities offered by the prospect of managing parts of local-authority housing stocks and of raising private finance to augment public resources from the Housing Corporation. Few of the organizations in the housing-association movement, even including the larger bodies, have finance managers or the skills required in raising private finance. The need for capacity building for a very different future again seems evident.

The spatial scales of development

The operation of local labour markets; the occupational and social composition of local populations; the political context within which local authorities operate; the inheritance of local skills, entrepreneurial experience in industry and commerce; the stock of industry, services, and infrastructure; and the environmental context within local areas: all these form a richly varied *mélange* within Britain. The needs and the potential of localities vary greatly from area to area (Cooke, 1988). Such local variability suggests the need for more locally informed and locally sensitive policies in fields such as training, the stimulation of enterprise through business and economic development, and the facilitation of community development. On the very smallest scale, it is clear that community development is something for which central-government departments are not well placed and for which they may not even recognize the necessity. This is to argue the need for a stronger and more autonomous input from local communities within the context of local governance, reinforcing the need for capacity building and fiscal autonomy at a local level. The early years of the Urban Programme offered opportunities for the development of voluntary-sector activities and for community development and provided some scope for the emergence of a *local* voice in determining priorities in the development and implementation of local schemes. The faltering growth of co-operatives, of tenants' groups, of community associations provides the seed-bed of a more broadly based participative democracy which adds legitimacy to decision-making if such groups are given a genuine voice in determining the circumstances of their own well-being; the further development of such local participation can only be welcomed.

There is also, however, a broader regional argument about the strategic needs of planning policy for urban areas. The scale and openness of labour markets reinforces the need to interpret and to plan at a scale larger than single local authorities. So too does the increasing plethora of new agencies and bodies in the field of training and economic development. Even though regions may make decreasing functional sense in terms of the operation of regional economies, they make great sense in terms of strategic planning, so as to avoid the zero-sum product of myriad authorities competing against each other for inward investment in a context of balkanized jostling. There is a need for regional strategic planning—more so in light of the demise of metropolitan authorities which, for all the many faults which justified their abolition, did play a valuable strategic role within conurbations. This is not to argue that we need to strengthen the local outposts of central-government departments, since the existing regional offices of such departments as DTI and DoE act too much as mere testing grounds for civil servants who, if successful, are generally sucked rapidly back to Marsham Street or Victoria Street, and, if not, tend to stay for long periods in the regions adjudged in a telling phrase by the centre as having 'gone native'. This is not real substitute for a permanent career-based devolution of functions to the regions. The contrast is most marked in comparing the experience of regional offices of central government in England with the relative autonomy of the Welsh and Scottish Offices under which have developed the Welsh Development Agency and the Scottish Development Agency. The latter in particular has had a stimulating impact on the turn-around of parts of central Scotland (Lever and Moore, 1986). The fortunes of Glasgow—long thought of as the most hopeless city in Britain and the first candidate for 'closure' in any suggested policy of triage—bears testimony to the success of the SDA as a co-ordinating and development agency for the area as a whole, and one which provides a surer context for establishing less fraught relations with local government. The fact of having a central co-ordinating body committed to and knowledgeable about the area and staffed with able, accessible, and relatively powerful civil servants, under whose auspices were mounted such projects as Locate in Scotland and the development of regional strategies (allied, it has to be said, with large sums of additional resources which were more generous on a per-capita basis than for the English regions), has had a considerable impact on the subsequent fortunes of central Scotland.

The limitations of present policy begin to suggest broad frameworks of alternative approaches to the development of a genuine urban policy in Britain. In looking to the future it is as well to remember that in considering what has happened so far 'it will do no good to search for villains or heroes or saints or devils, because there were none; there were only victims.'

6
What might now be done? *The Flower of Civilization*

> The city is the flower of civilisation. It gives to men the means to make their lives expressive. It offers a field of battle, and it could be made a livable place if its sons would stay and fight for it instead of running away.
>
> *Anon.*

In analysing the causes of the decline of our cities and some of our regions, in discussing the policies undertaken, and in assessing their degrees of success, it is easy to lose sight of the fact that 'people are living there'. One of the less endearing ploys of modern politicians is to talk glibly about 'our people': residents of those areas trapped by the incoming threatening tide of history can be forcefully pungent in their comments on this tendency. It is they who are at the receiving end of policy and it is they who, for the most part, feel alienated, forgotten, and threatened by the course of events. An apparently simple everyday occurrence like the arrest of a young man suspected of carrying drugs or of committing motoring offences can fan those feelings into flames of violence and disruption. In the hearts and minds of people damaged to the limits of endurance lies the real tragedy of the lack of a viable urban policy.

In an advanced and open economy, economic growth and social justice are dovetailed together. In the long run one can only maintain rigid and deep polarities in social conditions at the expense of overall national well-being—as the recent experience of South Africa and much of the developing world suggests. It costs money to police inequality and to sustain the inefficiencies which come from regional disparities and from underused resources of skills and infrastructure.

This forces us to a view of alternative futures which recognizes two dimensions: one is economic and the other is attitudinal (West Midlands County Council, 1982). On the one hand the effects of national growth are critical. Growth brings with it opportunities—opportunities which could be channelled into decreasing the levels of social inequality and ameliorating some of the disparities which now exist. Planners had grown used to couching their strategic thinking in terms of an assumption of growth, under which it becomes easier to plan for the redistribution of resources to areas in need. The no-growth economy of the period since the OPEC crisis in the middle 1970s is one to which we have still not become accustomed. Yet if, as seems likely, the next decade is one in which there *is* economic growth, but that growth is jobless growth, we need to adapt to the new tensions which derive therefrom. And the principal tension will be the exacerbation of the conflicting pull between the desire for growth and the failure of that growth to eradicate social inequality. Long-term national well-being requires that we resist the instinct to see *any* growth as something to be encouraged, wherever it may occur and whoever may benefit from it. It is clear, from all that has gone before, that growth in itself will not tackle the problems of inequality: those 'best' fitted are likely to benefit and those at the back of the queue of skills, or resources, and of political leverage are likely to suffer yet further absolute or relative deprivation. We therefore need also to consider the effects of a second dimension—of attitudes, of innovative social thinking informed by an awareness of the distress and unrest which can undermine national efficiency and the effectiveness of even the best-intentioned of programmes. Since social groups remain highly segregated in space both within cities and across regions of the country, any social dimension has a strong spatial basis. It is therefore important for policy to be couched in spatially sensitive terms.

There are diverse options on offer. We could do nothing and accept the market-driven lead of whatever transpires in the 'free' market. We could adopt a minimalist approach which merely trims at the edges. It could be argued that in due course the regional and spatial disparities reflected in house-price differentials, levels of unemployment, and economic and social buoyancy will be levelled out, in the style of neoclassical economics, by a process of 'trickle down' to the northern urban regions. Yet the potency of market-led and marginal adjustments of this sort seems implausible, given that the breadth of the existing disparities in land price, house prices, and other factor costs, and in levels of unemployment, have not led to any spatial readjustment of investment. Inflation nodes coexist with underused facilities, even in an island as small as Britain.

Both of these approaches are unacceptable responses to the palpable perversion of justice inherent in the prospect of growing inequality. All the evidence suggests that current trends would indeed increase inequality; there is no evidence of a widespread trickle down from national growth to counter the continuous widening of regional disparities and the increasing social polarities. Indeed, those in the North should beware the seductive argument that the prosperity of the South will eventually roll their way—that the rapid growth of house prices has already reached the southern outskirts of Birmingham and betokens the spread of economic prosperity throughout the country. This is merely the knock-on effect of the progressive extension of London's continuing spatial dominance of the national economy. So long as such growth emanates solely from the London command centre—is the result of the orientation of the economy to the high-wage and high-skill economy of the South East—the danger remains that the North will merely act as the low-wage, low-skill outpost; a kind of on-shore Taiwan.

So a more interventionist style seems called for. It could either be 'conventional' or 'innovative'. The first would attempt to recreate many of the familiar patterns of the early post-war years—an emphasis on manufacturing industry, a reinstitution of regional policy, a state-led emphasis on public investment as the lever of further growth and as a mechanism for redistribution, or some combination of parts of these. The experience of the 1960s leads one to be wary of such views: no convincing ways have been suggested as to how to break from the snare of galloping inflation associated with demand-led policy or how to avoid the limitation of a regional policy which in practice encourages the development of branch-plant economies and of capital-intensive establishments which create few employment opportunities in the 'assisted' areas. Nor can one be persuaded that the future lies in a return to manufacturing industry as a way of creating a more high-employment economy. The world has changed. And what has changed is not only the economic framework, but the political context and what one might call the expectational context. Before the midle 1970s, many idealized views of post-industrial society were widely canvassed. They presupposed a fall in productive industry, a growth in both personal and producer services, a rise in wealth, an increase in leisure, and a greater participation, democracy, and equality (Bell, 1973). That western nations have fallen short of such a vision is axiomatic in all that we have learned from urban decline. Much of the economic change postulated for the post-industrial society may indeed have occurred and, for those in work, may have been accompanied by rising real wealth and leisure. But the concomitants—of participation and equality through the growth of technology and the freedom from the grind of manual labour—have hardly proved to be the fruit of the pain of change through which advanced nations have gone over the last decade. Yet the *expectation* that those desirable accompaniments should be the right of everyone has undoubtedly grown and therein lies the tension to which policy needs to be addressed. In earlier years it was possible for Runciman to offer a powerful demonstration that the limited social reference groups used by the poor in making evaluations of their lot in the 1960s were the reason why relative deprivation did not lead to greater social discontent (Runciman, 1966). That agument has far less potency today. We are all more aware of the privileges and privations of others. It is now less easy to ignore the plight of the disadvantaged than it was in the depression of the 1930s or indeed in the relative affluence of the post-war decades. The claims of today's deprived—whoever they may be and wherever they may be found—have gained a political legitimacy which cannot readily be swept to one side. The context in which policy is formulated must therefore recognize the increasing long-term risks associated with promoting national economic competitiveness without addressing the issue of social fairness.

THE PRINCIPLES FOR POLICY

This leads us to some principles which should guide our thinking and our policy. The social dimension cannot be regarded as an optional extra to be tacked to the economic only if circumstances allow it. And the social dimension can only be addressed if certain conditions obtain: that development policy should be alive to the need to encourage genuine local participation in drawing up priorities and in their implementation; that policy should be sensitive to the variability in the experiences and inheritances of different local areas; and that it should be better able to target its resources to those most in need. These three principles are socially and spatially sensitive keystones which should guide us. Then, fourth, we need to ensure that policies and their various instruments are better co-ordinated so as to ensure greater efficiency in the delivery of resources on both the economic and the social fronts. These four principles may indeed lead to some conflict between the economic need to create and encourage growth and the social need to channel a significant part of what growth there is in order the better to ameliorate distress. It is a conflict which should be faced, since the tensions raised by too exclusive a concentration on economic growth are serious in both the short and the long term. In the long term, sustained growth seems feasible only in the context of a population which shares in its fruits and which offers a wide platform of support for its determinants. To bow to a purely market-led growth ethic and ignore the social implications is no recipe for long-term well-being. The alternative policy framework needs to involve both a recognition of the role of the new types of activity stimulated by the growth of high-tech. activities, by the central role of producer services, and by labour-intensive leisure activities, on the one hand, and the encouragement of smaller-scale community-based enterprise on the other. One thing is certain: a sustained attack on urban problems presupposes a national will to recognize the severity of the problems and to devote resources to combat them.

THE NEED FOR COHERENCE AND CONSENSUS

If government is serious in its stated desire to develop an urban policy, it needs to maintain a bending of resources over a considerable period of time, given the depth of the crisis which cities face. It needs to ensure that there is a greater consistency among the effects of the various policy arenas and in the incidence of spending benefits. Monitoring the spatial impacts of public spending must be one part of this. A set of regional accounts of the incidence of public spending by a range of departments is a prerequisite so as to provide the information on which to assess the unintended impact of policies which do not ostensibly discriminate spatially between different areas. This is no small task, not least because of the reluctance or inability of public bodies to make information freely available. Short's experience in this was instructive. Attempting to compile public-expenditure accounts for city regions extending the methods of his earlier regional-expenditure accounts (Short, 1981), he was unable to complete the task since the necessary central-government data for subregions were not forthcoming (Short and Howard, 1985). This is stark testament to the lack of awareness of or sensitivity to this dimension of public policy on the part of government departments. In the United States, under the Carter administration, there was a brief dalliance with a form of 'urban impact statement' whereby the differential effect of public spending on distressed urban areas was made one component of decisions on whether or not to proceed with a given policy (Hausner, 1983; Massey, 1980). For all its crudeness, such a device in Britain might at least awaken awareness to the issue.

The current reliance on a Cabinet subcommittee as a way of trying to achieve high-level policy co-ordination seems a poor substitute for a more formal structure through which the urban-related aspects of the policies of the variety of central departments might better be made less disparate. Central departments are large and relatively autonomous. It is difficult to see that they will ever voluntarily wish to bend 'their' programmes or 'their' expenditure in response to mere external exhortations or to the co-ordination which might be urged by a roving minister with overall responsibility for inner cities. In practice, co-ordination might only be achieved at a devolved level through the strengthening of regional and local governance.

Government could also do much to alter the perception of cities in the popular mind and to help to create a popular basis for a national will to sustain cities. No small part of the lemming-like piling-up of activity in the inflation nodes of the South East and of the flight from cities is the artificial creation of sentiments and myths which are manipulated at will by the unscrupulous. Whether it is the adman with his false but seductive image of fresh air and clean living away from the city or the politician massaging his voters to ensure majorities of one sort of another or the endless stream of pundits—some gently green from the groves of academe, some steaming magenta from the forcing-houses of competitive current-affairs programmes and supposedly informed journalism—or the speculative builder looking for quick profits, they are all in their own way 'conmen' to the public. Michael Heseltine showed something of the power of boosterism during his sojourn as maestro of Liverpool.

Pride in the city is a very real factor that could be used to advantage. The inhabitants of cities, whether rich or poor, deprived or affluent, have an innate willingness for *their* city to do well. Mixing with the crowds of a large city when their football team has won a cup or a championship or when the Christmas decorations have been switched on is to experience a totality of pleasure and pride in 'our city'. Recent suggestions from a Glasgow research team that Manchester was one of the least desirable places in which to live prompted a healthily virulent local indignation. Indeed it is that feeling which has been so effectively exploited for political ends by some local councils who have played on the idea that central government is somehow picking unfairly on a particular city. The local enthusiasm which backed Birmingham's abortive bid for the Olympic games may seem rather misplaced, but there is no doubting both its genuineness and the very real support that came from all walks of life. Glaswegians can already be heard positively purring (if such a term can be used of the sturdy inhabitants of that city) at the accolade awarded their city and no doubt much more will be heard when their year as European City of Culture dawns. Sheffield's success in attracting the World Student Games offers to the city not only the economic benefit of the spillover effects of new construction and trade, but also the psychological boost of linking the city with a major international flagship venture. 'Place marketing' can play an important role both in boosting local confidence and in spreading that infectious optimism to the perceptions of those outside the city concerned. Bradford's marketing has depended on more than selling the Brontës, but that has played an important role in its strategy; Wigan has more than a pier, but the dramatic regeneration of its canal area has acted as an important symbol of civic resurgence. The creation of such local confidence requires vision, the involvement of local communities, and the partnership that comes from strong networks between the private and public sectors and local institutes of higher education, together with the prompting of a strong public-sector lead. There is, of course, danger in this. What is today's fashion can readily become tomorrow's boredom. Placing too great an emphasis on local boosterism as a means of attracting mobile investment invites the fickleness of fashion; what comes can just as readily go, especially at a period when international capital is so mobile (Dicken, 1986). To counteract this, an important element of such strategy is what Stuart Gulliver, Regional Director of SDA, has called pacing devices; the aim of developing a sequence of events over time so as to maintain and re-channel local ebullience. In Glasgow's own case, the impact of the 'Glasgow's Miles Better' campaign is to be followed by the 1988 Garden Festival and the 1990 Year of the European City of Culture. Just as with community development, successful cities need constantly to reinvent themselves. Charismatic local figures can play an important role in releasing civic self-respect into creative channels. Civic pride has never been limited to the more prosperous burghers: it is only more difficult to sustain and express when pockets are empty and prospects are bleak.

POVERTY, LOW PAY, AND UNEMPLOYMENT

Lack of employment is clearly a principal determinant of poverty and low income. Yet, whatever initiatives might be developed it seems implausible that we will recreate the full-employment society which was taken for granted in the post-war decades. The relatively limited numerical successes of job creation through public assistance in the Newcastle area and in even the most active of the municipal authorities such as Sheffield do not suggest that such development schemes should be abandoned or lessened, but that even with the deployment of considerable sums of public money we need to recognize the limited scope for job creation. This is particularly so when in the foreseeable future greater productivity through the application of capital to production is going to continue to create jobless growth. If we accept that full formal employment is unlikely in any anticipated future, the blend of economic and social perspectives must lead to three particular concerns: the creation of an effective benefit system for those in continuing need; the creation of opportunities for *work* (in the absence of sufficient formal employment); and the more effective targeting of jobs and work opportunities to those most in need. If we are to create more work, in the absence of formal jobs, it is equally important that the distinction between the two does not carry with it damaging social overtones which decry the one and laud the other. That way yet deeper social divisions will occur.

Employment strategies

A unified benefit scheme offering a guaranteed minimum for those in or out of work would create great advantages over the present patchy and confusing system of benefits. All the costings of the various ideas that have been put forward show that it is a practical way forward, but one in which all of comfortable Britain have to accept a greater burden. Such a revolutionary but necessary approach would entail a new look at the concept of income support and indeed the right of the physically fit to receive an income for doing nothing. 'Workfare', as practised in America, has had an understandably hostile reception in Britain, but it might be possible to arrive at a more acceptable version. Workfare entails the unemployed being required to undertake social or community-based work of benefit to the local area as a pre-condition of the receipt of benefit. It has the potential merit both of encouraging responsibility in the individual recipient, and of tackling useful work in local areas. Its undoubted drawbacks are the social stigma attached to participation in such schemes and the element of compulsion which they entail. To meet the principle of eroding social polarization, it could be that the first of these objections might be met by combining a form of workfare with a parallel but *universal* scheme of 'civil service' which would involve all people at some stage between the ages of, say, 16 and 20 being required to spend one or two years undertaking community-based work. While such a scheme would be developed under the structure of central government, its implementation could be controlled essentially at community level through local authorities or the voluntary sector. The benefits of the universality of such a scheme would be the implicit removal of the stigma associated with involvement in 'government' projects and the breaking up of the treadmill of education for those involved in forms of higher education. Universities and polytechnics would thereby be encouraged to accelerate the process by which they are currently developing more flexible forms of educational provision on a cafeteria-based system, since they could no longer rely purely on the conveyor-belt principle of the brightest automatically moving *en bloc* from school to higher education. It would probably have the effect of encouraging a wider spread of entry into higher education and into the colleges of education. At a time when the 18-year-old population has just entered a period of long secular decline as the reduced birth cohorts of the late 1960s come of age, but when government has proclaimed its willingness to maintain or increase the intake into higher and further education (Department of Education and Science, 1987), there is a notable opportunity for higher education to broaden its base of intake and develop a more socially aware concern for those living in the vicinity of universities who traditionally have not qualified for entry. Particularly in those cities with big civic universities or polytechnics such as Manchester, Birmingham, Sheffield, Leeds, Liverpool, and Newcastle, such developments could impinge with especial benefit on the uban deprived. In Manchester, for example, access courses with agreed modules and syllabuses in further-education colleges have been devised by the local higher-education institutes so that adults and the young unqualified can gain accreditation for entry to the polytechnic and university. Shaking loose the traditional social and educational incestuousness of universities would offer the chance to develop their potential as local centres for capacity training. The social fairness of a 'civil service' scheme could therefore be accompanied by the inestimable benefit of producing a wider range of more educated, confident, and skilled people coming in due course to the job market.

Such a modified form of workfare in the shape of a 'civil service' scheme would therefore address the need to create 'work' as much as 'employment' in the context of a national economy which seems unlikely again to offer full employment in the face of a technologically driven need for fewer and fewer hands to make or to process products and information. The predictable response of 'slave labour' from the unions might hopefully be avoided once an associated development of a basic unified benefit or income support was seen as being both a fairer and a less complex way of helping the unemployed and low-incomed.

As far as formal jobs are concerned, the growing emphasis on the preservation of existing jobs in industry and services, in the face of uncertain growth, seems an important element of any strategy. It may in the longer term prove more effective than a more exclusive expenditure of resources to try to attract new enterprise in a competition between different authorities. This is a strategy which a few but an increasing number of local authorities are now more consciously pursuing. An important element of job creation and protection lies in public jobs. It has been the contraction of public employment which has dealt one of the most severe blows to the prospects of many of the more deprived inner-city residents. The boasts of many left-wing local authorities about creating jobs and preserving services may have a strong dose of slogan to them, and may in practice be more concerned with a self-interested preservation of public-service jobs than with the improvement of services to consumers, but they do address the twin needs of the most deprived urban residents in the large cities. For the unskilled there needs to be a range of work in caring for the old, the disabled, and children and for the small-scale environmental improvements and the variety of much-needed services. Local authorities have an important potential role in organizing such public employment and work; so too have the many voluntary-sector bodies through volunteer centres and community-development projects. Allied with easier access to further and higher education, schemes which provide work could offer eventual skills training to a presently unskilled population.

Targeting the deprived

Equally important, if we are to address the needs of the weakest in the formal labour market, is to consider better ways of targeting jobs and other benefits to the most needy. There are different routes by which more effective targeting might be achieved. On the one hand there are structural approaches which depend on enabling the deprived to achieve greater effective access to labour markets. This would entail a better co-ordination between skills training and job creation, which requires an intimate knowledge of local labour markets so that training courses can be more explicitly tied to the needs for labour. The changes in higher education discussed earlier would be of clear relevance. So too would an extension of the London Compact scheme in which, following the example of Boston, a group of private companies have concluded an agreement with three local schools in the East End of London, whereby in return for meeting defined standards (for example on attendance and placement experience as well as on more traditional educational performance criteria) the firms guarantee job interviews to pupils. Government has now recognized the potential of such schemes by announcing its intention to offer support to twelve inner-city Compacts (Cabinet Office, 1988). Other linkages can be just as important. For example, the constraints produced by rigid tenurially divided housing markets mean that housing policy and jobs need also to be linked more effectively. A regional scheme of council-house mobility would be of benefit by enabling those living in depressed labour-market areas to move more readily to the increasingly decentralized areas in which semi- and unskilled production jobs are now found; and at the same time it could help to achieve the limited and controlled reduction in densities from which cities would benefit. Conversely, the creation of an effective assured-tenancy scheme would help to enable young and childless households to find accommodation in more central areas where access to urban service jobs is easier. Housing associations have great potential to contribute to the freeing-up of mobility. The recent development of joint private-sector/housing-association schemes, as in Cardiff's introduction of a 30:70 split of private and public funding for housing-association schemes, is a presage of further growing involvement of this sector in house provision. The current Housing Bill aims to extend this process by giving housing associations a far greater role in the provision and management of housing through raising greater sums of public finance and through their possible involvement in tenants' opting-out of council housing. This has much to commend it, but doubts remain about whether private finance is readily available for the kinds of specialized and low-to-middle income housing which is now required and whether many housing associations other than the few already large ones have the capacity to expand their activity to the scale envisaged by government. Transport, too, needs to be planned with a strategic eye open to the increasing need for forms of reverse commuting by poorer inner-area residents to the peripheral job opportunities in suburban or non-urban areas.

On the other hand, there might be specific mechanical approaches to targeting. First, financial assistance could be given on a selective basis to firms which offer predominantly low-skill jobs. Second, the disadvantaged could be helped by the payment of a wage subsidy for inner-area residents. The drawback of both such approaches is that they are likely to perpetuate the competitive disadvantages of areas in decline. Third, training schemes could be focused on specific target groups, in the way that many local-authority and central-government schemes have increasingly come to recognize. While such schemes do not create long-term jobs, they can redistribute employment opportunities by breaking the vicious circle of economic and social disadvantage. Fourth, recruitment to new jobs could be spatially limited to people living in target areas, thereby achieving a partial closure of otherwise open labour markets. Here there could be objection from employers on the grounds of the restriction on their freedom to choose the 'best' for the job and there would be arguments about the equity of such discrimination.

Nevertheless this latter approach is of particular interest since such ring-fencing can be readily implemented and readily understood as beneficial by those in deprived areas. It involves a form of affirmative action, based on location. While one needs to recognize the open nature of labour markets, and to be alive to the legal and moral arguments against overtly positive discrimination, affirmative action to give equal weight or, at the margin, to give preferential treatment to those living close to new employment opportunities created in inner areas can go some way to avoiding the tendency merely to suck in the more prosperous commuters from outer areas. It is worth quoting the experience of one of the few existing examples as illustration. It is provided by the UDG-assisted expansion of a brewery in Manchester where agreement was reached with the company, Royal Brewery Scottish and Newcastle, that it should give preference to local residents in filling the 100 extra jobs associated with the publicly funded expansion. The managerial jobs were filled from outside, but of the 2,000 applications for the 64 new non-managerial jobs a principle of shortlisting only those living in the five adjacent postal districts meant that the number of applicants was reduced from 2,200 to 926. The final outcome was that all 64 jobs went to local people, of whom 39 were British/Irish, 23 of West Indian origin, 1 Asian, and 1 African (Robson, 1987). Doubts have been expressed about the success of this scheme on the grounds that some 10 per cent of those who gained jobs subsequently moved into private housing outside the area within the first year of the scheme (Haughton *et al.*, 1987). To this one can only respond that, nationally, annual residential mobility is approximately 10 per cent so that the scheme has in effect levered a group of previously immobile residents into mobility similar to that of 'comfortable' Britain and that it reinforces the argument for building more private housing in inner areas to cater for a broader choice in what is currently an institutionally suppressed demand for more private housing in inner areas. A similar ring-fencing approach was recently called for by Manchester City Council in a scheme of affirmative action to encourage council jobs to go to people living within the city boundary. Like many councils, currently some 80 per cent of its architects, almost 75 per cent of its planners, and 60 per cent of its teachers live outside the city. As a first step, school-leavers living within the city were to be taken on YTS trainee schemes or apprenticeship schemes. In the event, pressure from unions dented the council's initial resolve and the proposal has now been abandoned.

Some such schemes are at risk of running headlong into EEC

legislation which forbids positive discrimination in the recruitment practices of public bodies. The restrictions, however, are less rigid for private employment. Even within the constraints of legislation, forms of affirmative action can be developed to recognize the local employment needs of inner areas and to maximize the probability of recruiting local people. For example, Battersea Leisure Limited, the private company established to convert the disused Battersea Power Station into a leisure complex, having received planning permission from the local council, has worked with the Economic Development of Wandsworth, a multiracial inner London area of high unemployment, to develop a locally sensitive positive action programme for recruitment of the eventual 4,500 jobs which will be created. In the construction phase local companies will be encouraged to tender for contracts. In recruiting its workforce, the company has agreed the following procedures: identification of the skills of local labour and of the additional training needed to enable local labour to compete for jobs; development of preparatory training courses for local residents; implementation of recruitment and in-company training recognizing the needs of the target groups of school-leavers, the long-term unemployed, black people, women, and the disabled; and monitoring of the operation of the positive action programme (Battersea Leisure Ltd./Wandsworth Borough Council, 1986).

At the least, the need for greater sensitivity to the need for effective targeting holds a message for the advertising of jobs. The greater use of local libraries and of the ethnic Press, or the use of outreach workers, would be steps towards helping to target benefit more effectively to those in greatest need. Such schemes of affirmative action could be multiplied. They are not an argument for lowering the aptitudes of those appointed since many of the local residents often turn out to be as skilful and as committed as those who possess better formal qualifications. In the more depressed labour-market areas, most vacancies are flooded with applicants and consequently personnel managers often succumb to the temptation to cull applicants through the use of discriminatory criteria such as address and skin colour—a process that Boddy calls selection of the suitable rather than the competent (Boddy *et al.*, 1986, p. 150). Schemes of affirmative action can provide a context in which such local people are less likely to be discriminated against on the basis of inappropriate criteria.

SCALES OF GOVERNANCE

The needs for better co-ordination on the one hand and for more effective involvement of people on the other both suggest that forms of devolution of administration should be one of the priorities of urban policy. The guiding principle is that decisions should be taken at the lowest scale consistent with their effective and efficient performance. This should be the yardstick in determining which bodies and at what scales policy should be determined and implemented. Decentralization may involve forgoing some of the economies of scale associated with large organizations, but experience suggests that large scale has itself led to ineffectiveness through the inability to co-ordinate the policies and practices of the component sections of such organizations. It has also added to the estrangement of residents from involvement in decision-making and hence to the grumbling resentment both at local and at central government. The shunting-down of responsibilities from both central and local government suggests that there should be genuine regional strategic policy-making at one scale and equally that there should be devolution to community and resident groups at the other. To call such a prescription part of urban policy may at first sight appear odd. The fact is however that at the regional scale the interests of cities and regions have become increasingly consonant with each other. The poverty of the North is as much a product of the concentration of large old urban areas north of the Tees/Exe line as of the inherent imperatives of geography *per se*. To erode the overweening dominance of London and the South East would be to the advantage of the cities of the North as well as in the interests of greater efficiency of the country as a whole. At the other extreme, policies to devolve greater control to communities and neighbourhoods would be a step towards tackling the social and environmental distress found disproportionately in urban housing estates and hence towards providing mechanisms to reinvolve their increasingly alienated urban underclass.

Regional co-ordination

The experience of the Scottish Development Agency provides a pointer to the kinds of roles that could be played by regional authorities within England. They would clearly have an important role to play in developing networks amongst the various bodies with direct developmental roles: local authorities, regional offices of central government, Chambers of Commerce, and private-sector business. Such regional bodies should have limited revenue-raising powers through precepts on local rates (or on the Community Charge if it is introduced). They should assume the kinds of co-ordinating strategic planning role that had been played by metropolitan counties—a role made less effective by the artificially small boundaries within which the metropolitan counties used to operate. They should play an equally strategic role in housing, thereby making feasible the development of genuine systems of house transfer within and across regional boundaries so as to supplement the wholly inadequate levels of mobility currently promoted by the Tenants Exchange Scheme and the National Mobility Scheme (Champion, Green, and Owen, 1987). Such broader co-ordination of housing strategies will assume even greater importance if there is a range of types of landlord—housing associations, private companies, and the like—after the implementation of the current Housing Bill. The regional bodies could also play a co-ordinating role in developing economic strategies both to sustain and enhance existing activities and to provide one-stop shops for the attraction of new enterprise—in the way that Locate in Scotland has done.

The scope for developing such economic strategies is well illustrated by the experience of some of the enterprise boards which have acted at subregional level. Some of the most innovative of the job and training and enterprise schemes of the last decade have come from region-wide bodies such as the Greater London and West Midlands Enterprise Boards (GLEB and WMEB) or Lancashire Enterprise Limited (LEL). Their effectiveness is reduced both by their small size and by the fact that they are still in competition with the host of even smaller bodies based on individual local authorities. It is this 'balkanization' which has reduced the impact of any one of the contributing agencies. To create a small number of one-stop shop development agencies which would provide advice, information, and support for both existing companies and potential inward investment would add a valuable cutting edge to the development of local and regional economic strategies. Operation at a regional scale would avoid some of the unhelpful competition between adjacent towns in a region. Bodies at this scale would be more alive than centralized government departments to the peculiarities of the labour markets within their areas and able to tailor policy more sensitively than could national policy initiatives. Immediate objections would be raised in light both of government hostility to the implicit devolution and of more mundane arguments about where the boundaries of such bodies might be drawn. On the latter, the most logical divisions might be based on a very limited number of conurbations, ensuring that the regions were not so small as to be politically ineffective. It could well be, however, that the most appropriate framework would be the now long-established Standard Regions. There is no need for regional bodies to be established throughout the country. Indeed, to meet the seemingly implacable government opposition, it could be that a politically acceptable approach would be to introduce only one or two such agencies in 'demonstration' areas, so as further to expand the demonstration effect of the SDA and WDA. It is perhaps not without signficance that some Conservative MPs with northern constituencies have publicly voiced their support for such bodies (Brittan, 1988). An undoubted benefit of such bodies would be the framework that they would provide both to resolve some of the conflicts between the DoE and other government departments and to establish negotiations with local government and the private sector, less fraught with hostility and conflict. This certainly has been the experience of the Glasgow Eastern Area Renewal (GEAR) scheme in Scotland (Donnison and Middleton, 1987), where the co-ordinating role of the SDA and its long-established relations with local authorities undoubtedly helped to avoid the kinds of conflict so apparent in the London Docklands. GEAR was no less of an intrusion into traditional local government in Glasgow than were the UDCs in England. It was the fact that there was an established roving development agency able to act alongside district and regional authorities (which retained their planning responsibilities and whose councillors were therefore able to carry their electorates with them in the redevelopment area) which helped to ensure that GEAR was able to accomplish renewal with a degree of 'collaborative tolerance' (Wannop and Leclerc, 1987) that contrasts with the outright warfare which has characterized the English experience. Focused, as is suggested below, on some major northern cities with potential for economic growth, one or two such agencies could provide both the sustained and articulated momentum to revive regional economies and the alternative magnet to counteract the centralizing imperative of the South East.

One aim of such devolution would be to provide mechanisms for the development of effective regional strategy, for regional proselytizing, and for helping to argue the case for greater equity between regions in terms of public spending. In this latter regard, there would be a clear connection with the regional audits or monitoring of spatially differential public spending on goods and services, a need outlined above. Given the increased centrality of private-sector decisions, it would be important that, unlike the American development of urban-impact assessment, such monitoring and evaluation covered the private as well as the public sector (Massey, 1980). Monitoring of public-sector decisions—of procurement expenditure, of investment in health and the range of social goods and services, of expenditure on state-supported research and development—would not in itself do more than chart inequalities in benefit, but in the hands of large regional forums such information could be translated politically into an effective basis for ensuring greater spatial equality or for patterns of affirmative action on a regional basis. The examples of the Resource Allocation Working Party (RAWP) allocation formulae in the Health Service, with its incremental moves in the direction of levelling-up expenditures, or the new regional bias in funding from the Arts Council in its *Glory of the Garden* policy both provide models which could be followed in other such areas of public expenditure.

Sensitivity to the regional case could also be followed by a process of underscoring the regional remit of public utilities and quasi-public services—railways, gas, electricity, water—

even private companies such as the clearing banks. Antitrust legislation in America has created a devolution of companies to the level of states; in banking, for example, the effect of the inter-war McFadden Act has been to create state banks which both spread higher-level personnel more widely through the country and enable a greater sensitivity to the needs of local areas, and which do not necessarily prevent cross-state arrangements between banks in areas such as New York and California. In Britain such devolution could lead to regionally based operations across a range of service activities without necessarily undercutting the scale economies and network characteristics of much of their service delivery. Likewise, as part of regional monitoring, the Monopolies and Merger Commission should be given a specifically regional role, to consider the regional and spatial implications of proposed mergers and take-overs in a way that is currently not considered (Town and Country Planning Association, 1987). The eventual abandonment of the recent take-over bid for Pilkington in St Helens can be attributed in no small part to the clamour aroused by the local impact that might have ensued from the loss of involvement of a company more alive than most to its responsibility to its local community. The success of the Pilkington case was an exception; the arguments behind it should be more commonly applied.

It is here that the work of Business in the Community (BiC) provides a helpful role. Established in 1981 under the auspices of government, and comprised of major companies, trade unions, and voluntary organizations, it now has over 100 corporate members who include some of the largest of British-based businesses such as BP and the clearing banks. It acts as a forum and pressure group to encourage business to locate and invest in inner cities, to develop employment and training policies targeted to inner-city communities, to use their purchasing power to boost local economies, to develop local partnerships with local government and voluntary bodies, and to develop charitable support and community ventures (Business in the Community, 1986). The idea of a 'per cent club', through which business consciously aims to provide a slice of its profits to local community-based activity, is one of the ways in which BiC has tried to develop a greater sensitivity to businesses' responsibilities to the inner areas; a sensitivity prompted not merely by the arguments of equity, but also by the self-interest of companies who have historic investment in inner cities, and who have markets and labour forces which either are or profitably could be drawn from such areas. In these respects the British and the American experiences are vastly different. American business tends to have a much greater local involvement and attachment and local-community development agencies are much more forcefully present in American cities. Part of the former is due both to the federal structure of government and to the sheer size of the country; part of the latter reflects the historic development of ethnically segregated neighbourhoods and the long development of a more corporate social ideology of American life. The benefits are apparent in the greater ease with which schemes such as the linkage between business and the community have been developed in Boston; 5 per cent of profits of local companies being used to create a fund to assist housing, job, and training schemes and other community-based activities. In the context of the burgeoning economy in Massachusetts and the awareness of the local commitments of business, this provides a very real context for bridging the social and economic dimensions of regeneration. British ministers tend automatically to visit the United States to seek ideas for new initiatives. Given the structural differences between the two countries, one could argue that the United States makes a singularly inappropriate source of comparison. More positively, one could argue that ministers should be encouraged to return with a greater determination to create in Britain the fiscal and legislative context through which, in the United States, the decentralization of business involvement has provided the structural precondition for the success of many American schemes.

A similar case could be made for strengthening the role that local Chambers of Commerce could play. Again the contrasts with the United States are very marked, as is the relative insignificance of most British Chambers by comparison with those in Germany. Where they have energetic chief executives, some British Chambers have begun to show the positive functions they can play in local regeneration.

Throughout its history, Britain has been massively dominated by London and the Home Counties—to an extent far greater than any other European country. Even in France, where customarily one thinks of Paris as overwhelmingly dominant, 'le désert français' of the provinces is far more independent of the capital than is true of Britain's regions *vis-à-vis* the domination of the Great Wen of London. The reluctance of the great offices of state and other institutions to be based anywhere other than London means that there is always an imbalance between it and other cities. London's concentration of corporate and institutional power is of long standing (Robson, 1986). 'Provincial' Britain is in thrall to the financial strings of the capital. The rush to amalgamate the joint stockbanks at the turn of the century decimated the earlier provincial banking system so that 'the Big Five' which emerged from the struggle for banking power were all centred on London and controlled 80 per cent of domestic banking by 1918. And what is true of banking is as true of the range of less substantive but nevertheless influential powers; of the media, of central government (and the use of 'central' rather than 'national' cannot be without significance). 'To be out of London', said Samuel Johnson, 'is to be out of mind.' The ascendancy of the centre has provided the context out of which the strong and continuing regional inequalities have derived. Genuine devolution would entail the movement of the higher-level activities of corporations and agencies to the regions and thereby help to reverse the overweening dominance of London and the South East as the locus of managerial, professional, and higher technical personnel.

The community scale

At the small scale, local control is equally as important. The experience of Glasgow is once more worth quoting in the use that has been made there of community councils and of locally based small-scale housing associations as the cutting edge of the process of housing rehabilitation. Glasgow may have benfited from exceptionally high levels of housing resources—with £100 million per year over the decade 1974–84 (Maclennan, 1987)—but its success in turning around the chronic housing problems of the city would never have been so great had these not been tackled through an imaginative and alert housing authority *and* had the latter not involved small-scale developed agencies in the form of housing associations as a means of tackling the problems. Local control and local sensitivity are keynotes which help determine the longer-term success and the knock-on effect of expenditure. In England, the Priority Estates Project—with its demonstration cases in a diverse set of run-down council estates such as The Willows in Bolton, Wenlock in Hackney, and Tulse Hill in Brixton (Department of the Environment, 1981)—has shown consistently how locally based control of neighbourhoods offers a sensitivity which attracts a commitment from residents. The schemes have involved local residents of council estates being given powers over the selection and allocation of tenants and in determining local work on the improvement and upkeep of houses and the local environment. Turnover, dereliction, and arrears can all be reduced dramatically as a consequence of such schemes so that estates which have previously been hard to let can become newly oversubscribed popular areas as a result of such decentralized management. This is a world removed from the large-scale insensitive paternalistic bureaucracy of most local-authority housing management. Equally, it is worlds removed from what appears to be the intention in the government's proposed creation of Housing Action Trusts. It could, however, be allied with the proposed break-up of council estates where smaller-scale housing associations or companies *may* be better placed to incorporate opportunities for tenant involvement in the running of individual estates. Many local authorities are now beginning to take a more active interest in 'tenant control' and forms of decentralization. At present over 30 authorities are planning, or have in being, decentralization initiatives for service areas, with a particular emphasis on housing (Hambleton and Hoggett, 1984). Many housing co-operatives and efforts at self-help or self-build in housing have faced considerable political opposition from local authorities; one of the most dramatic examples being the obstacles placed in the way of the Weller Street and other housing co-ops by Liverpool's City Council (McDonald, 1986). Small schemes such as these—or such as the Town and Country Planning Association's support of self-build in its Conway and Lightmoor projects (TCPA,

1987)—may make little numerical impact on the scale of the housing problem. Multiplied to the extent that has begun to emerge in Glasgow, however, they do more than provide symbols of a more robust form of community involvement. The expected future growth of the 'third estate' of housing tenure could offer a valuable opportunity to expand this principle.

The suspicion lurks in many such schemes that they act as a guise for creating a yet more dependent and politically manageable population, by providing more ubiquitous state tentacles extended into local areas, and that they entail more the appearance than the substance of involvement by local people. On the other hand, they can be seen as radical moves to provide new structures within which a fresh relationship is forged between the state and residents so that politicians and officials can better respond to grass-roots initiatives and ideas. Ideally, the components of decentralization involve: devolving decision-making so that staff can better meet the needs of local people and incorporate their views into the development of policies; co-ordinating functions so that the often fragmented roles of service-delivery departments can be reintegrated at a local level through interdisciplinary teams working in a more flexible way across the boundaries which professionalization and departmental structures have produced within large organizations; localizing services so that they are more 'user-friendly', physically accessible, more sensitive, and more open to local people. Most local authorities are treading in largely uncharted waters in this field. There is much still to discover about the tensions involved in genuine local decentralization: how the respective roles of councillors and local chairmen of community groups might be resolved; how spending power can be devolved and yet some form of accountability be retained; whether indeed there is overall benefit in attempting to retain strict accountability for relatively small sums of money involved; whether there should be concern about the issue of representativeness—a concern which often sits oddly when coming from councillors who themselves owe their election to perhaps no more than one-quarter of the electorate; how the slow process of genuine participative democracy can be reconciled with the desire of those involved to see rapid implementation of their ideas. The conclusion hopefully to be drawn from such questions is not one of mistrust and opposition, but rather a desire to experiment with various models of local participation.

Existing schemes which could provide such models include neighbourhood councils, which are a form of statutory local council pressed for by the Association for Neighbourhood Councils, or the community councils such as exist in Stockport. Just before the end of the last parliament in April 1987, David Alton, MP for Mossley Hill Liverpool, introduced a bill whereby any 100 electors might be given the right to petition for the setting up of a parish council. It can only be hoped that other preoccupations and a new parliament do not prevent the idea from being revived. Following the pioneering scheme in Walsall in 1981, a number of authorities are decentralizing services to neighbourhood offices. Within Islington over twenty such neighbourhood offices have been opened. The largest city authority yet to experiment with such a model is Birmingham, where, by 1986, some eleven neighbourhood offices had been opened, even though the scheme has suffered through the speed with which it is being implemented and the varying interpretations of its objectives (Hoggett and Hambleton, 1985). Manchester is in the process of experimenting with a series of local neighbourhood-services offices, again based partly on housing but extending beyond this to a range of local-authority services. The Manchester scheme may be one of the sadder victims of the city's current financial crisis, in which it faces a shortfall of over £100 million and the impact of rate-capping through earlier overspending. Newcastle, as part of its inner-city programme, set up action teams, based on relatively large areas within the inner city, each of which had limited spending powers to undertake schemes based primarily on environmental improvements.

There has also been a growth of locally based schemes involving multi-agency approaches to tackling crime and domestic burglary in inner cities. Such schemes have been introduced by the Home Office with the support of local agencies, as in the 'Five Towns' project in Bolton, Croydon, North Tyneside, Swansea, and Wellingborough. The impacts of local schemes can be illustrated by the experience of the

Kirkholt Project in Rochdale. Here, in an estate of just over 2,000 households which had earlier been given priority status by the DoE, a Home Office scheme involving the police, the Manpower Services Commission, Manchester University, Rochdale's housing department, and the probation service has begun to work jointly with the local community to tackle crime in a run-down estate area. The Project claims that its installation of burglar alarms, window locks, and other 'target hardening' devices, and its involvement of victims and their neighbours within the context of multiple agencies offering advice, counselling, and practical assistance, have had the effect of reducing rates of domestic burglary from a monthly rate of 47 to one of 15 within the first year of its operation.

Once such schemes of local community development are in operation, devolution offers a new platform to councillors and a sounding board for tapping the views and preoccupations of the local residents. A danger is that such bodies can become as politicized as the local authorities within which they have been established and that they add merely another tier and another pressure group within the local state. The principal benefit, however, comes from the new involvement of local residents and the cracking of the mirror of extensive apathy which characterizes citizens who feel that, in the absence of such schemes, they have been rendered powerless to alter or influence the circumstances in which they live. It is as easy to deride as to romanticize the notions of neighbourhood and community. However, the reality of the power of residents' attachment to their locality should not be dismissed: it is a potential which can be used creatively or destructively, in community development or in rioting. Being outside, or being felt to be outside, society lies at the roots of much urban unrest (Benyon and Solomos, 1987, pp. 65–79, 185–6). The need for more appropriate political outlets for today's more aware and more bloody-minded electorate reinforces the potential value of locally based structures of governance. And if it is objected that neighbourhood-based schemes soon lose their vitality once the original pioneer participants have disappeared or lost interest, then that is an argument not for abandoning such schemes, but for the acceptance that they need constant innovative injections, that they need to be reworked to avoid the institutional sclerosis or communal apathy which come with time (Donnison, 1988).

Party politics

The third element of administration is the need to achieve some erosion of the party politicization of local-authority administration. Local economic development and the supply of goods and services must inevitably be political. It is from the debate of conflicting interests that decisions of who gets what must emerge. What is not inevitable is the strong party involvement in that debate. The strength of the control of party politics at the local level has heightened the head-on clash between central and local government, reinforced the sclerotic fiefdoms of party officials, and ridden roughshod over the often more subtle wishes of residents themselves. The 'extreme' authorities may indeed be small in number, but they are a significant part of the large local authorities who control the most deprived parts of the country. The Audit Commission's increasingy frequent assaults on the damage associated with the political hegemony of certain local authorities have demonstrated some of the inefficiency associated, in this case, with 'hard-left' authorities. Its comparison of the eight London boroughs of Brent, Camden, Hackney, Haringey, Islington, Lambeth, Lewisham, and Southwark with eight similarly deprived but 'better managed' London boroughs suggests that the first group spent £16·50 per house for refuse disposal as against £9·00 in the second group; that rent arrears were 20 per cent as against 7 per cent; that vehicle maintenance costs were over £1,000 per year as against under £700; and that the eight 'hard-left' boroughs had negotiated deferred purchase arrangements of some £550 million, a large part of which is to finance revenue expenditure (Audit Commission, 1987). Future mortgaging of assets through schemes of creative accounting have been prominent. Manchester instituted such a scheme in 1987 which involved leasing buildings to a local-authority company which in turn leases them back to the authority to borrow on their value. Interest payments can be rolled up and deferred usually for a period of three years, but such mortgaging of the future can only be a short-sighted response to the reductions in finance from which many authorities have suffered. Indeed, in

March 1988, the Secretary of State for the Environment summarily banned local councils from entering into such financial deals.

The excessive cost of managing and running services; the wide disparities in employment associated with such discrepant costs; the involvement of local authorities in 'political' projects on which they can have nothing but political persuasive powers—such as with police monitoring bodies in metropolitan districts, campaigns on Northern Ireland, nuclear-free zones, and the like—all of these may be relatively inexpensive as a proportion of total expenditure, but it is marginal expenditure which could be put to better effect in the direct mainstream services that local authorities provide.

Many of such activities are prompted more by a pure political stance reflecting distaste for the present government than as actions designed to offer direct benefit to local residents. They clearly increase the already fraught relations between central and local government. Much of the difficulty has come from the significant reductions in central-government support which have eroded the subsidy to local-authority housing and finances through the Rate Support Fund. Central government has itself helped to create the ogre which it now wants to lay to rest. The wish seems warranted, but the fiscal vacillation and overt hostility out of which the problem has derived have been much of central government's own making. Policy on Rate Support has led to the enormously effective campaigns of persuasion that local authorities have run on the basis of having been 'robbed' by central government.

Such politicization has created bastions of one-party rule in an increasing number of big-city local authorities. In Manchester, for example, Labour had 86 of the 99 council seats before the elections of May 1987, when the overwhelming control of the party was marginally reduced by the loss of 9 seats. Reforming local taxes—particularly in the regressive fashion of the currently proposed introduction of a per-capita Community Charge in place of property-based local rates—seems unlikely to offer a salve to the problems out of which such political bifurcation has derived (Department of the Environment, 1986a). Indeed the new proposals for a Community Charge will result in substantial increases in the level of local taxes for the residents of large northern cities and reduce those of the smaller southern places. The role of political parties, with the associated influence of pre-council party caucuses, is unlikely to disappear. Nevertheless, the introduction of proportional representation at local level would help to create a better-balanced representation of the mix of views of local electorates and would be a more effective way of encouraging local government to be more responsive to the wishes of its electorate. This would be one way of ensuring that fewer local councils were uniformly comprised of solid blocks respectively of Labour and Conservative councillors in urban and rural areas, able to create unresponsive fiefdoms which persist over many decades. The politicization of local politics might also be eroded by drawing stricter lines between officers and politicians; at the very least by introducing tighter restrictions on the increasingly common practice of the staff of one authority becoming political members in a neighbouring council. The Widdicombe Committee, which went some way to addressing these issues, was excessively cautious in its recommendations (Department of the Environment, 1986b). The political scene has changed as dramatically as has the economic; the response needs to be a bolder constitutional one.

Such changes are not attempts to downgrade the importance of local government. Local authorities have a vital part to play in the drawing-up, co-ordinating, and implementing of many policy areas and in delivering a range of local services. To argue that, in the face of current changes in their responsibilities (such as the proposed diminution of their direct role as housing landlords), they will no longer have an independent and central function is to ignore the new challenges of working within the fields of employment and local economic development, acting in these and related areas as the co-ordinators of joint activity beween the public and private sectors. Some of the more perceptive local-authority officers have begun to articulate such new roles. For example, Rochdale's Director of Housing has argued that it is possible to be a supporter of a strong and democratic system of local government without being committed to any particular list of municipal functions; indeed, that having acted as local landlord has created a politically unhelpful authoritarian relationship with the constituents of

Labour councils. It may be that 'a most proper and beneficial role for the council is as the initiator and developer of services and functions which, when established and consolidated, can and should be passed over to new agencies constituted and designed for their specific functions' (Simpson, 1987). Such a *strategic* role could be developed across a range of existing and newly emerged activities, not least in local economic initiatives. In all of this local councils would need to develop networks across the various agencies in local areas. To achieve this they need a more supportive and more secure context in which to operate. The running battle between central and local government has done neither credit nor service to either.

Local government should clearly remain a principal source of the delivery of policy as a multi-service agency. It could be argued that, with devolution to regional scales on one hand, and to local scales on the other, the current size of local authorities would maintain an unnecessary middle tier of local policy-making and administration. Nevertheless, administrative framework of between 8 and 12 regional bodies together with numerous 'neighbourhood councils' could well provide a robust, powerful, and yet sensitive framework of devolved authorities for local and regional administration. The gap between the regional and the local may, however, better be filled by multi-agency district councils not dissimilar to the present ones. Whatever the geometry, the importance of responsive and responsible local governance acting as more than mere agent of the centre cannot be doubted. It therefore becomes vital that two issues of such local governance are addressed: the training of its officials and the creation of fiscal frameworks within which they can operate more securely and effectively. Training is necessary because local authorities have now moved into areas for which most of their officers are less than adequately prepared. This is especially true of their emergent role in economic development. Mills and Young's survey of officers in charge of local economic development suggested the clear need for training specific to the requirements of stimulating and developing policy on economic development. While the Local Government Training Boards could provide a channel for such training, there would be merit in turning to local universities and polytechnics in order to encourage the development of new bridges between higher and further education, on one hand, and local authorities, on the other—a liaison which would have benefits over and beyond those of training *per se*. Courses could be piloted through one or more of the existing research centres which have tackled work on local economic development and subsequently extended to other local centres of higher education at a number of regional bases throughout the country. Such liaison would help to encourage the further development of general links beween the worlds of higher education and their local communities. It would also add to the base of continuing and part-time education and the science parks which many universities have now established. Education could provide one of the springboards for further collaboration between the public and private sectors by offering a relatively neutral base for collaborative effort.

A secure and long-term fiscal framework for local-authority economic development would be a second necessity. If central government assumes—as in part it appears to do—that the implementation of much urban policy is to lie in the hands of local authorities, this is to presuppose that local authorities are competent to execute the new economic thrusts of urban policy. They can only do this with legislation which is not merely permissive, but encourages local authorities to develop programmes within a framework of assured fiscal power. The sound bases of such fiscal power were laid down long ago in the Layfield Report (Department of the Environment, 1976). The proposed Community Charge will provide a less satisfactory source of local income even than the unjustly hated rates. There is still a strong argument for a local property-related tax and an even stronger argument for central government to be less arbitrary in its disbursement of central financial resources to local authorities. Current legislation assumes that local authorities are not expected to play a role in production as distinct from consumption. The local initiatives that have been briefly touched upon earlier have been made possible only through interpreting to their limit such Acts as the Local Government Act of 1972. There is clearly need for additional statutory powers for local governance in the field of economic development.

Within more assured financial frameworks, local authorities could more readily develop productive links with the private sector. The growth of partnership across the public/private sector has been a principal aim of government since the early 1980s and, although slowly and partly reflecting the 'new realism' of local authorities, it is beginning to achieve increasing success through incentives such as Derelict Land Grant and Urban Development Grant, and through Urban Development Corporations and local-authority-led developments such as those in Birmingham, Salford, Kirklees, and elsewhere. The learning curve both for the committed local authorities and for the building societies, developers, and private industry within local-authority areas has been slow, but valuable. The new agencies which have bypassed local authorities, such as the UDCs and the recent Urban Renewal Grants, have fuelled central/local tensions through their lack of direct accountability. In retrospect, the thrusting of such agencies on to local authorities will probably be seen as a necessary step to the achievement of more effective public/private collaboration. If this is so, it reinforces the importance of the view that such imposition of new agencies should only be of a short-term nature. Were the goals of this prompting—the attraction of private-sector investment—now attainable without the means by which they have so far been introduced, development could more readily be achieved without courting the hostility which has accompanied many of the inner-city developments. A less party-politicized local government which was more responsive to local demands, more accountable to its electorate, and more capable of making commercially relevant decisions through a firmer fiscal framework, through regional development agencies, and through the training of its officers, might meet the need for firmer bridges across the public/private divide and thereby help to create more effective networks between local government, central government, and the private sector.

INFRASTRUCTURE AND RESOURCES

Investment in new and rehabilitated infrastructure is a clear need if we are to reverse urban decline. All of the evidence suggests the importance of a continuing generosity of public funding, if only as essential pump-priming; private funding by itself seems unlikely to tackle urban problems. All of the most successful commercial developments illustrate this; whether in Glasgow or in London. Indeed, the London Docklands makes the point most forcefully since over the period 1981–5 the Docklands Corporation spent over £200 million on land acquisition, administration, promotion, and community services; no small sum when set against the £1,000 million spent on the total Urban Programme over the same period.

This need for public resources is nowhere more urgent than in the case of housing. New housing investment should play a central role in urban strategies. The huge reduction in housing resources—a reduction of 54 per cent in the years between 1979/80 and 1984/5, far greater than that in any other area of public goods and services—will store up further and massive needs for reinvestment in the decades ahead. The specific effects on the housing resources of Manchester, for example, are shown in Fig. 6.1. The results of current neglect lead inevitably to the deferment to the future of ever-larger bills for repair and replacement. The bill for the public housing sector alone has been tacitly accepted by government as being over £20,000 million. There is need for a considerable injection of new funds if the short- and long-term needs are to be more than scratched. Resources for housing would not only lead to the regeneration of the most extensive form of urban land use and be one of the most effective forms of environmental improvement, but would also create jobs for skilled and semi-skilled workers. New housing investment is an important part of the need for greater general targeted expenditure to help cities. It should provide additional scope for the development and involvement of housing associations whose small size and local sensitivity make them an ideal vehicle for desirable, decentralized forms of investment. The government's current Housing Bill has gone a long way towards recognizing the potential of housing associations. Its limitation is in the ambiguity of what public resources, both for new investment and through housing benefit, might be made available to realize this potential. Much of the housing need is now for 'specialized' housing—for the elderly, for ethnic groups whose

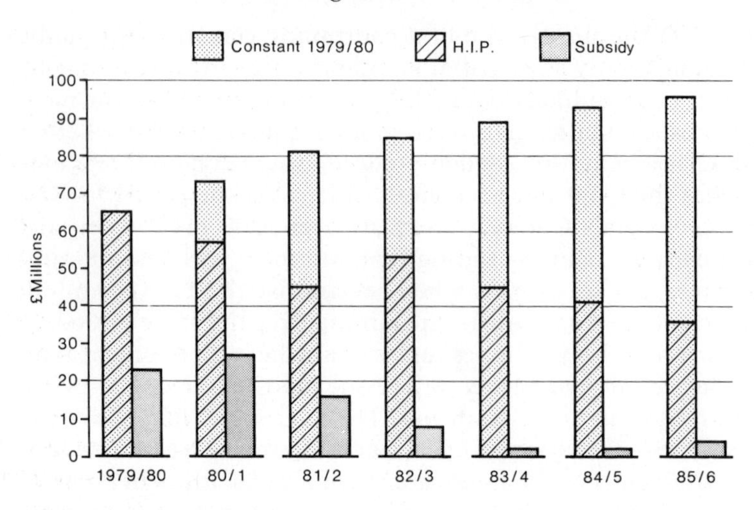

FIG. 6.1. Housing investment resources, Manchester, 1979/1980–1985/1986

Note: The highest bar shows the level of housing resources that would have been allocated to the city had the 1979–80 level been maintained in line with inflation. The size of the shortfall is shown by the gap between this level and those of the actual Housing Investment Programme and subsidy payments.

Source: Manchester City Council (1986).

families often need large houses, for the single, and the young. In only some of such cases is the reliance on raising private resources a realistic option. For the elderly with large houses to trade in for equity mortgages on purpose-built or sheltered accommodation, it may be perfectly realistic to look to private sources to provide capital; but for the elderly poor or the ethnic poor living in small, old, owner-occupied property in the inner areas of northern cities, those in need have neither the capital resources nor the ability to pay realistic rents in housing-association schemes where the associations are expected to raise significant sums of capital from the private sector.

Unless new public investment is forthcoming it seems inevitable that cities face the prospect of the need for large-scale urban renewal reminiscent of the experience of the 1950s and 1960s. In the 1990s, however, we would face the need for the replacement not merely of the large quantities of old private housing and of inadequate recent council housing, but also of the increasingly unsound areas of private inter-war housing which would then be over 60 years old—the period over which housing is customarily amortized. Since a fair amount of that housing is lived in by post-child couples or the single elderly, much of it suffers from inadequate private investment in its fabric. Were such large-scale clearance and replacement to happen because of the inadequancy of current expenditure, there is no guarantee that the mistakes of the 1950s and 1960s would not merely be repeated: the breaking-up of communities, the development of expensive but low-quality stock, the bureaucratic inefficiencies which led to such large sums of public resources being squandered in the post-war years (English, Madigan, and Norman, 1976). Smaller-scale refurbishment and infill and selective replacement, tackled now, would seem so infinitely preferable that the argument for more public housing resources must surely command wide support.

The other area of infrastructural investment for which there is equal need is the refurbishment of the basic services of large cities. Manchester, with a sewer system built in two waves in the nineteenth century, faces massive reinvestment needs as the system has reached a peak of dereliction. The city measures its increasingly frequent sewer collapses in units of DDBs—using the size of double-decker buses as a measure of the scale of each collapse. It is not that cities are unusually prone to infrastructural decay. There is merely a historical cyclical inevitability to the need to renew facilities, which echoes with varying time-lags the historic waves of initial investment or reinvestment (Barras, 1987). Rural areas and small towns will face not dissimilar needs in the future. To ignore the historic curve of current city needs is to turn a blind eye to the inevitable, in whatever location.

Public funds are only one part of the equation. The increased involvement of private developers in schemes within inner cities is a trend which is clearly to be welcomed because of the impact that it has begun to have on the social mix of urban residents, no matter how relatively insignificant it has so far been. The increased range of income groups slowly appearing in areas which had previously been almost uniformly lived in by the deprived is likely to exert a beneficial influence on the life of the city. The potential political articulateness and influence of a more mixed population can be brought to bear in fields such as the environment and education. In areas in which such schemes commandeer large proportions of inner areas there is a danger that the interests of the erstwhile indigenous residents will be ridden over roughshod and that social tensions will merely increase—a danger which is already apparent in London's Docklands and in some parts of the East End in general. Here again there is scope for a greater involvement of housing associations to ensure that local residents have opportunities to live within such areas. In the more typical case of provincial cities, however, such dangers seem remote indeed and any development of owner-occupied housing must be welcomed. The probability is that, as the economy and the housing market strengthen over the next decade, private developers will be increasingly reluctant to become involved in 'brownfield' development within inner areas and that renewed pressure will be placed on outer areas and peripheral villages and small towns. The question then arises, should such development be encouraged; should such pressure for development in peripheral areas lead to the progressive breaching of the protection offered by Green Belts and by planning restraint in areas beyond Green Belts? The arguments in favour of a greater relaxation of restrictions and of encouraging development in outer areas are that it would help to reduce the spiral of house prices by increasing the supply of housing, that it would increase the access of the less affluent to the semi-skilled and unskilled jobs which have become increasingly peripheral in their location, and that there is in any case insufficient urban land to accommodate the housing needs of the next decade, particularly if one aimed to achieve some greening of the city by lowering the overall density of development. These are powerful arguments, but they smack as ever of a London-dominated perspective.

There is a strong case for a regionally differentiated approach in this (a differentiation which would be feasible with regional bodies in place of the uniformity of Whitehall). In the London case, as Buck, Gordon, and Young (1986) argue, there is an argument for encouraging some outward movement of the deprived, given the relative ebullience of the regional economy, the related overheating of house prices in the region as a whole, and the relative decline in house prices as one moves to the Outer Metropolitan Area. Even in the absence of specific policy encouragement, there is sufficient pressure for development within the inner areas of London, as evidenced by the extent of gentrification and the success of Docklands, and by the resilience of the City and the overall growth of jobs within London. The thrust of urban policy in London should primarily be a matter of making provision for those who are weak in the labour market; some outward movement would be to the benefit of such groups without endangering the operation of London itself. Were such outward moves to and beyond the Green Belt to be given planning permission only in the case of people and firms from London itself, the relaxation could achieve some easing of the development pressure in the South East without merely reinforcing the investment divide between North and South. Furthermore, even in the London case, there may be strong arguments for resisting proposals within the Green Belt (as at Tillingham Hall) while adopting a more pragmatic view of some proposals outside it (as at Foxley Wood).

In most of the 'provinces', however, the case is very different. The policy need is to reform whole cities in the context of the economic decline of their containing regions. Green Belts in most northern metropolitan areas play a continuing role in encouraging developers to invest in inner areas; in their absence, it seems unlikely that much investment would happen. There is simply not the same pressure from the overall regional economy to make the inner areas reasonably attractive as is true of London. Within the regions there is insufficient overall investment to make it likely that new development would occur in both outer and inner areas. London's problems are narrowly urban; the problems of northern cities are more regional (Buck, Gordon, and Young, 1986). The argument in the northern cities must therefore be very different; to preserve the girdle of the Green Belts as one plank in the encouragement of investment within inner areas and to encourage that development to involve the private sector so that the social mix of inner areas can be increased.

FUTURE SCENARIOS

There is a way ahead. It is certainly not well charted. Its maps owe more to the pioneering sketchy work of Ptolemy than to the later skills of the Ordnance Survey. If its tracks are rough they are nevertheless passable. Scenarios of the future can be built out of journeys taken along these roads. Scenario-building is more than an exercise in self-indulgence. It can paint the dimensions of projected futures which policy might strive to avoid or to encourage and it can suggest the processes from which such future might derive. Alternative scenarios can be constructed in the boxes produced by the two dimensions which have alternated throughout this book: of national growth/no growth and of insensitive/sensitive social and spatial policy. The common view is that the path ahead requires national economic growth before change is feasible. The path to progress is therefore usually seen as the first track on Fig. 6.2. Yet, from all that has been learned it is clear that growth in itself can worsen the problems from which we start. Beloved it may be by both free-marketeers and interventionists, but growth does not necessarily help either the ailing city or the people trapped in the ranks of the urban underclass. They

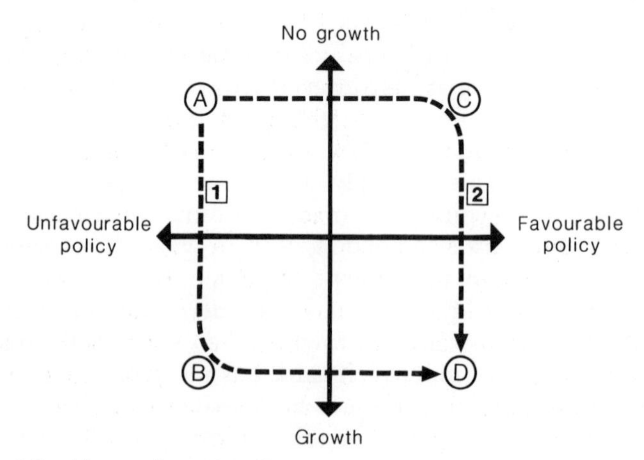

FIG. 6.2. Alternative scenarios

Note: Boxes A to D show the combinations of the two axes of growth and policy. Two different tracks from A to D are shown.

are 'out-landers' who are likely to be made more disadvantaged by those who benefit from growth. Flight from the city accelerates: it may be through the search for greenfield sites for new-style industry or through the desire to quit a landscape dominated by the constant destruction of old and new slums and the building of yet more vast swathes of council estates or even the simple following of fashion, lubricated by the unintended consequences of taxation policy.

Unbalanced growth, whether private or public, may well lead therefore to even more severe polarization than we currently experience in Box A, with large urban areas having growing concentrations of the poor, the unemployed, the black, the elderly, the vulnerable, and the criminal within them. The track through Box B may therefore take us yet further into polarization and distress to suggest one of the more horrifying worst-case scenarios. The danger is of a political response which tackles such social problems by formally enclosing the 'out-landers' in a sophisticated form of social and spatial apartheid. The current specialized policing now used for areas threatening problems of public disorder could be used to control such ghettos. The signs are already there in those cities where the police spend more time on such activities than on the ordinary matters of petty crime. Within these urban concentration camps an official blind eye might be turned to certain criminal activities, not least in the area of drugs. Those who make the real profits in this business would continue to ply their trade from the safe harbours of legitimate enterprises and the costs would continue to fall on the members of a ghetto population.

Once those perceived as inadequate and inept had been corralled into such areas they would be physically separated from the more manageable parts of Britain, the 'in-land', with its capacity for wealth creation and its technology, which would allow production with a minuscule labour force. Some of the helpless would be allowed out in order to perform menial tasks for the 'in-landers' and the ghettos would in turn be served by visiting professionals offering minimal state-provided services. Most of these 'out-lander' quarters would be in the old industrial cities of the North, but most large towns would have a small enclosure, if only to provide cheap unskilled labour. London might present a special problem since any possible threat from the scale of inner-area deprivation at the heart of the major urban engine of the economy would be difficult. The increasing gentrification of the inner city might make it awkward to cordon off large parts of the city. Perhaps the increasing displacement of the indigenous poor from areas such as the Docklands and Hackney could lead to the creation of an out-lander zone in the eastern suburbs—that same area where Eastenders were decanted in the 1960s. It does not take too strong an imagination to see how such 'Havens for the Helpless' could be developed and, worse still, accepted in a Britain dominated by economic growth and prosperity.

Such a gloomy scenario is not too fanciful. Those who argue that it could never happen here need only go to Belfast. Britain has already gone some way down this road with the increasing residualization of council housing over the last decade and the containing police methods used in many parts of inner cities. In most cities it is common for those who live in the affluent suburbs to shudder at the mention of the inner city. Suburban women—and men—tell with a salacious horror of the supposed happenings in such places and vow never to visit them, at least not after dark. The fact that, in Manchester at least, those very people descend on the leisure centres and the libraries of an area like Moss Side to avail themselves of its facilities makes little impression on the tales over cocktails. They accord with the accepted wisdom of decline and decay all around—the view expressed by Lord Hailsham in 1980: 'We are living in the City of Destruction, a dying country in a dying civilisation and across the plain there is no wicket gate offering a way of escape'.

The formalized ghetto is a future to be avoided. There is a need for a coherent, consensual, long-term urban policy so that growth, whether natural or engineered, is channelled into ways which decrease the polarization of our society. Rather than argue that we need growth to realize equity and thereby to see a path from Cell A through Cell B to Cell D, the argument should be for a path which, regardless of growth, develops policy which is sensitive to the social and spatial divides within the country; a track from Cell A through Cell C to Cell D (Fig. 6.2). Emphasis should therefore be placed on the development of socially and spatially sensitive policies through which a more positive scenario might be created. The kinds of policy emphasis discussed earlier in this chapter would therefore aim to create a context in which the disbenefits of recession or the fruits of growth were dispersed more equitably across urban and non-urban areas and across communities within our large cities. The hopeful scenario of Cell D would therefore incorporate both a more justly distributed prosperity through income support and more effective targeting of resources and would promise a growth which would offer hope for positive economic re-formation of the beleaguered and reeling cities and declining regions.

The immediate question is what economic rationale those cities would have. The stock response is to emphasize their potential for general and business tourism and for leisure-related activities and to stress the importance of their idea-creating potential in association with their higher-education functions. Dock and riverside renewal would bring an influential and high-spending residential population to leaven the uniformity of the urban underclass; physical renewal and the reuse of historic buildings would provide tourist honeypots; science parks would provide the links between enterprise and education; environmental improvement would offer greater incentive for new investment. As we have seen, it has been the leisure-related track which more and more cities have pursued. All of this is plausible, but it does not go far enough.

To it one can now add the prospect of attracting 'real' service and industrial activity to large cities. This rosy view is prompted by recent developments in the organization of production. One of the trends of the most recent years has been the tendency for large companies to *fragment* their activities. Part of the growth of the small-firm sector and of the development of forms of flexible labour which were noted earlier in Chapter 3 (see above, pp. 72–4) has been associated with this trend. The process has had three elements: decentralization, devolvement, and disintegration (Shutt and Whittington, 1987). Decentralization has involved the retention of ownership but the hiving-off of production into small plants; devolvement has involved the transfer of the responsibilities of ownership to smaller firms but the retention of revenue control through licensing of franchising agreements; disintegration has involved fragmentation into separate ownership but the retention of influence by large companies through either their power of market dominance or their ability to repurchase the independent companies. The latter process of disintegration has been most strikingly illustrated by the increase in worker and management buy-outs. Each of these types of fragmentation can be seen as a way in which companies have tried to externalize the risks associated with rapidly changing technologies and rapidly fluctuating market demand to exert control over the labour process by the creation of more flexible workforces. The fragmentation has been accompanied both by the increasing tendency for firms to move from large production runs to small customized batch runs—now made possible by rapid computer-driven modifications to the specification of control machinery—and by the development of just-in-time delivery systems which avoid the costly stockpiling of products. Such changes clearly require sophisticated application of computer control both in the production process and in marketing.

All of these developments increase the importance of *linkages* between sets of firms, between manufacturing and services, and between firms and customers. With more small firms, with a greater need to identify potential customer demands and to monitor changes in those demands in a rapidly changing market context, with greater need for professional services such as accountancy, stock control, marketing, response to changing legislation, and the opportunities of new schemes of public assistance, with the associated need for advice and maintenance and upgrading of computer systems, and with the heightened significance of access to the cutting edge of technical change, firms need access to information, to services, and to each other. The experience of 'the Third Italy', the area of Veneto and Emilia Romagna in which large numbers of small firms in the footwear and clothing businesses have developed considerable growth through a co-ordinated and flexible system of putting-out backed by communal technical and marketing expertise, may have much to teach us about the importance of fragmentation and linkages in creating employment opportunities (Brusco, 1982). Much of this linkage could, of course, be a-spatial and therefore lead merely to further decentralization of investment away from cities. With good telecommunications, physical proximity has become less necessary. But it is precisely from the creation of an information-rich environment that large cities *could* benefit. It has been argued that the development of advanced telecommunications has worked against the interests of less favoured regions such as the North East since advanced digital transmission of data through telecommunications networks has favoured those places which were first tied in to the evolving network (Goddard and Gillespie, 1987). However, the nodes on those networks have consistently included most of the large cities. Whichever of those cities is ready and able to install a dense local network of broad-band telecommunications to link companies, services, decision-takers, and higher education into an effective information network could help to create local linkages, especially for value-added network services, so as to capitalize on the technical and organizational changes in production. Therein lies a hope for cities to offer new locational attractions for business investment (Hepworth, 1987). Nowhere in Europe has yet developed such a 'wired-up' city with a dense mesh of advanced telecommunications; London's Docklands has partly—and accidentally—developed the basis of one with its ring of broad-band lines for Mercury and Telecom linked to satellite receivers. The closest approach to such development is, significantly, in the Tokyo suburb of Kawasaki, which has invested in precisely this kind of dense fibre-optic network offering firms access to information and to services (Batty, 1987). There is clear scope for public investment in one or more demonstration projects based in some of the large northern cities which offer a strong potential base of commercial, producer-service, and industrial firms (Town and Country Planning Association, 1987; Breheney, Hall, and Hart, 1987). It is not too fanciful to envisage information-rich production centres—industrial clusters—within some of our large cities, with the spin-off benefits that would accrue. The UDC in Trafford Park could be an example. Historically, part of the attraction of Trafford Park as the first purpose-built industrial estate, which employed at its peak some 75,000 people, was the *physical* linkage represented by its now rusting and abandoned railway system running throughout the road network of the industrial park. The challenge for the new Development Corporation should be to develop, in place of this physical linkage, a non-physical advanced telecommunications network to respond to today's information needs of industry and commerce. Pump-priming by public investment in one or more such areas could create powerful demonstration effects. Such developments would come about only in those places whose city fathers were ready to recognize the potential and were prepared to develop the necessary physical infrastructure in a commercially sensitive political context, jointly with the private sector. Such communication-linked and spatially concentrated clusters could help to establish a new economic rationale for cities.

The hopeful scenario can therefore be based on more than the arguments about the leisure and tourist potential of cities, important though these may be. If linkage is of growing importance to production, cities could play a pivotal role in the new high-tech. adaptation to the changing world economy. Vision and foresight are needed in the local leadership of entrepreneurs and of governments and such vision can only be harnessed if all of the agencies are prepared to develop effective partnerships between central government, local government, the higher-education sector, the local communities, and the private sector.

The future of our old proud cities is bedevilled by the crude simplicities of the adversarial nature of parliamentary democracy coupled with an innate selfish greed. A concern for civil liberties needs to be married to the encouragement of an enterprise culture—no mean feat in a nation long characterized by an individualism which Michael Young called 'a virulent form of defensive–offensive acquisitiveness carrying all before it' (Young, 1983). Research can point the way. Occasional good practice can pave part of the road, but it is neither an impossible nor a fantastical dream to aim for something more than this—a comprehensive long-term urban policy well resourced, well supported, free from the petty wrangling of party politicians, and energized by joint activities from networks of local leaders in business, government, and education. The book of Jonah describes how the city of Nineveh was saved from destruction because its citizens turned 'every one from his evil way and from the violence that is in their hands'. This was taken as a message of hope by the Chief Rabbi in his reaction to the publication of *Faith in the City* (Jakobovits, 1986). More apposite, however, may be the final fate of Nineveh as foreseen in the book of Nahum: 'The shatterer has come up against you . . . Woe to the bloody city! . . . I will throw filth at you and treat you with contempt, and make you a gazing-stock. . . . You increased your merchants more than the stars of the heavens . . . there is no assuaging your hurt, your wound is grievous.' If for Nineveh the grievous wound which justified the laying to waste of 'the city of hope' was unscrupulous commerce, therein lies a message for our contemporary way ahead. Commerce is vital, is indeed the life blood of the city, but the drive to restore commercial vitality need not entail so unscrupulous and single-minded a preoccupation as to exclude the citizenry from the drive for renewal and regeneration. It is clear that the choices are not foreclosed by the imperatives of economics, that there *are* options open to us which would better sustain and revitalize cities and offer them surer prospects of a new economic and social rationale. Each missed opportunity, like the damp squib of *Action for Cities*, diminishes the possibility of hope. It grows ever more clear that the 'big job to be done in some of those inner cities' was not a rallying cry for an all-out effort to help those people and places caught in a trap which will need skill, co-operation, and patience to prise open. A cynic might wonder why, if that big job was a shrewd assessment of the political landscape, such anxiety should have been expressed about a group of voters who may not even register as they seek to evade the regressive Community Charge: a realist might answer that the present government was probably taught history after the old-fashioned manner of causes, events, and results, amongst which would loom large the proposition that revolutions occur when a country is turning the corner from bad times and an articulate, prosperous group, opposed to the established regime, is primed to provide leadership for the worst-off. A more progressive 'empathetic' approach to the past would recognize the hopes and fears of ordinary people and identify the moments when bloodshed and violence could have been avoided. Riots, ghettos, despair, disease, crime, and vandalism:

these have already scarred our cities. More shopping malls, more small businesses, more high tech., more housing are essential parts of the framework for improvement, but the human dimension of our cities cannot blithely be ignored. If that dimension *is* ignored the prognosis for the future has already been made apparent. The choice must be ours.

Bibliography

ADAMS, C. D., BAUM, A. E., and MACGREGOR, B. D. (1987). 'Land Prices and Land Availability in Inner City Redevelopment', in B. T. Robson (ed.), *Managing the City: The Aims and Impacts of Urban Policy*, Croom Helm, London, pp. 154–77.

ALLON-SMITH, R. D. (1982), 'The Evolving Geography of the Elderly in England and Wales', in A. M. Warnes (ed.), *Geographical Perspectives on the Elderly*, Wiley, Chichester, pp. 35–52.

Archbishop of Canterbury's Commission (1985), *Faith in the City*, Church of England Commissioners, London.

ATKINSON, J., and GREGORY, D. (1986), 'A Flexible Future: Britain's Dual Labour Force', *Marxism Today*, Apr. 12–17.

Audit Commission (1987), 'The Management of London's Authorities: Preventing the Breakdown of Services', Occasional Paper 2, Audit Commission for Local Authorities in England and Wales, London.

BARRAS, R. (1987), 'Technical Change and the Urban Development Cycle', *Urban Studies*, 24, 5–30.

Battersea Leisure Ltd./Wandsworth Borough Council (1986), *Employment and Training Positive Action Policy Statement and Programme*, Economic Development Office, Wandsworth.

BATTY, M. (1987), 'The Intelligent Plaza is only the Beginning', *Guardian*, 17 Sept.

BEGG, I., and EVERSLEY, D. (1986), 'Deprivation in the Inner City: Social Indicators from the 1981 Census', in V. Hausner (ed.), *Critical Issues in Urban Economic Development*, vol. 1, Clarendon Press, Oxford, pp. 50–88.

——MOORE, B., and RHODES, J. (1986) 'Economic and Social Change in Urban Britain and the Inner Cities', in V. Hausner (ed.), *Critical Issues in Urban Economic Development*, vol. 1, Clarendon Press, Oxford, pp. 11–49.

BELL, D. (1973), *The Coming of Post-industrial Society: A Venture in Social Forecasting*, Basic Books, New York.

BENTHAM, G. (1986), 'Socio-tenurial Polarization in the United Kingdom, 1953–83: The Income Evidence', *Urban Studies*, 23, 157–62.

BENYON, J. T. (ed.) (1984), *Scarman and After: Essays Reflecting on Lord Scarman's Report*, Pergamon Press, Oxford.

——and SOLOMOS, J. (eds.) (1987), *The Roots of Urban Unrest*, Pergamon Press, Oxford.

BIRCH, D. (1980), *Job Creation in Cities*, Massachusetts Institute of

Technology, Cambridge, Mass.

Boddy, M. (1987), 'High Technology Industry, Regional Development and Defence Manufacturing: A Case Study from the UK Sunbelt', in B. T. Robson (ed.), *Managing the City: The Aims and Impacts of Urban Policy*, Croom Helm, London, pp. 60–83.

—— Lovering, J., and Bassett, K. (1986), *Sunbelt City? A Study of Economic Change in Bristol's M4 Corridor*, Clarendon Press, Oxford.

Boyle, R., and Rich, D. (1984), *In Pursuit of the Private City: A Comparative Assessment of Urban Policy Orientations in Britain and the United States*, Department of Urban and Regional Planning, University of Strathcylde.

Breheney, M., Hall, P., and Hart, D. (1987), *Northern Lights: A Development Agenda for the North in the 1990s*, Derek Wade & Waters, Preston.

Brittan, L. (1988), 'View from the Back Benches', *Town and Country Planning*, 57, 54–6.

Brusco, S. (1982), 'The Emilian Model: Production Decentralisation and Social Integration', *Cambridge Journal of Economics*, 6, 167–84.

Buck, N., and Gordon, I. (1987), 'The Beneficiaries of Employment Growth: An Analysis of the Experience of Disadvantaged Groups in Expanding Labour Markets', in V. Hausner (ed.), *Critical Issues in Urban Economic Development*, vol. 2, Clarendon Press, Oxford, pp. 77–115.

—— —— and Young, K. (1986), *The London Employment Problem*, Clarendon Press, Oxford.

Business in the Community (1986), *Business and the Inner Cities*, BiC, London.

Cabinet Office (1988), *Action for Cities*, HMSO, London.

Champion, A. G. (1987), Momentous Revival in London's Population', *Town and Country Planning*, 56, 80–2.

—— and Green, A. E. (1985), 'In Search of Britain's Booming Towns: An Index of Local Economic Performance for Britain', Discussion Paper 72, Centre for Urban and Regional Development Studies, University of Newcastle.

—— —— (1988), *Local Prosperity and the North–South Divide: Winners and Losers in 1980s Britain*, Institute for Employment Research, University of Warwick.

—— —— and Owen, D. (1987), 'Housing, Labour Mobility and Unemployment', *Planner*, Apr. 11–17.

Charters, S. (1986), *Louisiana Black*, Marion Boyars, London.

Checkland, S. G. (1976), *The Upas Tree*, University of Glasgow Press, Glasgow.

CHESHIRE, P. (1987), 'Economic Factors in Urban Change: European Prospects', Discussion Paper 30, Department of Economics, University of Reading.

—— CARBONARO, G., and HAY, D. (1986), 'Problems of Urban Decline and Growth in EEC Countries: Or Measuring Degrees of Elephantness', *Urban Studies*, 23, 131–49.

CHISHOLM, M. D. I., and KIVELL, P. (1987), 'Inner City Waste Land: An Assessment of Government and Market Failure in Land Development', Hobart Paper 108, Institute of Economic Affairs, London.

CIPFA (1987) *Paying for Local Government: Beyond the Green Paper—a Detailed Analysis*, Chartered Institute of Public Finance and Accountancy, London.

CLARK, D. (1984), *Post-industrial America: A Geographical Perspective*, Methuen, London.

COLEMAN, A., BROWN, S., COTTLE, L., MARSHALL, P., REDKNAP, C., and SEX, R. (1985), *Utopia on Trial*, Hilary Shipman, London.

COOKE, P. (ed.) (1988), *Localities: A Comparative Analysis of Urban Change*, Hutchinson, London.

Coventry Community Development Project (1975), 'Coventry and Hillfields: Prosperity and the Persistence of Inequality', Final Report, CDP.

CRAWFORD, P., FOTHERGILL, S., and MONK, S. (1985), 'The Effect of Business Rates on the Location of Employment', Final Report to the Department of the Environment, Department of Land Economy, University of Cambridge.

CROSSMAN, R. (1975), *The Diaries of a Cabinet Minister*, vol. 1: *Minister of Housing 1964–66*, Hamish Hamilton and Jonathan Cape, London.

CROWTHER, S., and GARRAHAN, P. (1988), 'Corporate Power and the Local Economy', *Industrial Relations Journal*, 19, 51–9.

Department of Education and Science (1987), *Higher Education: Meeting the Challenge*, Cm. 114, HMSO, London.

Department of Employment (1987), *Action for Cities: Building on Initiative*, HMSO, London.

Department of the Environment (1976), *Local Government Finance: Report of the Committee of Inquiry*, Cmnd. 6453, HMSO, London (The Layfield Committee).

——(1977), *Policy for the Inner Cities*, Cmnd. 6845, HMSO, London.

——(1981), *Priority Estates Project 1981: Improving Problem Council Estates*, HMSO, London.

——(1982), 'Urban Deprivation', Information Note 2, Inner Cities Directorate, DoE, London.

——(1986a), *Paying for Local Government*, Cmnd. 9714, HMSO, London.

Department of the Environment (1986b), *The Conduct of Local Authority Business*, Cmnd. 9797, HMSO, London (The Widdicombe Report).

——(1986c), *The Urban Programme, 1985*, HMSO, London.

——(1987a), *DoE Report on Research and Development, 1984–86*, HMSO, London.

——(1987b), *The Urban Programme 1986/87: A Report on its Operations and Achievements in England*, HMSO, London.

Department of Health and Social Security (1980), *Inequalities in Health: Report of a Research Working Group*, DHSS, London (The Black Report).

Department of Trade and Industry (1988), *DTI: The Department for Enterprise*, Cm. 278, HMSO, London.

DICKEN, P. (1986), *Global Shift: Industrial Change in a Turbulent World*, Harper and Row, London.

DONNISON, D. (1988), 'Secrets of Success: What Makes some Community Projects Work, while Other Collapse?', *New Society*, 83, No. 1309, 11–13.

——and MIDDLETON, A. (eds.) (1987), *Regenerating the Inner City: Glasgow's Experience*, Routledge and Kegan Paul, London.

——and SOTO, P. (1980), *The Good City: A Study of Urban Development and Policy in Britain*, Heinemann, London.

EDWARDS J., and BATLEY, R. (1978), *The Politics of Postive Discrimination: An Evaluation of the Urban Programme, 1967–77*, Tavistock, London.

ENGLISH, J., MADIGAN, R., and NORMAN, P. (1976), *Slum Clearance: The Social and Administrative Context in England and Wales*, Croom Helm, London.

ERICKSON, R. A., and SYMS, P. M. (1986), 'The Effects of Enterprise Zones on Local Property Markets', *Regional Studies*, 20, 1–14.

FIELDING, A. J. (1982), 'Counterurbanisation in Western Europe', *Progress in Planning*, 17, 1–52.

FOTHERGILL, S., and GUDGIN, G. (1982), *Unequal Growth: Urban and Regional Employment Change in the United Kingdom*, Heinemann, London.

——MONK, S., and PERRY, M. (1987), *Property and Industrial Development*, Hutchinson, London.

FRANK, C. E. J., MIALL, R. H. C., and REES, R. D. (1984), 'Issues in Small Firm Research of Relevance to Policy Making', *Regional Studies*, 18, 257–66.

GALE, D. E. (1984), *Neighborhood Revitalization and the Postindustrial City: A Multinational Perspective*, Lexington Books, Toronto.

GIBSON, A. (1987), 'Learning the Economic Lessons of Lightmoor', *Town and Country Planning*, 56, 304–5.

GOODARD, J. B., and GILLESPIE, A. E.(1987), 'Advanced Telecommunications and Regional Economic Development', in B. T. Robson (ed.), *Managing the City: The Aims and Impacts of Urban Policy*, Croom Helm, London, pp. 84–109.

GORDON, P. (1979), 'Deconcentration without a Clean Break', *Environment and Planning*, 11, 281–90.

Greater Manchester Council (1981), *Report of the Moss Side Enquiry Panel to the Leader of the Greater Manchester Council*, Manchester (The Hytner Report).

HALL, P., and HAY, D. (1980), *Growth Centres in the European Urban System*, Heinemann Educational, London.

HAMBLETON, R., and HOGGETT, P. (1984), 'The Politics of Decentralisation: Theory and Practice of a Radical Local Government Initiative', Working Paper 46, School for Advanced Urban Studies, Bristol.

HAMNETT, C. (1983), 'Regional Variations in House Prices and House Price Inflation, 1969–1981', *Area*, 15, 97–109.

—— and RANDOLPH, W. (1982), 'The Changing Population Distribution of England and Wales, 1961–1981: Clean Break or Consistent Progression?', *Built Environment*, 8, 272–80.

—— —— (1986), 'Tenurial Transformation and the Flat Break-up Market in London: The British Condo Experience', in N. Smith and P. Williams (eds.), *Gentrification of the City*, Allen and Unwin, London, pp. 124–55.

HARRISON, P. (1983), *Inside the Inner City: Life under the Cutting Edge*, Penguin Books, Harmondsworth.

HAUGHTON, G., PECK, J., and STEWARD, A. (1987), 'Local Jobs and Local Houses for Local Workers: A Critical Analysis of Spatial Employment', *Local Economy*, 2, 201–7.

HAUSNER, V. (1983), 'Urban and Regional Policy in the United States: The Experience of the Carter Administration', *Regional Studies*, 17, 366–89.

HENNESSEY, P. (1988), 'Precision Lacking in Latest Plan to End Urban Blight', *Independent*, 21 Mar.

HEPWORTH, M. (1987), 'The Information Cities', *Cities*, 4.

HESELTINE, M. (1987), *Where there's a Will*, Hutchinson, London.

HOGGETT, P., and HAMBLETON, R. (1985), 'Decentralisation in Birmingham', Final Report to ESRC, School for Advanced Urban Studies, Bristol.

HOLTERMANN, S. (1975), 'Areas of Urban Deprivation in Great Britain: An Analysis of 1971 Census Data', *Social Trends*, 6, 33–47.

Home Office (1981), *The Brixton Disorders 10–12 April 1981: Report of an Enquiry by the Rt Hon The Lord Scarman*, Cmnd., 8427, HMSO, London (The Scarman Report).

House-builders Federation (1986), *Inner City Consortium: Report of the Salford Local Study Team*, Technical Services Department, Salford.

Jacobs, J. (1970), *The Economy of Cities*, Jonathan Cape, London.

Jakobovits, I. (1986), *From Doom to Hope*, Office of the Chief Rabbi, London.

Keeble, D. E. (1976), *Industrial Location and Planning in the United Kingdom*, Methuen, London.

—— (1986), 'The Changing Spatial Structure of Economic Activity and Metropolitan Decline in the United Kingdom', in H.-J. Ewers, J. B. Goddard, and H. Matzerath (eds.), *The Future of the Metropolis*, de Gruyter, Berlin, pp. 71–99.

Kilroy-Silk, R. (1987), 'Riots that go Unremarked', *The Times*, 22 Aug.

Kirwan, R. (1986), 'Local Fiscal Policy in Inner City Economic Development', in V. Hausner (ed.), *Critical Issues in Urban Economic Development*, vol. 1, Clarendon Press, Oxford, pp. 200–28.

Law, C. (1987), 'Waterfront Redevelopment and the Cityport Economy: The Redevelopment of Mancheter Docks', Unpublished conference paper, Department of Geography, University of Salford.

Lawless, P. (1986), *The Evolution of Spatial Policy: A Case Study of Inner City Policy in the United Kingdom, 1968–81*, Pion, London.

Lever, W. F., and Moore, C. (eds.) (1986), *The City in Transition: Policies and Agencies for the Economic Regeneration of Clydeside*, Clarendon Press, Oxford.

Lloyd, P. E. (1980), 'Manchester: A Study in Industrial Decline and Economic Restructuring', in P. White (ed.), *The Continuing Conurbation: Change and Development in Greater Manchester*, Gower, Farnborough, pp. 53–76.

—— and Dicken, P. (1982), 'Industrial Change: Local Manufacturing Firms in Manchester and Merseyside', Inner Cities Research Programme Reports 5, Inner Cities Directorate, Department of the Environment, London.

—— and Mason, C. (1984), 'Spatial Variations in New Firm Formation in the United Kingdom: Comparative Evidence from Merseyside, Greater Manchester and South Hampshire', *Regional Studies*, 18, 207–20.

—— and Shutt, J. (1985), 'Recession and Restructuring in the North-west Region, 1975–82: The Implications of Recent Events', in D. Massey and R. Meegan (eds.), *Politics and Method: Contrasting Studies in Industrial Geography*, Methuen, London, pp. 16–60.

McArthur, A., and McGregor, A. (1987), 'Local Employment and Training Initiatives in the National Manpower Planning Context', in V. Hausner (ed.), *Critical Issues in Urban Economic Development*, vol. 2, Clarendon Press, Oxford, pp. 116–59.

McDonald, A. (1986), *The Weller Way: The Story of the Weller Streets Housing Co-operative*, Faber and Faber, London.

Maclennan, D. (1987), 'Housing Reinvestment and Neighbourhood Revitalisation: Economic Perspectives', in B. T. Robson (ed.), *Managing the City: The Aims and Impacts of Urban Policy*, Croom Helm, London, pp. 110–41.

Manchester City Council (1986), *Housing Defects in Manchester*, Manchester City Council.

——(various dates), *Planning and Economic Bulletin*, Planning Department, City of Manchester.

Manpower Services Commission (1984), *Community Programme Postal Follow-up Survey*, Employment Division, MSC, Sheffield.

Massey, D. (1980), 'Urban Impact Analysis: The Potential for its Application in the United Kingdom', *Built Environment*, 6, 131–5.

——(1984), *Spatial Divisions of Labour: Social Structures and the Geography of Production*, Macmillan, London.

——(1987), Geography Matters, Open University Books, Milton Keynes.

——and Meegan, R. (1978), 'Industrial Restructuring Versus the Cities', *Urban Studies*, 15, 273–88.

Mawson, J., and Miller, D. (1986), 'Interventionist Approaches in Local Employment and Economic Development: The Experience of Labour Authorities', in V. Hausner (ed.), *Critical Issues in Urban Economic Development*, vol. 1, Clarendon Press, Oxford, pp. 145–99.

Mills, L., and Young, K. (1986), 'Local Authorities and Economic Development: A Preliminary Analysis', in V. Hausner (ed.), *Critical Issues in Urban Economic Development*, vol. 1, Clarendon Press, Oxford, pp. 89–144.

Moore, B., Rhodes, J., and Tyler, P. (1986), 'Geographical Variations in Industrial Costs', Final Report to the Department of Industry, Department of Land Economy, University of Cambridge.

Murphy, D. (1987), *Tales from Two Cities: Travel of Another Sort*, John Murray, London.

National Audit Office (1986), *Report of the Comptroller and Auditor General: Enterprise Zones*, HMSO, London.

National Council for Voluntary Organisations (1986), *Inter-city Network*, No. 39.

Nationwide Building Society (1987), *House Prices: First Quarter 1987*, Nationwide Building Society, London.

Pahl, R. E. (1984), *Divisions of Labour*, Blackwell, Oxford.

Parkinson, M. (1986), 'On Liverpool's Waterfront', *New Society*, 77, No. 1227, 10–12.

PARRY, G., MOYSER, G., and WAGSTAFFE, M. (1985), 'The Crowd and the Community: Context, Content and Aftermath', Unpublished paper presented to ESRC Conference on 'The Crowd in Contemporary Britain'.

PATEL, S., and HAMNETT, C. (1987), 'How Insurers Strangle Cities', *New Society*, 82, No. 1987, 16–18.

PEARSON, G. (1981), *Hooligan: A History of Respectable Fears*, Macmillan, London.

PRAIS, S. J. (1976), *The Evolution of Giant Firms in Britain*, Cambridge University Press, Cambridge.

ROBERTS, S., and RANDOLPH, W. (1983), 'Beyond Containment: The Evolution of Population Distribution in Great Britain, 1961–1981', *Geoforum*, 14, 75–102.

ROBINSON, F., WREN, C., and GODDARD, J. B. (1987), *Economic Development Policies: An Evaluative Study of the Newcastle Metropolitan Region*, Clarendon Press, Oxford.

ROBSON, B. T. (1985), *Where is the North? An Essay on the North/South Divide*, North of England Regional Consortium, Manchester.

——(1986), 'Coming Full Circle: London Versus the Rest, 1890–1980', in G. Gordon (ed.), *Regional Cities in the U.K. 1890–1980*, Harper and Row, London, pp. 217–31.

——(1987), 'Local Employment: A Success Story?', *Business in the Community*, No. 4, Spring, 16–18.

——and BRADFORD, M. G. (1984), Urban Change in Greater Manchester: Demographic and Household Change, 1971–1981', Report to Greater Manchester Council, GMC, Manchester.

————(1988), 'The Impacts of Privatisation: Housing Refurbishment in Salford Estates', Working Paper 4, Centre for Urban Policy Studies, Department of Geography, University of Manchester.

RUNCIMAN, W. G. (1966), *Relative Deprivation and Social Justice*, Routledge and Kegan Paul, London.

Salford City Council (1986), *Salford Quays: First Annual Review*, City of Salford.

SCOTT, A. J. (1982), 'Locational Patterns and Dynamics of Industrial Activity in the Modern Metropolis', *Urban Studies*, 19, 111–41.

SHORT, J. (1981), *Public Expenditure and Taxation in the UK Regions*, Gower, Aldershot.

——and HOWARD, J. (1985), 'The Developmental Role of Public Expenditure in Regions and Subregions', Unpublished paper for ESRC Inner Cities Research Programme.

SHUTT, J., and WHITTINGTON, R. (1987), 'Fragmentation Strategies and the Rise of Small Units: Cases from the North West', *Regional Studies*, 21, 13–23.

SIMPSON, D. (1987), 'Swedish Attractions', *Roof*, July and Aug., 42–3.

SOLESBURY, W. (1986), 'The Dilemmas of Inner City Policy', *Public Administration*, 64, 389–400.

SPENCER, K., TAYLOR, A., SMITH, B., MAWSON, J., FLYNN, N., and BATLEY, R. (1986), *Crisis in the Industrial Heartland: A Study of the West Midlands*, Clarendon Press, Oxford.

STEDMAN-JONES, G. (1971), *Outcast London: A Study of the Relationships between Classes in Victorian Society*, Clarendon Press, Oxford.

STONE, P. A. (1973), *The Structure, Size and Costs of Urban Settlements*, Cambridge University Press, Cambridge.

STOREY, D. J. (1982), *Entrepreneurship and the New Firm*, Croom Helm, London.

STRETTON, H. (1978), *Urban Planning in Rich and Poor Countries*, Oxford University Press, Oxford.

Town and Country Planning Association (1986), *Whose Responsibility? Reclaiming the Inner Cities*, TCPA, London.

——(1987), *North–South Divide: A New Deal For Britain's Regions*, TCPA, London.

TOWNSEND, A. R. (1983), *The Impact of Recession*, Croom Helm, London.

TOWNSEND, P., PHILLIMORE, P., and BEATTIE, A. (1987), *Health and Deprivation: Inequality and the North*, Croom Helm, London.

TYLER, P., and RHODES, B. (1986), 'The Census of Production as an Indicator of Regional Differences in Productivity and Profitability in the United Kingdom', *Regional Studies*, 20, 331–9.

TYM, R., & Partners (1984), *Monitoring Enterprise Zones: Year Three Report*, DoE, London.

VINING, D. R., and KONTULY, T. (1978), Population Dispersal from Major Metropolitan Regions: An International Comparison, *International Regional Science Review*, 3, 49–73.

WANNOP, U., and LECLERC, R. (1987), 'The Management of GEAR', in D. Donnison and A. Middleton (ed.), *Regenerating the Inner City: Glasgow's Experience*, Routledge and Kegan Paul, London.

WARD, C. (1978), *The Child in the City*, Architectural Press, London.

WARD, R. (1987), 'London: The Emerging Docklands City', *Built Environment*, 12, 117–27.

WEINER, M. J. (1981), *English Culture and the Decline of the Industrial Spirit, 1850–1980*, Cambridge University Press, London.

West Midlands County Council (1982), *West Midlands Futures Study*, Managing the Metropolis Working Party, Birmingham.

WRAY, I. (1987), 'The Merseyside Development Corporation: Progress Versus Objectives', *Regional Studies*, 21, 163–7.

YOUNG, M. (1983), 'Inflation, Unemployment and the Remoralisation of Society', Tawney Pamphlet No. 2, The Tawney Society, London.

Index

abolition of metropolitan counties 107, 168, 170
Action for Cities vii, 96, 170–1, 225
Adams, D. 74–6
additionality in housing rehabilitation 102
affirmative action 42, 138, 167, 193–6
agricultural land use 47–8
Allon-Smith, R. 86
Alton, D. 205
Arts Council 199
Association for Neighbourhood Councils 205
Atkinson, J. 74
Audit Commission 207

Banham, R. 48
banks 72, 83, 171, 200, 202
Barras, R. 215
Barratt Ltd. 122, 126, 146
Bassett, K. 64, 172
Batley, R. 99, 101
Battersea 195
Batty, M. 223
Baum, A. 74–6
Beattie, A. 23
Begg, I. 11–12, 28, 32, 40
Belfast 220
Bell, D. 184
Bentham, G. 23
Benyon, J. 37, 45, 46, 206
Birch, D. 92
Birmingham 8, 11, 14, 16, 29, 31, 37, 45, 70, 86, 93, 102, 120, 137, 150, 163, 165, 190, 212
  City Action Team 134
  Heartlands and UDC 124, 128–9
  labour market 176
  Olympic Games 187
  neighbourhood office 205
  shift-share analysis 69
  Task Force 134
  unemployment 9–10
  Urban Development Grant 119–20
birth-rate change 85–6
black religions 5, 25
Boddy, M. 63–5, 172, 195
Bolton 24, 203, 205
Boyle, R. 117
Bradford 109, 187
Bradford, M. 23, 90, 123
Breheney, M. 1, 223
Bristol 16, 31, 45, 86, 89, 94, 128, 134
  defence spending 172–3
  industrial restructuring 63–5
  UDC 124
British Technology Group 154
Brittan, L. 198
Brixton 203
brownfield sites 36, 53, 74, 76, 121, 122, 216
Brusco, S. 222
Buck, N. 6, 7, 45, 65, 71, 98, 126, 216, 217
Business in the Community 171, 200–1

Cambridge 38, 94, 172
Carbonaro, G. 19–20
Cardiff 47, 192
chambers of commerce 129, 138, 197, 201
Champion, A. 12–14, 15, 22, 197
Channel tunnel 174–5
Charters, S. 19
Checkland, S. 70
Cheshire, P. 19–20, 89
Chisholm, M. 36, 79
City Action Teams 134, 167, 169, 171
City Grant 121, 171
civil service scheme 189–91
Clark, D. 27
Clarke, K. vii, 96, 167
Clydeside *see* Glasgow
Coleman, A. 37
comfortable/uncomfortable Britain 2, 4, 41, 48, 52
  see also North/South divide
Commercial/Industrial Improvement Areas 110
Community Development Programme 59, 61, 116

community involvement 134–5, 140–1, 149, 165, 171–2, 179, 190, 196, 200–1, 202–7
Confederation of British Industry viii
Consortium Developments Ltd. 50
contract compliance *see* affirmative action
Cooke, P. 143, 179
Corby 115
corporate sector 50, 93
costs per job 139, 151, 152, 157–8, 165
Coventry 59
Crawford, P. 90
crime, vandalism and social unrest 3, 37–9, 45–7, 148, 160, 177, 205–6, 225–6
 in rural areas 38, 47
 see also riots
Crossman, R. 59
Crowther, S. 74
Croydon 205

decentralization of population and industry 49, 50, 84, 85–7
Department of Employment 116, 134, 167
Department of Environment 9, 36, 90, 96, 99, 106, 107, 109, 116, 117, 119, 121, 122, 130, 134, 138, 147, 152, 154, 167, 180, 198, 203, 208
Department of Health 23, 169
Department of Trade 106, 107, 116, 134, 154, 157–8, 165, 167, 171, 180
derelict land 35–6, 47, 53, 76–9, 148
Derelict Land Grant 78, 117, 121, 122, 130, 140, 212
Dicken, P. 66, 93, 188
Donnison, D. 14–16, 45, 198, 207

Ealing 106
economic change, restructuring 62–9
 sectoral shifts 25–7, 28–9, 67
economic vs. social priorities 176–7, 181–2, 185, 218–21, 225–6
education 161, 163, 170, 192
 higher education role 190–1, 206, 210–11, 221, 224
Education Priority Area 101, 102
Edwards, J. 99, 101
employment change, and industrial premises 79–83
 and firm size 92
 and job loss 27–9, 39–40
 shift-share analysis 67–9
 spatial division of labour 25, 62–3
employment impacts of financial aid 150–3, 159
 deadweight, displacement, duration, duplication and distribution 150–1, 156–7, 159, 168
English, J. 215
English Estates 154, 157, 170
English Heritage 144
Enterprise Allowance 168–9
enterprise boards 108, 139, 197–8
enterprise trusts 136
Enterprise Zones 119, 151
 areas 113
 costs 116
 displacement 115
 financial incentives 111–13
 job impact 115
environmental rehabilitation 147–8
Ericksen, R. 113
Estate Action 124
ethnic groups 4–5, 24–5, 29, 39, 46–7, 99, 135, 160, 161–4, 194, 195
 and demographic change 24–5
European cities 19–20, 111, 222
European Regional Development Fund 107, 140
European Social Fund 107, 140
Eversley, D. 11–12

female labour 25, 72
fibre optics 53, 223
Fielding, A. 21
Financial Investment Group 117
Fothergill, S. 79–83, 90, 92
Fox, Sir Cyril 14
Frank, C. 92

garden festivals 110, 111, 127, 148
Garrahan, P. 74
Gateshead 111, 113, 116
gearing ratios 118, 120, 121, 125, 127, 131, 139, 156
General Improvement Areas 101
ghettos 219–20
Gillespie, A. 223
Glasgow 2, 8, 11, 14, 27, 31, 36, 41, 70, 89, 187, 190, 213

City of Culture 111, 187, 188
community role 202–3, 204
industrial restructuring 63–4
financial aid 121–2, 168
Garden Festival 111, 188
GEAR 198–9
housing rehabilitation 102–3
Miles Better campaign 186
privatization 121–3
shift-share analysis 67–9
urban vs. regional aid 106–7
Goddard, J. 66, 68, 153–9, 168, 223
Gordon, I. 6, 7, 45, 65, 71, 98, 216, 217
Gordon, P. 21
government, central/local relations 24, 91–2, 98, 116–17, 120, 126, 127–9, 131, 142, 164, 166, 177, 180, 208, 209–12
devolution 196–202, 210
Greater London Train Board 140
Greater London Enterprise Board 108, 139
Greater Manchester *see* Manchester
Green, A. 12–14, 15, 197
green belts 47, 48, 216–17
Gregory, D. 74
Groundwork Trust 147
Group of Eleven 120, 171
Gudgin, G. 79–83, 92
Gulliver, S. 188

Hackney 9–10, 109, 203, 207
Hackney, R. viii
Hailsham, Lord 220
Hall, P. 19, 48, 223
Hambleton, R. 203, 205
Hamnett, C. 21, 24, 33, 39
Hart, D. 223
Haughton, G. 194
Hausner, V. 186
Hay, D. 19, 20
headquarters location 66, 83, 153, 202
health 23, 116, 199
Hennessey, P. 98
Hepworth, M. 223
heritage 54
Heseltine, M. 51, 111, 117, 127, 148, 187
high-tech firms 93–4, 172–3
Hoggett, P. 203, 205
Holtermann, S. 41
Home Office 163, 164, 205–6
House Builders Federation 78
household mobility 7, 22, 23, 33, 35, 86, 90, 102, 175, 192, 194, 197
housing:
council sales 23
decentralization 203–4
and demographic change 85
and labour markets 35, 192
dereliction 148–9, 203
enveloping 102
financial cuts 124, 160, 165, 173, 213
gentrification 23–4, 86–7
investment needs 213–15
local authority roles 209–10
local authority sales 123
mortgage defaults 44
price changes 31–5, 49, 85–6, 122–3, 126, 131
privatization 121–4, 146–7
sectoral changes 3, 23, 213–14
see also household mobility
Housing Action Areas 101, 121
Housing Action Trusts 203
housing associations 117, 124, 146, 178, 192–3, 197, 202–4, 213–14, 216
housing development 48–9, 51–2, 87–8, 217
Howard, J. 186
Hull 2, 11, 88
Hytner Report 37, 46

Imperial Tobacco Ltd. 64–5
industrial floorspace change 79
industrial fragmentation 221–3
industrial linkage 222–3
informal economy 43, 56
infrastructural investment 213–15
infrastructure decay 47, 53, 54, 66, 74, 82, 94
Inner Area Studies vii
insurance in inner city areas 38–9, 43
Investors in Industry 83, 171
Ipswich 64
Islington 205, 207

Jacobs, J. 70
Jakobovits, I. 225
job preservation 191
jobless growth 182, 189

Keeble, D. 27, 84, 92
Kilroy-Silk, R. 38

Kirklees 138, 212
Kirwan, R. 113–15
Kivell, P. 36, 79
Kontuly, T. 20

Lancashire Enterprises Ltd. 139, 197
labour costs 70–2
labour flexibility 63, 66, 72–4, 95
labour markets:
  balance sheets 31
  and housing 35, 192
  leakage 166, 175–6, 193
  ring-fencing schemes 194–5
land availability 79–83, 95
land development:
  and legal problems 77
  and plot size 76, 95
land register 78–9, 171
land values 51–2, 74–9, 90, 121
  comparative vs. residual methods 74–6
  in Enterprise Zones 113–15
  and local authorities 76, 78
Law, C. 129
Lawless, P. 99
Layfield Report 211
Leclerc, R. 199
Leeds 8, 11, 124, 134, 137, 190
Leicester 102, 120, 134
Lever, W. 27, 68, 98, 106, 150, 180
leverage 152, 156
Liverpool 2, 8, 11, 14, 18, 36, 41, 45, 64, 66, 88, 89, 91, 117, 187, 190, 205
  City Action Team 134
  Garden Festival 111
  housing co-ops 203
  Mersey Development Corporation 111, 127–8, 131, 170
  unemployment 9–10
Lloyd, P. 29, 66, 93, 94
Local Government Training Board 210
local authorities:
  capacity 177–8
  economic development roles 136–40, 177–8
  efficiency 207–8
  mobility schemes 192, 197
  multi-purpose role 141–2
  see also government
local variability 143, 178–9
Locate in Scotland 180
London 2, 7, 9, 11, 14, 16, 17, 18, 23–4, 31, 56, 73, 86, 87, 88, 89, 174, 220
  City Action Team 134
  Docklands Development Corporation 116, 125–7, 131, 177, 198, 213, 216, 217, 223
  dominant role 183, 196, 199, 201–2
  Green Belt 216–17
  house prices 33–5
  industrial restructuring 65
  labour costs 70, 71–2
  local authority expenditure 137, 207
  population turnaround 21–2
  riots 37, 45–6
  schools Compact 192
  Task Force 134
  Urban Programme and rate resources 98
Lovell 120, 131
Lovering, J. 64, 172

M4 Corridor 94, 172
McArthur, A. 140, 169
McDonald, A. 203
MacGregor, A. 74–6, 140, 169
Maclennan, D. 102–3, 121, 202
Macmillan, H. 58
Madigan, R. 215
Manchester:
  Castlefield 144–6
  City Action Team 134
  comprehensive planning 4
  derelict land 148
  employment loss 29, 93
  ethnic groups 4–5, 24–5, 29, 161–2, 163–4
  financial schemes 207
  firm size 66, 70
  G-Mex 144
  higher education role 190
  housing cuts 213
  labour market ring fencing 194–5
  land transactions 74–6
  local pride 187
  Moss Side/Hulme 4–5, 29, 45, 135, 149, 169, 220
  neighbourhood offices 205
  Phoenix 120, 144
  political control 8, 91, 119, 208
  population loss 18
  refurbishment 110–11, 120, 143–9

retirement migration 86
riots 36, 45–6, 111
sewers 215
Ship Canal Company 124
social unrest 36–7
Task Force 134–6
unemployment 5, 9–10, 29–30
Urban Development Corporation 124
urban services 56
Victoria Park 17
voluntary sector ix, 109
well-being 3–5, 11, 16, 41
Manpower Services Commission 73, 91, 98, 134, 139, 140, 141, 151, 168, 206
Mason, C. 94
Massey, D. 25, 62, 66, 143, 186, 199
Mawson, J. 138, 139, 150
Medway 169
Meegan, R. 66
mergers and take-overs 95, 200, 202
Merseyside *see* Liverpool
Merseyside Enterprise Board 139
Miall, R. 92
Middlesbrough *see* Teesside
Middleton, A. 198
migration *see* household mobility
Miller, D. 138, 139, 150
Mills, L. 137, 178, 210
Milton Keynes 56
Ministry of Defence 172
Moore, C. 27, 28, 32, 40, 68, 70, 98, 106, 150, 180
Moyser, G. 45
Muggeridge, M. 58
multi-agency approaches 59, 205–6
Murphy, D. 163

National Council for Voluntary Organisations 110
Nationwide Building Society 34–5
NCVO 170
new realism 119, 136, 142
new towns 13, 18, 19, 21, 58, 124, 154
private development 48, 50, 217
Newcastle 2, 11, 14, 16, 31, 66, 70, 72, 74, 86; 188, 190, 205
City Action Team 134
economic vs. social aims 107–9
financial aid 154–8, 168
industrial structure 153
job impacts of aid 153–9
labour market 175–6
urban vs. regional aid 107
Urban Development Corporation 124
Newport Pagnell 47
non-plan 48, 50
Norman, P. 215
North/South divide 2–3, 6–8, 11, 12–16, 27, 32–3, 62, 67, 92, 172–5, 183, 196, 208–9, 217
Nottingham 64, 110, 120, 134

Oldham 24, 45
outer estates 11, 30, 41, 52
outlanders 219–20
Owen, D. 197

Pahl, R. 56
Parkinson, M. 127
Parry, G. 45
Patel, S. 39
Pearson, G. 39
Phillimore, P. 23
Phoenix 120, 144
place-marketing 187–8
Plymouth 11, 16, 21, 41
polarization, social 23–5, 192, 219–20
police policy 46, 160–1, 162, 219, 220
policy coherence 95, 106, 166–72, 185–7
political control in localities 7–9, 24, 91–2, 137, 163, 206, 207–9
Poll Tax *see* taxation
population change:
and counterurbanization 20–1
and ethnic groups 24–5
in European towns 19–20, 37
urban loss 17–23, 39–40
urban turnaround 21–3
in USA 19–21
Portsmouth 16
post-industrial society 184
poverty:
poverty policy 42, 188–9
spatial concentration 43
Prais, S. 62
Prime Minister vii, 96, 169, 170–1
Prince of Wales 175
Priority Estates Project 203
private sector involvement 91–2, 117–24, 128, 131, 135–6, 138, 142, 149, 165, 171–2, 211–12, 215

privatization 117, 121–4, 141–2, 146–7, 173, 203
probation service 206
PROBE 120

R & D location 62, 94, 153, 159, 172
Randolph, W. 21, 24
rate capping 98
Rate Support Grant 98, 208
RAWP 199
Rees, D. 92
regional agencies 179–80, 197
Regional Development Grant 106, 154, 156–9
Regional Health Authorities 116
regional policy 51, 66, 98, 101, 106, 153–6, 158–9, 172–3, 179–80, 182, 183
Regional Selective Assistance 106–7, 154, 156–9
relative deprivation 42, 184
Rhodes, J. 28, 32, 40, 68, 70, 71
Rich, D. 117
Ridley, N. 167, 170, 208
riots 37–9, 45, 59–60, 177
  in 1930s 45, 47
Roberts, S. 21
Robinson, F. 66, 68, 107, 108, 153–9, 168, 176
Robson, B. 2, 36, 90, 123, 194, 202
Rochdale 123, 134, 206, 209
Royal Town Planning Institute viii
Runciman, W. 184
rural development 51–2
rural/urban myth 175

St Helens 200
Salford 8, 88, 91, 212
  Enterprise Zone 113
  land transactions 77–8
  Phoenix 120–1
  privatization 122–3, 146–7
  Quays and UDC 123, 124, 128, 129–31
scales of governance 179–80
Scarman Report 37, 160, 161–2, 163
scenario-building 182–5, 218–21
schools compact 170, 192
Scott, A. 71
Scottish Development Agency 180, 188, 197, 198
Section 11 Grants 164
Section 137 funds 139, 140, 211
service provision 55–6
Sheffield 8, 14, 45, 120, 137, 138, 178, 187, 190
  Lower Don and UDC 128, 170
Sheppard, Revd D. 2
shift-share analysis 67–9
shopping 53, 56–7, 84, 116, 147
Short, J. 186
Shutt, J. 29, 221
Simplified Planning Zones 110
Simpson, D. 210
slum clearance 14, 18–19, 58, 214–15, 220
small firms 69–70, 71, 83, 92–4, 150, 153, 156, 170, 171
  recession-push/technology-pull 93–4
social and economic indicators 9–16, 23, 103, 106
social mix 123, 215–16, 221
Solesbury, W. 60
Solomos, J. 37, 45, 46, 206
Soto, P. 14–16, 45
South Yorkshire *see* Sheffield
spatial monitoring 185–6, 199
Spencer, K. 29, 120, 176
Stedman-Jones, G. 45
Stockport 205
Stoke 11, 111
Stone, R. 54
Storey, D. 94
Stretton, H. 60
Syms, P. 113

targeting job benefits 101–3, 103–6, 110–11, 152, 175–6, 189, 192–6
  spatial logic 101–3
Task Forces 91, 134–6, 162, 167, 169, 171
taxation policy 50–1, 89, 95, 211–12
  local rates and Community Charge 89–91, 94, 123, 173–4, 197, 208–9, 211, 225
Teesside 11, 14, 134
telecommunications 223–4
Third Italy 222
Tokyo 223
tourism and leisure 127–8, 144–6, 221, 224
Town & Country Planning Association viii, 1, 200, 203, 223
Townsend, A. 66
Townsend, P. 23

trade unions 72, 191
Trafford 113, 115, 116
  Urban Development Corporation 123, 223–4
training 138, 140, 141, 150, 168–9, 177–8, 193, 210, 223
transport 52–3, 55, 84, 172, 193, 223
trickle-down 182–3
Tyler, P. 70, 71
Tym, Roger & Partners 115
Tyne and Wear *see* Newcastle

underclass 162, 169, 189, 219, 221
unemployment 29–31, 39–40
unified benefit schemes 189, 191
unintended impacts of policy 172–5
United States comparisons viii, 18–19, 27, 37, 51, 53, 86–7, 88, 92, 119, 186, 189, 192, 199, 200, 201
Urban Development Action Grant 119
Urban Development Corporations 111, 116, 120, 124–34, 142, 177, 198, 212, 223–4
Urban Development Grants 91, 117, 118–20, 165, 171, 212
urban impact assessment 186
Urban Programme:
  current objectives 100
  vs. DTI funds 106–7
  economic/social inconsistency 100–1
  financial resources 154–6
  Management Initiative 152
  Other Designated Districts 103
  Partnership/Programme authorities 96, 103, 116–17, 119, 134
  resources 96–8, 103–6
  switch to economic aims 61, 99–100, 107–9
  Traditional Urban Programme 96, 106
  and voluntary sector 109–10
Urban Renewal Grants 117, 120–1, 171, 212
urban/rural myth 49–50, 51, 84, 87–8
urban services 191, 199–200

vandalism *see* crime
venture capital 83–4
Vining, D. 20
voluntary sector role 101, 103, 107, 109–10, 116, 140–1, 160, 170, 171, 179, 191

Wagstaffe, M. 45
Walsall 205
Wandsworth 119, 195
Wannop, U. 199
Ward, C. 57
Ward, R. 125
waterside sites and redevelopment 88–9, 127, 134, 146, 221
Weiner, M. 51
well-being 6–7
  see also social indicators
Welsh Development Agency 180, 198
West Midlands *see* Birmingham
West Midlands Enterprise Board 139, 197
West Yorkshire *see* Leeds
West Yorkshire Enterprise Board 139
Whittington, R. 221
Widdicombe Committee 209
Wigan 44, 188
Wilson, Sir H. vii, 99
Winchester 44
workfare 189
Wray, I. 127
Wren, C. 66, 68, 153–9, 168

Young, K. 7, 65, 71, 98, 136, 178, 210, 216, 217
Young, M. 224
Youth Training Scheme 5, 160, 194